Franchising

Franchising

Its Nature, Scope, Advantages,
and Development

Second and Revised Edition

Charles L. Vaughn
The Vaughan Company

Lexington Books
D.C. Heath and Company
Lexington, Massachusetts
Toronto

Library of Congress Cataloging in Publication Data

Vaughn, Charles L.   1911-
 Franchising: its nature, scope, advantages, and development.

 Includes index.
 1. Franchises (Retail trade) I. Title.
HF5429.V36 1979   658.8'4   78-24841
ISBN 0-669-02852-5

Second printing, January 1982

Published simultaneously in Canada

Printed in the United States of America

International Standard Book Number: 0-669-02852-5

Library of Congress Catalog Card Number: 78-24841

To W. Seavey Joyce, S.J.
Friend of Innovation

Contents

List of Figures

List of Tables

Preface to the
First Edition

The purpose of this book is to present in consolidated form the results of the seven annual international conferences on franchising sponsored by Boston College from 1965 through 1971, as well as other pertinent information on franchising gleaned from research into the problems of franchisors and franchisees.

To accomplish these objectives, a thoroughgoing content analysis was made of the proceedings of the conferences, of which five have been published in full. The general literature on the subject of franchising was carefully reviewed, with special attention being paid to published research directly pertinent to problems of franchisees since the conferences were franchisor-oriented.

Emerging as the topic of greatest interest today was international franchising, and a chapter on this subject is included in the book. Other topics covered at some length in the conferences were advantages and disadvantages of franchising, recruitment and selection of franchisees, training, finance, and real estate. These are all covered herein, and because of the many misunderstandings surrounding the nature, scope, and history of franchising, considerable attention has been directed to this topic. The topic is also, of course, one of intrinsic interest to a scholar.

Several subjects, however, have not been treated at length because of space limitations and their adequate coverage elsewhere. Two of these topics are minority business enterprise and legal problems in franchising. One should also hasten to add that practically any chapter in the book could be expanded into book form itself—for instance, training, recruitment and selection, finance.

In reviewing the material on franchising one cannot escape the conclusion that franchising, albeit beset with many legal and public relations problems, is a dynamic marketing method which

1. Combines the advantages of big and little business to the benefit of the small businessman.
2. Produces capital for the franchisor at perhaps a high cost but enables him to expand rapidly.
3. Seemingly entices an undue number of "promoters" with little substance behind their promotions, although the number of such purely promotional schemes has probably been grossly exaggerated.

Legitimate fortunes have been made in franchising by franchisors and franchisees alike. I hope that this book will serve to generate an understanding of how such achievements have been accomplished.

The book should prove valuable to diverse groups: franchisors and would-be franchisors, as well as personnel in franchisor firms; potential and actual franchisees; suppliers to franchisors and franchisees, including bankers, lawyers, accountants, and insurance salesmen as well as manufacturers and wholesalers; legislators; college and university teachers of marketing and other business subjects; and the general public.

Acknowledgments are made specifically to Joyce E. Nelson and to Joan F. Hong, who nursed this manuscript along, to the many chairmen, speakers, and panelists at the Boston College conferences, and to the many authors of publications on franchising. All their contributions have been invaluable.

Preface to the
Second Edition

In teaching a course in franchising at Boston College with the first edition of this book as a text from 1974 through 1977, I found that U.S. Department of Commerce figures on franchising were changing so fast that my lecture notes constantly needed revision. So when copies of the first edition ran out, it seemed only natural to submit a revision of the text.

It is possible as a result of the government studies to portray the growth of franchising in the United States for a decade, from 1968 through 1977, and to note that rather than being dead, as even some of my graduate students insisted when entering the course, franchising has continued to expand in both numbers of units and sales. When one stops to consider that franchising is a systematic means (and probably the only means) of creating new businesses, as the U.S. Department of Commerce notes, there is little wonder that it continues to grow.

In this revision I have added a chapter on marketing the product or service and spelled out franchising's role in the marketing process. This chapter should help introduce the neophyte franchisor or franchisee (as well as others) to the interdependent and necessary components of the total marketing program. In professional marketing circles franchising is designed primarily to secure physical distribution of the product or service and comes under the technical heading channels of distribution. I hope that as a result of this new chapter the prospective franchisee as well as the franchisor will be acutely aware of the need to review all components of the marketing mix before concluding that a particular franchise is viable.

Because of the work we have done to lead minority groups (principally blacks) into business as entrepreneurs through the franchise route, I have also added material on that subject. Entrepreneurship should help open the doors to opportunities that seem closed to these groups in tightly structured organizations. I have not devoted a great deal of space in the main text to legal problems in franchising but have included four appendixes pertinent to those problems, with one appendix on the Federal Trade Commission's new trade regulation rule on disclosure in franchising. However, I suspect that overemphasis on these problems may kill this golden goose known as franchising. I have also expanded coverage of international franchising, a subject that has grown greatly in the past few years.

Aside from its use as a university text, this book has served me best as an answer to multitudinous queries about franchising from people with ideas they want to franchise, from others who are thinking about buying a franchise, and from lawyers thrust into a field with which they are not familiar and to which they want some introduction before they seek the services of a specialized legal firm or provide the client with advice themselves. The book has also served to acquaint lenders, that is, banks and other financial institutions, with the subject of franchising. I hope that it will be found in the reference departments of libraries so that access to the subject will be free to all who might be interested in the topic.

Finally, many thanks are due the countless authors and others who have sent me their publications, particularly authors in Europe and Asia, and those who have called my attention to articles about franchising in general or some particular franchise. For some unconscious reason, perhaps, I would like to extend special thanks to those behind the Iron Curtain, whose research into franchising has led them to communicate with me. Also, my special gratitude is due to Garth Henzler for her persistence in typing the manuscript and my wife, Kathleen Thayer Vaughn, for her aid in proofreading it.

1

The Nature, Scope, and History of Franchising

The Nature: Illustrations of Franchises

McDonald's hamburg stands and Kentucky Fried Chicken units are so common-place today that a discussion of franchising can start with them as illustrations of what is meant by the word, and the reader will pretty much understand immediately.

But there are many other kinds of franchises as well in fields other than fast foods and with different types of contractual arrangements. Laundry and dry-cleaning establishments are often, if not usually, franchised. Likewise, campgrounds (for example, Kampgrounds of America), gasoline service stations, automobile dealerships, income tax services (H&R Block), motels (Holiday Inns), soft drink bottlers (Coca-Cola), rental services (Hertz for cars and United Rent-All for various things), and business aids (Postal Instant Press and General Business Services), real estate sales offices (for example, Century 21 and Gallery of Homes) and now professional services such as law and dentistry.

The word *franchise* is also applied in many noncommercial or quasi-commercial ways. For example, during discussions regarding the legal voting age or women's suffrage, reference is frequently made to the franchise to vote, that is, to the privilege, or right, to cast a ballot. In professional sports' leagues— baseball, basketball, hockey—a particular team is said to have the franchise for the city in question—Boston, New York, Los Angeles.

Still another type of franchise was illustrated by an article in *The Wall Street Journal:* "American Television & Communications Corp. said it was awarded four new franchises to construct and operate cable television systems. The contracts were awarded by Sioux Falls, S.D., Apopka, Fla., and by Aberdeen and Pinehurst, N.C."[1]

Although cable television and professional sports franchises are certainly commercial in nature, they are sufficiently provocative to be treated apart from this study.

The Scope: Definition of Franchising

Franchising as it is generally known today is a form of marketing or distribution in which a parent company customarily grants an individual or a relatively small company the right, or privilege, to do business in a prescribed manner over a

1

certain period of time in a specified place. The parent company is termed the *franchisor;* the receiver of the privilege the *franchisee;* and the right, or privilege itself, the *franchise.*

The privilege may be quite varied. It may be the right to sell the parent company's products, to use its name, to adopt its methods, and to copy its symbols, trademarks, or architecture, or the franchise may include all these rights. The time period and the size of the area of business operations, which are specified, may also vary greatly.

The rights that are granted and the duties and obligations of the respective parties, the franchisor and the franchisee, are usually, but not always, spelled out in a written contract. Unfortunately, franchise contracts vary greatly in their completeness, and some contracts are purely oral.

In McDonald's hamburg chain the sign, the architecture, the menu, and the service from place to place are nearly identical. Similar statements may be made about Howard Johnson's, Kentucky Fried Chicken, Burger King, Burger Chef, Dunkin' Donuts, Mister Donut, Pizza Hut, Bonanza Steak Houses, and many other chains in the restaurant field, and Holiday Inns, Quality Court, Travelodge, Sheraton, Ramada, and so on in the motel field.

Many parent companies, or franchisors, grant area franchises for rather large territories, such as an entire state or even a region, where several retail outlets may be established. These retail outlets may be operated by the area franchisee, or they may be subfranchised. A&W Root Beer originally franchised out large territories such as a state; McDonald's, also, originally sold sizable geographic areas, although they have been buying back the larger areas. The unsuccessful Performance Systems (originally Minnie Pearl) sold large territories, and some correspondence schools have franchised in a similar way. In the international field it seems to be the rule to franchise a whole area, often a country, rather than deal from the United States or some other country with each individual in the foreign state.

When a whole area is franchised and the area franchisee has the right to subfranchise, the area franchisee himself is sometimes called a *franchisor.* He may also be referred to as a *distributor,* and the operator of the individual unit as a *dealer.* Automobile and gasoline outlets are generally termed *dealerships,* although they come within generally accepted definitions of franchises.

Franchising, Licensing, Agency, and
Employee Relationships

A franchise may and frequently does involve a license, but on the subject of licensing there is a broad literature that has no reference whatsoever to franchising. The major literature on licensing arises from the field of patents. The distinction between franchising and licensing has been described thus by Kenneth W. Brown:

... a franchise involves primarily retail, service, or wholesale operations operated by one or several *individuals.* Franchise holders are independent businessmen—not employees, not agents and not contractors to the franchisor. In a broad sense they do *not* operate as licensees. Current use of the word franchise seems always to involve geographic areas of operations. ... licensing is based upon patents, trademarks and industrial type technology and it relates generally to manufacturing processes or manufactured products, often in million dollar corporate endeavors. Thus, franchising can be said to be to the individual as licensing is to the corporation. ...[2]

There is also another relationship somewhat similar to the franchise, and that is the agency relationship. Hewitt explains the agency relationship thus:

... Typically, the goods would be shipped on consignment with the title of the goods remaining in the manufacturer unless and until the goods were sold to consumers by the retailer.

The agent owes strict duties of loyalty, good faith, obedience, honesty, and care to the principal as to how he (the agent) carries out the agency. The principal (the manufacturer) owes certain duties in connection with reasonable expenditures the agency may have to make. The principal must indemnify the agent for liabilities that the agent incurs in carrying out the principal's business.

... agency law is brought into sharp focus by the fact that a principal may be liable to third parties for the negligent acts of fraudulent misrepresentations of his agent, even though the principal was in no way negligent or fraudulent himself. ...[3]

The agent is thus an extension of the principal, whereas the franchisee is in fact an independent businessman, albeit tied to the parent company but in looser and different ways from the agent. The French term *concession* has the same meaning as franchise, although in the United States, at least, the concession is almost a lease arrangement such as that held by a nonintegrated unit in a department store, without more control by the store than could be exercised by any lessor.

In certain borderline cases it is easy to confuse the franchisor-franchisee relationship with the employer-employee relationship. The franchisee is an independent businessman; he is a contractor to the franchisor. The employee, on the other hand, is under the complete control, in the work situation at least, of the employer. The difference between the franchisee and employee can be of considerable importance in dealings with government agencies, for example, in the payment of withholding taxes, federal insurance contributions, and the like. The employer is responsible for these payments for an employee; the franchisor is not responsible for them for his franchisees. Generally, if the individual has an investment in the business and can sell it, he is a franchisee. However, some interesting legal cases have arisen in the past few years as a result of state franchise termination acts. Managers under incentive pay programs who have invested in inventories have insisted that they are franchisees and not employees and cannot be terminated except in accordance with the cognizant state's franchisee termination laws. The situation requires investigation of the amount of control that the parent company has over the individual. Generally, if the sole responsibility of the individual is to supply consumers with a product or service that meets certain requirements, then the relationship is that of an independent contractor to the franchisor, or that of a franchisee. On the other hand, if the parent dictates the methods by which the product or service is generated, then the relationship becomes that of employer to employee. In borderline cases, however, such as in the fast food field, the franchisor may exercise tight control over the franchisee to assure standards of cleanliness and service and the ephemeral qualities of taste that are important; in the food field relationships that might otherwise be termed employer-employee ones are regarded as legitimate franchisor-franchisee relationships. A company's branch office managers and assistants are all employees of the company, and the company is responsible for them in the same way as it is for any other employee-manager.

The Size and Impact of Franchise Systems

The network, or chain, of retail units individually owned by franchisees and headed by a parent firm, or franchisor, is called a franchise system. Such systems may be large international networks such as those of the petroleum and auto marketers, the car rental agencies, the temporary-help giant, Manpower, or they may be small and confined to a region or even a single metropolitan area. U.S. government research indicates that there were more than 1,100 franchise chains and 380,000 franchised outlets in 1978 in the United States.[4] About $239 billion worth of goods and services flowed through these franchised outlets in 1978. Almost 4 million persons were employed in franchise-related businesses in 1976, and 31 percent of all retail sales in the United States flowed through franchisee and company-owned units in franchise chains in 1977. About 90 percent of all receipts of firms in franchise chains were accounted for by retail sales in 1977.

Among 116 (out of a total of 136) fast food chains cooperating in a 1969 survey, Vaughn found that the median number of units in chicken chains was 17; in hamburg/hot dog chains, 60; in pizza chains, 50; in roast beef chains, 18; in sandwich shops, 32; and in seafood chains, 9.[5] By and large, the chains were not mammoth networks, but there was and is considerable concentration of establishments and sales volume in the largest chains.

A later study found that the "four largest fast food franchisors (ranked by number of franchised units) have 26.1% of all fast food franchised units and 21.2% of all franchise sales."[6]

On the basis of a 1976 analysis of U.S. government statistics in reference to fast food chains, Vaughn concluded: "The big chains are taking over. The top seven [fast food chains] in the United States have almost half of all units and sales."[7]

Types of Franchise Systems

Since franchises do differ so greatly from one another, they should be subgrouped and discussed separately. The legal, real estate, and other franchise problems of a Mobil Oil gasoline station are quite different from those of a Holiday Inn; those of a Coca-Cola bottlership are different from those of a drug or automotive aftermarket store. Some authorities would even say that certain of these business relationships are not franchise relationships (for example, those between the petroleum marketer and the proprietor of the gasoline station), even though traditionally they may have been considered under franchising.

Actually, franchise systems may be grouped into four broad categories, as shown in table 1-1. Also, so that comparisons of the relative importance of different types can be made, table 1-2, together with table 1-3, provides rough estimates of the number of establishments (units or outlets) of each type as well as estimates of their sales volume in terms of the percentage of the total franchising market.

The Type I Franchise System: The Manufacturer-Retailer System. The manufacturer-retailer system includes automobile manufacturers and their dealers,

Table 1-1
Types of Franchise Systems

Type	Businesses Included
I: Manufacturer-retailer systems	Mainly automobile and truck dealerships and gasoline service stations
II: Manufacturer-wholesaler systems	Soft drink syrup manufacturers and their bottlers (Beer distributors should probably also be included here, although they have not been.)
III: Wholesaler-retailer systems	Sellers of automotive products and services (including appliances, lawn furniture, and so forth) and retailers in drugs, hardware, and paints
IV: Trademark/trade name licensor-retailers	Business aids and services, construction, remodeling, home cleaning, convenience grocery stores, educational products and services, fast-food restaurants, other food retailing, hotels and motels, laundry and dry cleaning, recreation, entertainment and travel (including campgrounds), and some miscellaneous businesses.

Table 1-2

Types of Franchises and the Frequency of Units, 1978

(Franchised Units Only)

Franchise	Thousands of Units	Percent of Total
Type I: Manufacturer-retailer	168	44%
Automobile and truck dealers	31	8
Gasoline service stations	137	36
Type II: Manufacturer-wholesaler	2	0.04
Soft drink bottlers	2	0.04
Type III: Wholesaler-retailer	83	22
Automotive products and services (including appliances, lawn furniture)	47	12
Retailing (including drugs, hardware, paints, but excluding food)	36	9
Type IV: Trademark/trade name licensor-retailer	126	33
Business aids and services	27	7
Accounting, credit, collection agencies, and general business systems	4	1
Employment services	3	1
Printing and copying services	2	0.5
Tax preparation services	5	1
Miscellaneous business services	13	3
Construction, remodeling, home cleaning	14	4
Convenience grocery	5	1
Educational products and services	1	0.3
Fast-food restaurants	43	11
Food retailing (non-fast foods or convenience grocery)	14	4
Hotels and motels	5	1
Laundry and dry cleaning	3	1
Recreation, entertainment, and travel (including campgrounds)	6	2
Rental services	7	2
Miscellaneous (beauty salons, carpet cleaning)	2	0.5
Total: All franchising	380	100.0

Source: U.S. Department of Commerce, Industry and Trade Administration, Office of Consumer Goods and Service Industries, *Franchising in the Economy 1976-1978* (Washington, D.C.: U.S. Government Printing Office, 1978), p. 30.

Note: Estimates made in 1976. Data grouped by types of franchises by Charles L. Vaughn and rounded off. (Rounding may produce some slight discrepancies in sums.)

petroleum marketers and their dealers, and a few other very small groups. This is truly the automotive group of franchised outlets. The General Motors, Ford, Chrysler, Volkswagon, Exxon, Texaco, Mobil Oil, Citgo, and other manufacturer-dealer chains fall into this category.

Type I franchise systems have long dominated the franchise field, and of the $239 billion in sales through franchised outlets in 1978, $188 billion flowed through the manufacturer-dealer type systems, according to figures adapted

Table 1-3
Types of Franchises and Their Sales Volume, 1978
(Franchised Units Only)

Franchise	Sales (billions of dollars)	Percent of Total
Type I: Manufacturer-retailer	188	79%
Automobile and truck dealers	142	60
Gasoline service stations	46	19
Type II: Manufacturer wholesaler	12	5
Soft drink bottlers	12	5
Type III: Wholesaler-retailer	13	5
Automotive products and services (including appliances, lawn furniture)	5	2
Retailing (including drugs, hardware, paints)	8	3
Type IV: Trademark/trade name licensor-retailer	26	11
Business aids and services	2	1
Accounting, credit, collection agencies and general business services	0.2	0.08
Employment services	1	0.4
Printing and copying services	0.2	0.08
Tax preparation services	0.1	0.4
Miscellaneous business services	1	0.4
Construction, remodeling, home cleaning	1	0.4
Convenience grocery	2	1
Educational products and services	0.2	0.08
Fast food restaurants	14	6
Food retailing (non-fast foods or convenience grocery)	2	1
Hotels and motels	4	2
Laundry and dry cleaning	0.2	0.08
Recreation, entertainment, and travel (including campgrounds)	0.3	0.1
Rental services	1	0.4
Miscellaneous (beauty salons, carpet cleaning)	0.4	0.2
Total: All franchising	239	100

Source: U.S. Department of Commerce, Industry and Trade Administration, Office of Consumer Goods & Service Industries, *Franchising in the Economy 1976-78* (Washington, D.C.: U.S. Government Printing Office, 1978), p. 30.

Note: Estimates made in 1976. Data grouped by types of franchises by Charles L. Vaughn and rounded off. (Rounding may produce some slight discrepancies in sums.)

from the U.S. Department of Commerce Survey (USDC).[8] Also, 169,000 of the total of 380,000 franchised outlets in 1978 were of the manufacturer-dealer type. In other words, 44 percent of all franchised outlets and about 79 percent of all sales volume through franchised outlets were of Type I, as shown in tables 1-2 and 1-3. The tables omit certain manufacturer-operated franchises, such as Mode O'Day Corporation, or franchises that consign lines of merchandise to their franchised departments in stores.

The Type II Franchise System: The Manufacturer-Wholesaler System. The manufacturer-wholesaler system is exemplified by the Coca-Cola, Pepsi-Cola, and other bottler-syrup supplier chains. This type of system is another important one but with a relatively small number of units (the USDC report estimated two-thousand franchises for 1978; figures in table 1-2 are rounded off), although 1978 sales volume was large at $12 billion.

The Type III Franchise System: Wholesaler-Retailer Franchises. The wholesaler-retailer system includes hardware chains, drug store chains, automotive after-market chains, and so on. Collectively, these had an estimated 83,000 units in 1978 with sales volume in the neighborhood of $13 billion, according to USDC figures. According to the USDC report, about 70 percent of all Type III and IV franchisor product sales to franchisees were in Type III systems.

The auto aftermarket chains such as Western Auto Stores, Firestone, Goodyear, and Goodrich are an important segment of the Type III group. Besides auto tires and accessories, the outlets carry seasonal home furnishings, some sports equipment, lawn care tools, bicycles, and so on. William P. Hall wrote an excellent article on this type of system in the *Harvard Business Review* in 1964.[9] The growth of this type of system was especially noticeable in the 1930s.

The Type IV Franchise System: The Trademark/Trade Name Licensor. This licensor system has grown much in the United States in the past two decades and has been penetrating European and Oriental markets. In this system the franchisor, who is seldom a manufacturer and usually not a wholesaler, generally has a common trade name and standardized methods (or business format as it is often termed) for successful operation of retail units. The retail units may market a product or group of products, a service or group of services, or some combination of these under a common trade name. Architecture of the units is usually standardized and attention-getting.

Among the well-known Type IV systems are

Motel chains: Holiday Inn, Sheraton Inn, Quality Courts

Restaurant chains: Howard Johnson's, McDonald's, Kentucky Fried Chicken, Dunkin' Donuts, Mister Donut, Burger King, Burger Chef, Wimpy's, A & W, Baskin Robbins, Wendy's, Pizza Hut

Auto and truck rental firms: Hertz, Avis, Budget Rent-a-Car, National

As one will note from this list of motel, restaurant, and car rental chains, and as I have pointed out elsewhere,[10] the origin and development of these chains and the units composing them are associated with the great personal mobility of the American public. In other words, one might conclude that the success of these operations stems from the successful distribution of automobiles; the full parking lots surrounding the units tend to confirm the validity of this conclusion.

In the case of the motel chains and some of the earlier restaurants, successful locations are along the highways, although great headway has been made by restaurant chains in penetrating central city markets in recent years. Initially fast food chain patronage was thought to come primarily from people traveling the highways, but it is now apparent that the continued operation of restaurant units has resulted in an increase in customers from the adjacent neighborhoods.

Type IV systems are particularly interesting, not only because of their great growth in the past decade or so in the United States, but for other reasons as well. What is being sold by the franchisor in Type IV systems is generally a subsystem of a retail operation and a trade name with consumer recognition and attractiveness. The systems concept is especially important in the Type IV category. The franchisor in these systems is in a sense a management consulting firm possessing a trade name to sell.

According to figures developed from the USDC study, Type IV systems included about a third (33 percent, table 1-2) of all franchised units in 1978, but only a ninth (11 percent, table 1-3) of all franchise sales.[11] Fast food unit sales accounted for more than half of all Type IV system sales, and the numbers of units about a third of all Type IV units. Because franchising is popularly identified with fast foods, it should perhaps be stressed that fast food units accounted for only 11 percent of all franchised units in 1978 and no more than 6 percent of all sales through franchised outlets.

History and Growth of Franchising

Ten Years of Growth in Franchising, 1969-1978

Franchising witnessed a dramatic growth during the ten-year period from 1969 through 1978: the number of franchisors increased; the number of franchisees, or establishments, grew; and sales volume skyrocketed, according to survey results.

The number of franchising companies increased from about 600 firms in 1969 to more than 1,100 firms in 1978, excluding the automobile, gasoline, and soft drink companies, according to United States Department of Commerce figures. During this same decade the number of franchisee-owned establishments grew from 315,000 to 380,000, reflecting a 21 percent increase during the ten-year interval, or more than 2 percent per year. The trend is shown graphically in figure 1-1. There was also a significant increase in the number of company-owned, or nonfranchised, establishments in franchise firms during the decade.

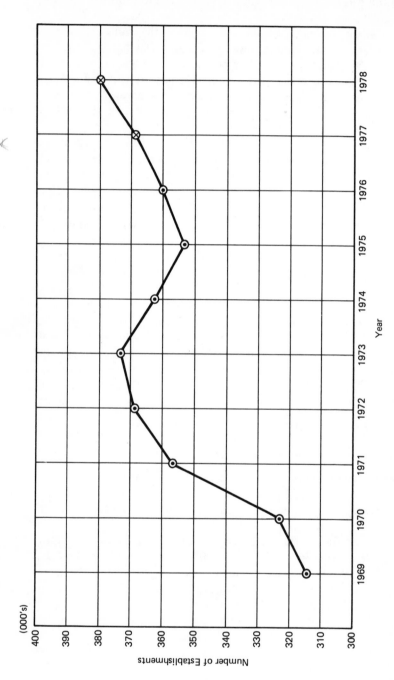

Source: U.S. Department of Commerce *Franchising in the Economy 1975-77, 1976-1978.*
Note:

All Franchises: Franchisee-Owned Only
⊙ Actual as Reported
⊗ Projections

Figure 1-1. A Decade of Growth in Franchising: Number of Franchisee-Owned Establishments, 1969-1978

More dramatic, however, was the increase in dollar sales volume during the 1969-1978 decade—from about $95 billion in 1969 to more than $239 billion in 1978. That increase of more than $144 billion in sales reflects, of course, an increase of more than 150 percent, or 15 percent a year on the average in sales through franchised outlets. Figure 1-3 depicts the situation graphically.

Further inspection of these graphs and two others (figures 1-2 and 1-4) reveals several other trends. First, the number of franchised units rose sharply from 1969 to 1973 (figure 1-1), when the number of establishments peaked. Then there was a sharp decline in number of units until 1975, when the uptrend in numbers of units resumed.

Some insight into the reasons for the sharp downturn in total number of units may be inferred from figure 1-2, which shows the trend in numbers of franchised units by type of franchise. Apparent from this latter graph is that the 1969-1973 uptrend in the total number of franchised establishments camouflaged a steady downtrend in the number of Type I franchisees (gas stations, auto dealerships). In 1973 there was a sharp drop in Type I franchises, coinciding with the Arabs' boost in petroleum prices and Americans' awakening to the energy crisis.

On the other hand growth in dollar sales continued to mount after 1970, barely showing even a slowdown (figure 1-3) from 1973 to 1974. As depicted in figure 1-4, even Type I franchises continued to increase their sales volume: in fact, sales volume through Type I franchises showed by far the greatest increase of any type, both in absolute terms and in percentages during the decade.

Nor did the growth in franchised units and sales volume show any signs of abatement at the end of the decade. As one may observe in figures 1-3 and 1-4, the uptrend in the curves was just as sharp at the end of the decade as it had been at the beginning. One should note, however, in figures 1-2 and 1-4, that the different types of franchises were growing at different rates, and the downturn in numbers of type I franchised units (largely gas stations) seemed to be gaining momentum, although sales volume spurted, no doubt due in large part to higher prices.

Of particular interest to those who have followed franchising closely is the situation of the Type IV franchises, the ones that have attracted the most attention since the late 1950s. Type IV franchises grew in numbers at a rather uniform rate, with perhaps a hint of a slowdown in the 1973-1974 period, but no more than a hint. Fast foods, a significant segment of this type of business format franchise, grew in numbers at a fairly uniform rate too, as isolated and shown separately in figure 1-2. Fast foods did not show a slowdown in growth at the end of the period. A similar picture is depicted for sales volume (figure 1-4): steady year-by-year growth in sales volume (which is unimpressive when compared with that in Type I) with no indication of a slowdown near the end of the decade.

Fast Food Franchising

Since the Type IV, or business format, franchise systems are so heavily weighted with fast food firms, the latter deserve some further special treatment. In 1978,

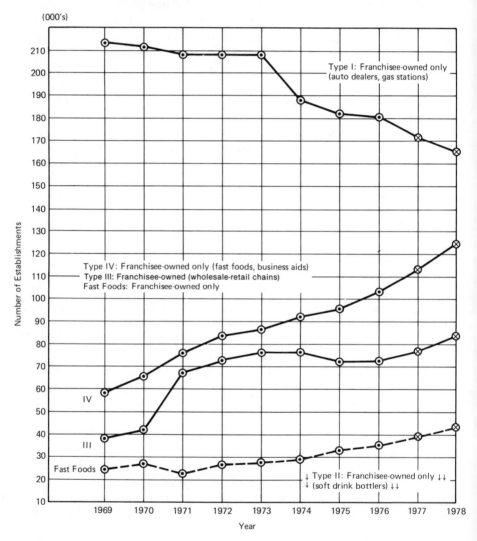

Source: U.S. Department of Commerce *Franchising in the Economy 1975–77, 1976–1978.*
Note:
⊙ Actual as reported
⊗ Projections
Figure 1-2. A Decade of Growth in Franchising: Number of Franchisee-Owned Establishments, 1969-1978, by Type of Franchise

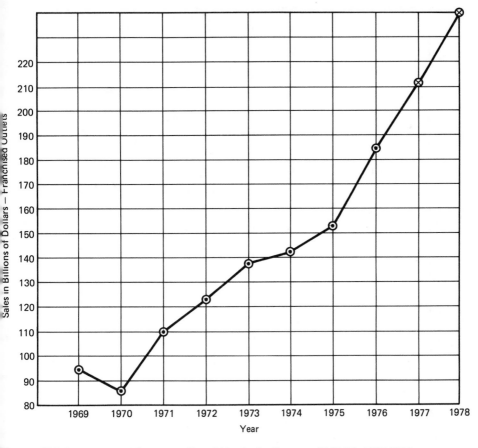

Source: U.S. Department of Commerce *Franchising in the Economy 1975-77, 1976-1978.*
Note:
All Franchises
⊙ Actual as Reported
⊗ Projections

Figure 1-3. A Decade of Growth in Franchising: Sales through Franchisee-Owned Establishments, 1969-1978

for example, about a third of all Type IV units were in the fast food field (table 1-2), and more than half of all Type IV sales went through franchised fast food outlets (table 1-3). Figures for fast foods do not include those from doughnut shops, ice cream stores, and other specialty food stores, which the U.S. Department of Commerce does not consider fast food restaurants. Moreover, growth in fast food franchised units and sales was pretty consistent during the 1969-1978 decade, except for a brief small decline in number of units in 1971. By 1978 sales through fast food outlets alone surpassed all Type II and Type III sales. The graphs are in figures 1-2 and 1-4.

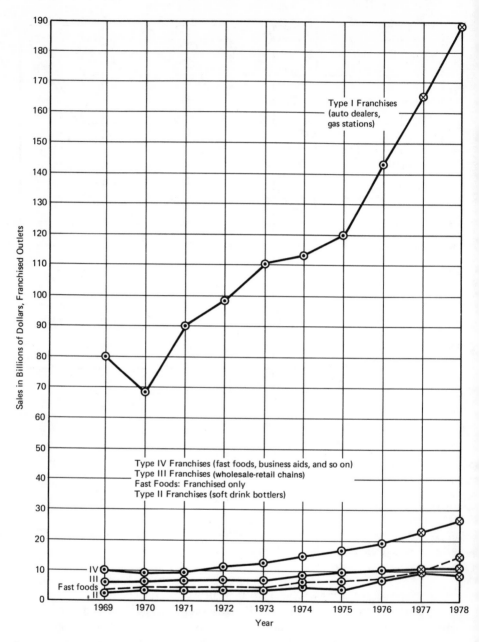

Source: U.S. Department of Commerce *Franchising in the Economy 1975-77, 1976-1978.*

Note:

⊙ Actual as Reported

⊗ Projections

Figure 1-4. A Decade of Growth in Franchising: Sales through Franchisee-Owned Establishments, 1969-1978, by Type of Franchise

The 1970s also marked the successful penetration of inner city markets by fast food chains, in particular by McDonald's and Burger King. Sales volume through their downtown units has been tremendous, perhaps nullifying the early conclusion that highway traffic is necessary for the success of a fast food operation. In the central cities fast food units are in direct competition with "atmosphere restaurants," but for several reasons the fast food chains have done well there, especially during lunch hours, and the fast food chains are successfully varying their menus and altering their decor, by adding breakfasts for example, in order to maintain their momentum.

Each year *Institutions Magazine* publishes a report on the 400 largest food service organizations (away-from-home feeders). In 1977, 33 of the largest of these food service organizations were involved in franchising, not including 8 additional hotel-motel franchise chains that were ranked in the top 100 on the basis of their food service activities alone.[12] Interestingly, 4 of the top 33 franchise food service organizations were franchisees (as distinct from franchisors).

Largest in sales volume of all food service organizations in the United States was McDonald's, with more than $3 billion in sales in 1976. Although McDonald's had 4,225 food service units by 1977 (about two-thirds of which were franchised), McDonald's was not the largest in numbers of units. Kentucky Fried Chicken Corporation (often referred to as Colonel Sanders), which was second in sales volume (about $1.6 billion in sales in 1976), had the most units of any franchise organization with 6,015 food service establishments, according to the *Institutions* survey.

Curiously, despite the leading position that franchise chains enjoyed in the food service field, no one franchise chain had a large share of the food service market. *Institutions* estimated this market at $86.2 billion in 1976. McDonald's 1976 sales volume of about $3 billion would be about 3.6 percent of the 1976 food service market and Kentucky Fried Chicken's sales of about $1.6 billion would be about 1.8 percent. Thus, despite the high position of franchise firms, both in terms of sales and public recognition, individual firms certainly did not dominate the field.

Some changes in ranks among franchise food service chains deserve mention. Wendy's International, featuring a special type of hamburg, for example, moved from a rank of 213 among *Institutions'* 400 in 1974 to 48 just two years later, in 1976, despite the fact that McDonald's, Burger King, and other hamburg chains were also growing (a phenomenon which should be noted by those experts who in the early 1970s, and even before, feared that saturation by fast food chains was at hand). It is noteworthy that four different menu items were featured by the top five franchised fast food chains: McDonald's and Burger King, of course, featured hamburgs; but Kentucky Fried Chicken, which featured chicken, was in second position; International Dairy Queen, which ranked among the top five franchise chains in volume, featured various soft ice cream dairy products; and Pizza Hut, as the name indicates, featured pizzas, "thick and chewy" and otherwise.

The 33 franchised food service chains which fall in *Institutions'* 400 largest food service organizations improved their position considerably in the two-year span from 1974 to 1976. Their average rank in 1976 was forty-fifth among *Institutions'* 400; in 1974, just two years before, their average rank was fifty-fifth. Some chains, of course, went down in rank. In fact, 10 of the 33 did, the most notable of which was Shakey's, whose rank went from forty-ninth position in 1975 to seventy-third in 1977.

I have depicted the growth of the industry menu item by menu item elsewhere in more detail.[13] In brief, fast food units featuring hamburgers, franks, and roast beef dominate the field and showed a consistent growth from 1972 to 1976. Pizza items, although they had far less in total sales volume, also sustained growth, and seafood appeared to be gaining acceptance in America. Continued rapid growth is anticipated on the basis of government figures newly released, although this growth may be negated by an oil crunch.

Other Indicators of Activity in Franchising

Recruitment advertising for franchisees continued at a fast pace even at the end of the decade. For example, the Thursday, 17 November 1977, issue of *The Wall Street Journal* carried forty-five advertisements offering readers new businesses. Although not all the offerings would qualify technically as franchises, they could be considered such for practical purposes. Another example of the continued active search for franchisees was shown in the Sunday, 27 November 1977, issue of *The New York Times*, which had thirty-six franchisee recruitment advertisements. These two issues of *The Wall Street Journal* and *The New York Times* were not unique: practically every Thursday edition of the *Journal* and Sunday edition of the *Times* (the two days on which the respective papers feature this type of advertising) carried similarly large volumes of franchise advertising. In February 1979, *The Wall Street Journal's* companion publication, *Barron's* (*National Business and Financial Weekly*), introduced a franchise and business opportunities section, to appear at periodic intervals during the year.

Moreover, public relations people were quite active, and some companies' advertising was indeed grandiose. For example, at about the same time (latter 1977), the *Boston Herald* had a long feature story on Weight Watchers and Diet Workshop, two franchisors in the weight reduction field. A full-page advertisement in *The Wall Street Journal* the same day played up the Midas franchising program, and about two months later the *Journal* carried a two-page advertisement for Holiday Inns, which claimed to be "the number one hotel franchise in the world." The 25 July 1977, issue of *Business Week* devoted an entire page to "Franchisees Tune in to Tune-ups," that is, the $5 billion annual tune-up business; and the 17 July 1977, issue of *The New York Times* carried a half-page article "A Mom and Pop Business Rings up $2 Billion," the story of Southland

and its 7-Eleven convenience grocery stores. In February 1979 *The New York Times* carried a banner headline on the first page of its business and finance section titled, "Corporate Giants Invade the Residential Market" and then proceeded to discuss the large and fast-growing real estate agency franchises, of which Century 21 is probably the most prominent. Possibly of even more importance was the two and one-half column lead story in the 5 April 1978, issue of *The Wall Street Journal* headed "Whopper War". It described the hamburger fight between McDonald's and Burger King and characterized their strategies together with hints at others.

A total of 244 column inches of space was devoted to advertisements for franchisees in the 17 November 1977, issue of *The Wall Street Journal.* That number represents about a page and a half of advertising. Types of franchises offered were in diverse fields. Nine of the forty-five *Wall Street Journal* advertisements were in the automotive aftermarket: for example, recruiting franchisees to provide a service designed to install an attachment to a truck; another, to operate transmission repair shops; another, to run a rust-proofing enterprise; another, a post-collision body repair service; and still another, muffler repair shops.

Employment agency and other personnel-type franchises were next most frequently offered in *The Wall Street Journal* advertisements, with seven of the forty-five ads for these. In the government classifications such franchises come under the heading Business Aids and Services. Personnel-type franchises were followed in frequency by recruitment for franchisees to run fast food shops (with five advertisements), quick copy shops (five), business-counseling services (two), carpet-cleaning services (two), and twelve miscellaneous types of services (rental agencies, furniture restoration units, giant-screen television, personal grooming, flower sales, home nursing services, bookstores)

Each year for more than a decade the U.S. Department of Commerce in conjunction with the Office of Minority Business Enterprise has published the *Franchise Opportunities Handbook*, which lists and describes briefly currently offered franchises that are not discriminatory on racial and other grounds. The 1977 edition[14] listed 745 such franchises, as contrasted with only 253 offerings in the 1968 edition. The 745 firms were in some forty business categories, ranging from automotive products and services to water-conditioning businesses. Most but by no means all of the franchises listed were in the Type IV category. Table 1-4 is a list of the forty business categories included in the 1977 *Handbook*.

The table indicates the extent to which franchising is retail oriented and has penetrated the retail field. In fact, to repeat, more than 90 percent of all gross receipts from franchising were in the retail field in 1977, and 31 percent of all retail sales in the United States in 1977 flowed through outlets of franchising companies.

Table 1-4

Categories of Franchises Listed in 1977 *Franchise Opportunities Handbook*

Automotive products and services
Auto, trailer rentals
Beauty salons, supplies
Business aids, services
Campgrounds
Children's stores, furniture products
Clothing, shoes
Construction, remodeling materials, services
Cosmetics, toiletries
Drug stores
Educational products, services
Employment services
Equipment rentals
Foods: Donuts
Foods: Grocery, specialty stores
Foods: Ice cream, candy, popcorn, beverages
Foods: Pancake, waffle, pretzel
Foods: Restaurants, drive-ins, carry-outs
General merchandising stores
Health aids, services
Hearing aids
Home furnishings, furniture: Retail, repair services
Laundries, dry cleaning services
Lawn and garden supplies, services
Maintenance, cleaning, sanitation: Services, supplies
Motels, hotels
Paint and decorating supplies
Pet shops, guard dogs
Printing
Real estate
Recreation, entertainment, travel: Services, supplies
Retailing, not elsewhere classified
Security systems
Soft drinks, water bottling
Swimming pools
Tools, hardware
Transit service
Vending
Water conditioning
Miscellaneous wholesale, service businesses

Early History of Franchising

Thompson has an excellent summary of the development of franchising.[15] As Thompson notes, Ernest Henderson, Sr., speaking at Boston College's Second Annual Management Conference on Franchising, traced the early history of franchising thus:

Historically, franchising in one form or another dates back to quite early days. During the Middle Ages, when separation of Church and State had not yet been generally accepted, important personages were frequently granted what today might be called franchises. These usually conferred the right to collect revenues, in return for various services or considerations. This early manifestation of franchising came to an end four hundred years ago, when, in the year 1562, the Council of Trent discouraged these activities.

The term "franchising" did not become prevalent in England until more recent centuries. Franchises were usually granted by royalty, or by legislative bodies. Franchising in the Eighteenth and Nineteenth centuries usually involved the acceptance of certain specific obligations on the part of a grantee, in return for certain specified privileges, usually of a long-term nature, and frequently involving some monopolistic advantages.[16]

In its modern form franchising probably originated with the Singer Sewing Machine Company, which developed an elaborate franchising system in the United States following the Civil War.[17] This system gradually declined, and it was not until the franchise methods entered the automobile and soft drink fields at the beginning of the twentieth century that franchising became an integral part of the distribution system. "The honor of being the first franchised [automotive] dealer has been attributed to William E. Metzger of Detroit, who established a dealership to handle steamers in 1898."[18] "By 1910 the basic pattern found in modern automobile franchise agreements had been established," according to Hewitt,[19] and a decade later found the manufacturers very jealous of their product lines. Cancellation of the franchise on ten days' notice was instituted if the dealer handled competing products. The trend in subsequent years was toward more control on the part of the manufacturers, until pressures against the manufacturers from several sources began to mount, and in 1949 exclusive representation, territorial security, and antibootlegging provisions were dropped from franchise agreements.[20]

Quoting from Thompson:

As was true with the beginning of automobile franchising, the answer to why the franchise form has been perpetuated seems to have been primarily economic. A financially independent franchisee can be forced to absorb part of the costs of overproduction or styling errors made by the manufacturer. These costs would have to be borne by the manufacturer in a system of manufacturer-owned outlets. Franchised dealers absorb the first impact of any price fluctuations at the retailing level, as the manufacturer's price fluctuates much less frequently and less strongly than do retail prices. The problem of used car trade-ins and resale introduces further financial uncertainties that are borne by the franchisee rather than by the manufacturer. There are additional state taxes and fees to be paid where a nationwide manufacturer-owned retail system is involved. Also, branch managers are not felt to have the same degree of motivation to succeed as the independent franchised dealer who has both his income and business investment to lose in case of business failure. Finally, franchised dealers are felt to have a stronger attachment to and rapport with the local community than would salaried employees of a manufacturer.

The continuation of the franchise system in automobile distribution can be partially explained by the immense amount of capital that would be required by a franchisor who wished to buy back franchisees and establish a wholly owned system. . . .[21]

These paragraphs not only succinctly summarize the reasons for the continuance of the franchise system in the automobile field but also cover the advantages of franchising as seen in fields besides the automotive. Alfred P. Sloan, Jr., in his autobiography, stated: "I believe that the franchise system, which has long prevailed in the automobile industry, is the best one for manufacturers, dealers, and consumers."[22] An excellent theoretical and empirical treatment of the restrictive franchise system in automobile distribution is provided by Pashigian.[23]

Parallel with the development of franchising in the automotive field was the granting of franchises in the soft drink industry. Shih and Shih in their discussion of franchising in the American soft drink industry state:

Application of franchising in the soft drink industry started in the 1890s. . . . In practice, a bottling franchise conveys the exclusive privilege of using a proprietary syrup, concentrate, or a copyrighted formula of manufacturing and packaging a brand-name beverage in a defined area. A franchise bottler is obliged to purchase certain raw materials, particularly the syrup, exclusively from the parent company, to produce the finished products according to a quality-controlled standard, and to maintain such unique quality at all times. . . . In return, the franchising company is usually obliged to provide a variety of supporting services for its franchise bottlers. . . .[24]

These services are in the areas of production, marketing, and management.

The underlying reasons for the continuance of franchising in the soft drink industry are explained thus by Ginsberg:

The bottling business is fundamentally a local one. The vast majority of plants are owned and operated by men who have grown into maturity in their respective communities. Various factors, of which perhaps the outstanding one is the returnable bottle with its refundable deposit, act to limit the profitable distribution radius of bottled beverages from any given site. The uneconomic aspects of bottled soft drink shipment over great distances is another reason. A natural result has been the localization of the business . . . giving it a "sheltered" quality comparable to many of the service trades.

While essentially local in nature, the industry has assumed a national character through the development of the franchise system. The franchise trend—which had its beginnings around 1900—is constantly increasing in importance. There are less than 50 bottlers today who do not own a franchise of some kind and the number grows smaller with each passing year. It is obvious that except in a relatively few instances, the soft drink manufacturer needs the support of brand-name merchandising to successfully compete in the marketplace.[25]

Shih and Shih list seventy-six soft drink franchisors; the major ones include Coca-Cola, Pepsi-Cola, Royal Crown Cola, Seven-Up, and Dr. Pepper.[26]

Ginsberg makes an interesting observation. "It's probably a safe estimate to assume that more than 350 companies have attempted franchising in the soft drink field since the idea was first conceived. Less than 100 exist today. . . ."[27]

To understand franchising it is important to realize that the most successful franchise chains were started by individuals, working initially with little capital but having a zealous, almost evangelical, regard for their products or services and successful experience in operating one or more retail units of the type franchised or in selling the products they manufactured to satisfied customers. For more complete details on this point, one should refer to Harry Kursh's book, *The Franchise Boom*.[28] Large companies, on the other hand, often seem to stumble and falter in trying to start franchise operations, or for that matter, in trying to operate ones that they may have acquired, possibly because of their basic orientation toward production and intermediary buyers rather than toward the ultimate consumer, or retail customers. Despite the astounding financial success of many individuals with limited resources in expanding through the franchise route, there is no doubt in my mind that oftentimes their lack of knowledge in regard to the sound management methods necessary in the larger enterprises which they become, has contributed greatly to the many legal and public relations problems which have been associated with franchising.

The origin and development of the Coca-Cola Company is an early illustration of the successful effort of the individual with limited resources. The formula for Coca-Cola was created in 1866 by John S. Pemberton, an Atlanta druggist, for a beverage to be sold at soda fountains. Asa G. Candler assumed complete ownership of the company in 1891, and in 1899 he granted bottling rights for most of the United States to Benjamin F. Thomas and J.B. Whitehead.[29] The Woodruff family took over the company in 1919.

The Pepsi-Cola Company began similarly just before the turn of the twentieth century. C.D. Bradham founded and headed the company until 1923.[30] In 1968 Harry Kursh noted that the franchise for the Georgia Coca-Cola Bottling Company had been held by one family since 1901.[31]

With the establishment and continued development of franchising in the automotive and soft drink fields, this method of distribution achieved a solid position in American marketing. In the automotive industry the franchise relationship was that between the manufacturer and the retailer, or what I have termed the Type I franchise system. In the soft drink field the association is between a syrup manufacturer and a wholesaler, or bottler, what I have termed the Type II system. The automotive and soft drink industries adopted the franchise method of distribution almost from their very beginnings.

The petroleum industry, on the other hand, represents a field in which manufacturer-owned outlets were supplanted by dealerships franchised by the manufacturers; this type of franchise is quite similar to that in the automotive field.

Until about 1930 the large petroleum marketers owned most, if not all, of their service stations, but they had been having profitability problems with these outlets. These problems resulted in part from price wars in which independently owned stations had a distinct advantage over company-owned and operated stations. That is to say, it was impossible for central management in the giant company-owned chains to set competitive prices in the multitudinous locales across the nation. On the other hand, the small independent operator had great flexibility in this matter. Add to these problems the fact that Iowa and other states were growing increasingly antagonistic to "foreign chains," and conditions were ripe for the establishment of franchising in the petroleum industry.

What was termed the Iowa plan was instituted in 1930, when the first gasoline station was leased to the salaried manager for his independent operation.[32] The practice gained momentum, and by 1935 the movement peaked, when new costs were added to those already imposed on company-owned stations. As large chains, the petroleum marketers were obliged to pay social security taxes and overtime. In addition, Iowa and other states imposed license taxes depending on the number of stores in the chain and an additional tax keyed to gross receipts.

This is what Standard Oil Company (Indiana) reported:

> Our company operated outlets are no longer competitive. Efforts to check declining sales have been unavailing under our present price and discount policies. . . . By placing our stations in the hands of independent dealers and by giving them the flexibility and private initiative of the independent operator, their sales trend should be reversed and our profits increased.[33]

Subsequent to the development of the Iowa Plan in the 1930s, most companies found that independent dealers provided a more effective means for handling the retailing function than did company employees, according to McLean and Haigh.[34]

Gross receipts actually increased 11.78 percent under the franchise plan, and the dealer could work longer hours while bringing in family members.

Definite evidence also accumulated that personal attention to the customers by the dealer was greater than it had been under salaried managers. The franchise system was thus cemented into the petroleum industry.

Since the oil companies already owned the service station properties, they continued to control them even though operators became "independent." One side benefit to the petroleum marketers was the property rentals which accrued to them, and this was income which they had not received when the stations were company owned. This conversion to franchised dealerships had a double-barrel effect on company income: gasoline gallonage and rental income both increased.

Another line of manufacturer-retailer franchising began early, with manufacturers licensing departments in stores. Mode O'Day Corporation is an example; it began to license departments in apparel stores in 1933. This method of franchising single departments in stores has been used successfully in the appliance, radio, and television fields.

Also in the 1930s another type of franchise system developed, in which a wholesaler serves as a franchisor of retail outlets. This is what I have termed the Type III system, and Hall describes five examples in some detail.[35] The growth of these wholesaler-retailer franchise systems was brought about by

1. The expansion of mass discount merchandising
2. The continued growth of corporate chains
3. Growth of shopping centers whose lease requirements shut out many smaller independents
4. Decline of the population of small, country towns and the concurrent decline of independent stores serving these communities

Hall adds, "Compounding these economic, external problems are the historical shortcomings of doing business which are common to small independent retailers."[36]

After discussing several alternatives to these problems Hall goes into what he terms the "most complete answer." "It is through well-run franchise programs that independent wholesalers and retailers have found one of the most complete answers to their problems."[37] Walgreen Co., Western Auto Supply Company, Super Valu Stores, City Products Corporation (Butler Brothers), and Ace Hardware Corporation are five examples of early wholesaler-retailer franchise systems. The five companies illustrate the drug store, automotive parts, food, variety goods, and hardware franchised chains, respectively.

By 1963 Walgreen already had 1,900 franchised drug stores, and company sales were $353 million, having risen from a figure of $182 million in 1953. Western Auto was a pioneer in the franchise field, selling its first dealer store in 1935; Western Auto had nearly 4,000 stores by 1963. Super Valu, faced with chain store competition, started its voluntary franchised operation in 1930.

Butler Brothers was an early operator of franchised variety goods stores called Ben Franklin Variety Stores, and 2,400 units were in existence by 1963. Ace Hardware was another early entry into wholesaler-retailer franchising, with 550 stores and $40 million in sales by 1963 according to Hall.[38]

Independent Grocers' Alliance (IGA) and National Automotive Parts Association (NAPA) were also early initiators of the franchise method in wholesaling: they franchise wholesalers, who in turn may franchise retailers. Somewhat allied, but not strictly franchisors, are the cooperatives Associated Grocers and Certified Grocers of America.

Now let us turn to the franchise boom of the last twenty years. This boom has been in the Type IV franchise systems, or the trade name (service sponsor) retailer systems, of which McDonald's, Dunkin' Donuts, Mister Donut, Kentucky Fried Chicken, Howard Johnson's, Holiday Inns, and Hertz and Avis auto rentals are classic examples. In this system the franchisor has a trade name and a system of doing business, which he licenses, or franchises.

Here is a brief history of probably the first franchised restaurant chain, Howard Johnson's, as provided by Burton M. Sack, vice-president.

> The Howard Johnson Company began in 1925 when Howard D. Johnson took over a debt-ridden drugstore and, with borrowed capital of $500, he turned the money-losing drugstore into a profitable ice cream parlor.

> Within a year he opened his second operation, a beach stand on nearby Wollaston Beach. On opening day, with a 22-foot counter, he sold 14,000 ice cream cones and his second operation turned out to be as successful as the first.

> Three years later—in 1928—the Granite Trust Company in Quincy, Massachusetts, loaned Mr. Johnson $50,000 to open a restaurant on the first floor of the bank's new building. This was his first venture into the restaurant business with waitress and table service and it met with moderate success.

> It was not until 1935 when the next and greatest advance in the company's history took place. At that time there lived in Orleans, Massachusetts—a pleasant, small Cape Cod village—a master mariner by the name of Reginald Sprague. Sprague had been a classmate of Johnson's in grammar school, and he and his family had left Quincy to reside on the Cape, which in those days was approximately eight hours driving time from Boston. In January of 1935, Sprague came to Quincy and had dinner in Johnson's new restaurant.

> He told Mr. Johnson that his father, the owner of a summer hotel in Orleans, had lost some money in recent years and that his father thought that a Howard Johnson's restaurant would do very well on a piece of land which the elder Sprague owned in the center of Orleans.

Johnson, however, had no money to build another store but he was sure that another restaurant would be profitable.

He suggested that the younger Sprague buy the land from his father; build a restaurant; and make his fortune by selling Howard Johnson's ice cream under a franchise from Johnson. Johnson agreed to provide other supplies and to assist in the design, furnishing, and supervision of the new enterprise. In February of 1935, Sprague raised $7,500 and started to build. The store opened in May. A few minutes after the first ice cream was sold, Sprague went below to fix a leaking faucet. A neighbor came down to help him, and said: "The place is crowded Reggy, you are a rich man!" In 1940, *Fortune Magazine* stated that Sprague's restaurant netted him $13,000 a year. (A tidy sum 28 years ago!)

Sprague's immediate success proved two things to Johnson: first, that he had struck on a device to tap private capital; and second, that the profit from franchises—added to earnings of his own restaurants and beach stands—would enable him to expand in his own right.

. . . This double expansion began at once. He granted another franchise to a man in Dedham, Massachusetts; converted an old inn at Middleboro Circle; and built a restaurant in North Weymouth, Massachusetts. By the opening of the summer season of 1936, there were four profitable franchise stores and Johnson's company operated thirteen small roadside stands in addition to his restaurant in downtown Quincy. During that year, Johnson made the decision to convert many of his roadside stands into larger restaurants by adding tables and chairs.

These successes caused a sensation in the food industry. Several vice presidents and managers of the A&P grocery chain asked for franchises and received them. Many men and women who had no experience in the food industry—an electrical engineer, an editorial writer, a doctor, an ex-army officer, an accountant—made their applications. They bought land and put up buildings. By the end of 1936, Johnson opened 39 new franchise operations, and he himself opened only 2 for a grand total of 61 Howard Johnson's restaurants. The next year, 20 more restaurants opened and of these 17 were franchised and 3 were operated by Johnson's company.

At the close of 1938, Johnson had 93 operations and in 1939, there were a total of 107 Howard Johnson's restaurants operating in a half-dozen states. This accelerated expansion could not have taken place if it had not been for the franchising system which Johnson introduced to the restaurant industry.

Back in those days, no payments were made by the franchise agents or licensee operators as we call them today. In 1940, the licensees paid a fee of $1,000 upon signing the contract. Today, they pay $25,000.

Years ago, Mr. Johnson received no other direct payment from his licensee operators. In other words, there were no royalties. His profits came solely from the items which he manufactured and sold to his licensees. This same procedure holds true today. The Howard Johnson Company does not receive any royalties on the sales which our licensees make. Our profits today come from the licensee fee of $25,000 and the manufacturing profit on the items which the licensees buy from our commissary.[39]

Here again was an illustration of a new use for an old marketing technique (franchising), introduced in the early 1930s, during the severe American depression.

The franchise boom in Type IV systems, however, did not begin until the early 1950s, when Holiday Inns, Dunkin' Donuts, Mister Donut, McDonald's, Chicken Delight, and many trade name franchisors got their start.

Wallace Johnson, president, Holiday Inns, Inc., recorded this history of that company:

My business associate Kemmons Wilson and I began building Holiday Inns back in the early 1950's. Together we dreamed about a nationwide system of motor-hotels which could be depended on to give good food, lodging, and services . . . at rates which the American family could afford.

We also wanted to introduce a number of new features . . . including no charge for children under twelve when they share a room with their family. . . .

Our objective was to emphasize guest comfort and convenience.

We built several Holiday Inns in Memphis, Tenn., and they were quite successful. But Kemmons realized that to build this nationwide system, we would have to start a franchise program.

Kemmons and I were both homebuilders. So we invited seventy-five of the nation's leading homebuilders to Memphis to hear about our plan. About sixty showed up. They were enthusiastic. Said they would begin as soon as they got home, and would send their franchise checks for $500 and five cents per room per night for advertising.

But they got busy with other projects and had not caught the Holiday Inn vision. A year later only three of them had made any progress in developing a Holiday Inn.

We kept plugging away and slowly the franchises began to sell. But believe me, it wasn't a landslide!

The system did begin to grow . . . and it developed out from Memphis in a circle. We built our Inns and backed them up with our reservation and referral system.

In the beginning it was simple for an Innkeeper to phone ahead for a guest reservation at the next convenient Holiday Inn.

As we grew and travel patterns crisscrossed, this became complicated. So we set up regional reservation centers, still using telephones. The volume became so great, that we installed a teletype network.

Then in May 1965—some five years ago—our Holidex computerized reservation system was introduced. It was revolutionary. It was the first computerized reservation system in the history of the Innkeeping industry.

By using this network, every Holiday Inn, every Metropolitan Reservation Office and many large corporations with a heavy volume of reservations have instant on-line communication with our Memphis headquarters.

Today a Holiday Inn franchise—which once sold for $500.00—costs $100.00 per room with a minimum of $10,000 and a royalty fee of 15 cents per night or three percent of gross room revenue, whichever is greater.[40]

Although McDonald's hamburg stands were started by members of that family in California, it was not until Ray Kroc founded the *chain* in April 1955 and expanded nationally through the franchise route that this synonym of franchised fast food restaurants became a major factor in the franchise industry. *Time* magazine's cover story in the 17 September 1973 issue starts off with this quotation from Brillat-Savarin and follows it with two sentences that suffice to portray the impact of McDonald's chain:

"The destiny of nations depends on the manner in which they nourish themselves." *The Physiology of Taste.* Jean Brillat-Savarin (1826).

If so, America's destiny manifestly depends to no small degree on the hamburgers, French fries and milkshakes served beneath the arches of McDonald's. Last year the chain of drive-ins and restaurants rang up sales of $1.03 billion, passing the U.S. Army (1972 food volume: $909 million) as the nation's biggest dispenser of meals. . . .[41]

(Incidentally, Holiday Inns, with Kemmons Wilson featured, was the subject of *Time* magazine's cover story 12 June 1972.)

Colonel Harland Sanders is the creator of Kentucky Fried Chicken, and he literally started the operation on his social security check, when a new highway was constructed some distance away instead of passing directly by his restaurant. In 1964 an infusion of new blood—Jack C. Massey and John Y. Brown—started the company into "big time," and a year later they took the company public. Today, Kentucky Fried Chicken, like McDonald's, is one of the largest feeders in the world.

Here is what Colonel Sanders himself had to say about the origin of Kentucky Fried Chicken:

One time we had a fellow who franchised chicken in the rough, and it was too rough to be called chicken really, but he made a couple of million dollars on it, and I knew that. I knew that to be a fact. He had his own private airplane. He had a pilot and a co-pilot, and he was just living in glory. So I said, "Well, he made money on that chicken. Surely I can get mine to go if I tried." The wife and I discussed it. We decided we would sell the business that we had. We tried to sell it at a private sale, but we could not. Everybody else knew the road was going to change? they usually find that out! So, we put it up at auction, sold it, and got enough out of it to pay our bills and leave there clean.

Of course I was only 66 years old then, but I had to live, and I had $105.00 social security. I used it for traveling money. I usually slept in the back of the car wrapped up in a big red blanket to save money so I could buy a cooker for my franchisee the next day, if I happened to have one come along.

Now mind you, I did not sell my franchise. I gave it away, and I would go to a man's store and ask him to let me demonstrate my chicken and tell him how good it was. Well, that was an entrance if his chicken was not good as it ought to be. I got thrown out of more good restaurants than any man in the United States. I never would hit a restaurant with plate glass doors in front because they just would not do. I had to take the little fellows. My numbers gradually grew, but I always had in mind to keep my product good, because we did not fear competition from anybody in the world!

I worked at it faithfully, I knew my job, I knew what I wanted, and all I was getting was a nickel a head on the chicken. Now that came in awful slow, you know, but I got them in the business as quick as I could with as little investment as possible for the franchisee. I bought his equipment for him from the manufacturer, marked it up seven percent and sold it to him. When he got to making dollars, I got to making nickels, and they got to coming in good. I did not have a thing to fear. It was an honest franchise. The franchisee actually had something that he could sell.[42]

So much for these individual firms. "Better indications of the history of Type IV franchising can be obtained from tabulating the year in which 253 firms listed in *Franchise Company Data,* 1968 edition, started. Of the 253 firms, 60 percent started in 1955 or later. There was a sharp spurt in the five-year period 1955-1959 over the prior five-year period, 1950-1954. In fact, in the 1955-1959 period more than twice as many firms began as had started during the previous five-year period. . . .[43] And the franchise companies have continued to increase in numbers. The peak year, 1968, saw the birth of more fast food franchisors than in all previous history.

Fast food caters to a highly mobile customer public, one which is constantly on the move, not only on trips but during the course of the regular day. The growth in this type of franchising is associated with the greatly increased mobility of the housewife, acting as a chauffeur for the working husband and the children and also for herself as an employee away from home. Undoubtedly, the early growth of fast food franchising stemmed from trips on which the tired driver with a carload of youngsters wanted some place to eat for a reasonable price, a place whose name he was familiar with and which would not eject forthwith the bickering family. However, the continued uptrend in fast food franchising during the sixties was no doubt in a large measure due to America's move to the suburbs and to housewives' employment away from home, as well as to a high volume of intercity travel. It would be easy to conclude that Type IV franchising is actually newer than it is. However, *"Franchise Company Data,* published by the United States Department of Commerce, in the 1968 edition, lists sixteen franchise companies which started prior to 1915,"[44] and these were almost all Type IV franchises.

As figure 1-5 illustrates for five Type IV franchise companies, growth between 1961 and 1971 was indeed great. However, not all outlets were franchised.

Special Trends in Franchising

Dual Distribution, Penetration of Central Cities

Many if not most franchise chains engage in what is termed *dual distribution* in marketing circles, or in other words, they maintain company-owned as well as franchised units. In fact, in the decade from 1969 through 1978, depending on the year, from 17 percent to 19 percent of all units were company owned among companies which franchised any units. Variation from year to year was thus quite small, contradicting the claim that companies were generally buying back their franchises, or at least reducing their emphasis on franchising.

However, in the fast food field there was a steady downtrend in the percentage of franchised units for the period 1969-1976.[45] That is, about 87 percent of all fast food units were franchised in 1969, whereas only 74 percent of all units were expected to be franchised in 1976. The last percentage was a projection made by franchisors in 1974. The actual figures developed later indicate that by 1976 the percentage of units franchised had dropped to 73 percent of total units in the fast food field,[46] but this percentage was expected to stay about the same through 1978. Several things were responsible for this trend toward relatively more company ownership in the fast food field. One reason, of course, is the ability of the parent company to exercise greater control over company units; another is simply the greater profitability of company-owned units. Some companies emphasized, however, that they were not reacquiring franchised units but were keeping any new units under company ownership.

Other Special Trends in Franchising

Several other special trends in franchising are worth noting. The first is the growing attention which politicians and law enforcement officials have given franchising as it has developed. The second is the association of public figures with trade name franchising. A third trend has been toward mergers, acquisitions, and public offerings of stock. A fourth is the growth of the franchisee associations (for instance, the National Automobile Dealers Association) and the franchisor group, the International Franchise Association, which, founded in 1959, is rather heavily dependent on Type IV franchisors. A fifth has been the increase in books, articles, and research on the subject of franchising, this latter being primarily the annual studies by the U.S. Department of Commerce.

Worthy of mention is the brief flurry created in accounting circles by the treatment of initial franchise fees as current income in earnings statements, even though certain services promised by the franchisor had not yet been performed and payments by the franchisee had been deferred.

In one way or another, franchising seemingly has always been associated with a high level of legal activity. In fact, according to Hewitt, the franchise device in the automotive field arose in part during the early years of the twentieth century as a means of avoiding liabilities imposed on the manufacturer by the true "agency relationship."[47] Subsequent friction between dealers and manufacturers over the years coupled with an obvious bias of franchise contracts toward the manufacturer led to the "Automobile Dealers Day in Court Act," signed by President Dwight D. Eisenhower on 8 August 1956.

The act apparently had little positive effect, however, until 1970 when the United States Court of Appeals, Second Circuit, affirmed a decision of the lower court which granted the plaintiff (a franchisee) $611,000 because the defendant, Peugeot (the franchisor), had canceled the franchise for unsound reasons. Reverberations of the decision will be quite widespread, according to Tighe.[48]

Other noteworthy court cases in recent years have largely been in connection with Type IV franchise systems. Prominent cases are Carvel, Schwinn, Chicken Delight, Midas Muffler, and GTE-Sylvania, and lawyers have had a heyday injecting shadings and nuances of meanings into the court findings. The outcome of these cases has been, in brief, that the trade name licensor cannot require the licensee, or franchisee, to purchase supplies from the franchisor, except possibly in certain instances (for example, soft ice cream) in the food field. This finding, of course, is so obvious that it should not have required litigation to test its validity. Other controls by the franchisor were struck down by the Schwinn decision. Generally, the findings have been that the franchisor cannot tamper with the external relations of the franchisee, in buying or in selling. Thompson's book is a detailed review of franchise operations and antitrust.[49]

Committees of the U.S. Senate, noting the growing importance of franchis-

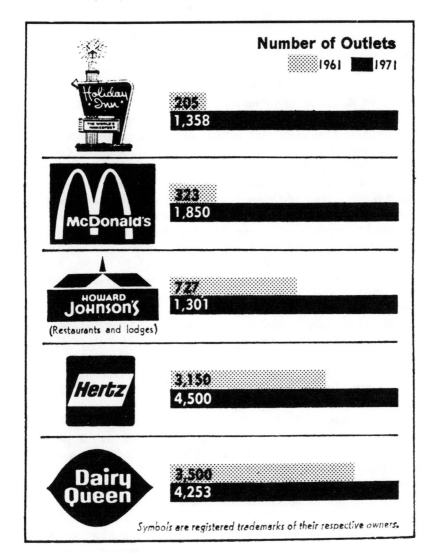

Number of Outlets

1961 ▓ 1971

Holiday Inn: 205 / 1,358

McDonald's: 323 / 1,850

Howard Johnson's (Restaurants and lodges): 727 / 1,301

Hertz: 3,150 / 4,500

Dairy Queen: 2,500 / 4,253

Symbols are registered trademarks of their respective owners.

Source: The New York Times, 28 November 1971.

Figure 1-5. Growth of Five Franchise Companies, 1961-1971. © 1971 by The New York Times Company. Reprinted by permission.

ing, have held several hearings on the subject; Senator Philip A. Hart in 1965 first introduced a bill in the Senate regulating franchise terminations. The bill was redrafted and reintroduced several times since then, the latest occasion being 6 August 1971, but was never passed. After extensive hearings Senator Harrison

A. Williams, Jr., in 1971 proposed the Franchise Fair Practices Act, which would require disclosure by franchisors of a number of items about the franchise, the franchisor company itself, and the principals of the franchisor company. The act was not passed.

Also in 1971 the Federal Trade Commission proposed the Trade Regulation Rule on the disclosure of information during the initial contact between franchisor and franchisee. After many revisions and requests for public comments, the Trade Regulation Rule was finally promulgated in December 1978, as discussed in chapter 4 and appendix D.

State governments have also been active with respect to legislation in the franchise field, as shown, for example, by Krischer.[50] The first and most widely emulated laws are those of California and Washington. These laws require full disclosure by the franchisor to the prospective franchisee. By 1973 eleven states had established regulations pertaining to termination and nonrenewal, and forty-two states had passed laws relating to franchise termination and renewal such as in the automotive and petroleum fields; and the Midwest Securities Commissioners Association in 1975 formulated the Uniform Franchise Offering Circular, which standardizes disclosure requirements for the fourteen participating states, as discussed in chapter 4 and appendix D.

Several other special trends have appeared in franchising in recent years, particularly in trade name franchising. Vaughn noted in 1968 that "the day of acquisitions and mergers is at hand in the franchising field. . . . General Foods acquired Burger Chef Systems; Pillsbury, Burger King; Consolidated Foods, Chicken Delight; United Fruit, Baskin Robbins and A&W Root Beer—just to name a few. In other words, large nonfranchise companies are acquiring smaller franchise companies."[51] Within a few years after these acquisitions Heublein acquired Kentucky Fried Chicken; Pillsbury, Steak and Ale; Royal Crown Companies, Arby's; Pepsico, Taco Bell and Pizza Hut; Pet, Stuckey's; and more recently Dunhill Personnel System was acquired by Canteen Corporation of America, a subsidiary of TWA; Manpower, by Parker Pen Company; Weight Watchers, by H.J. Heinz; and Midas International Corporation, by IC Industries Company.

Some franchise companies tried their hand at acquiring nonfranchise companies, such as International Industries' ill-fated courting of the former Delaware and Hudson Railroad. Small conglomerates of Type IV franchisors rose and fell in the late 1960s—for example, Nationwide Industries, Electronics Computer Programming Institute, and International Industries. Some large, fully integrated companies attempted, usually unsuccessfully, to generate their own franchise companies during the same period, and many of the early franchisors such as Ford and Coca-Cola began to look into the boom in franchising with the fear that they had missed an exciting resurgence of the form of marketing which they had pioneered.

Many public figures from the sports and entertainment world entered the franchise field as principals in the 1960s—Mickey Mantle, Minnie Pearl, Mahalia Jackson, Joe Namath, Arthur Treacher, Fred Astaire, Edie Adams, and others. Without strong product and service support for the names, many if not most of these franchises floundered and disappeared.

Another trend was the founding and growth of franchise associations. Although various soft drink, petroleum, and automobile dealers and manufacturer associations had been in existence for many years, the International Franchise Association was founded late in 1959, and by 1978 it had more than three-hundred members, mostly Type IV franchisors, about a third of whom were in the restaurant field. IFA conducts an annual symposium on legal problems facing franchisors, which has received considerable favorable comment. The association is growing in membership at about 18 percent per year and has an annual budget of well over a million dollars. For a brief period in the late 1960s and 1970s an association of Type IV system franchisees, the National Association of Franchised Businessmen, flourished; but it was superseded by an Illinois group attempting to achieve permanence. The French Franchise Federation is a strong influence in Europe, and just recently a German Franchise Association, with Dr. Walther Skaupy as its first president, was formed. Noteworthy, also, is the recent purchase by the German firm, Wienerwald, of the American fast food franchisors, Lums and IHOP (formerly International House of Pancakes).

Interestingly, Ginsberg states:

Years of growing unrest by the bottlers culminated in the formation of a new national group in 1919 known as American Bottlers of Carbonated Beverages. Today, A.B.C.B. has a membership of more than half of the industry's numerical strength and fully 90 percent of the total production.

It was a time, too, for organization at the local level. Bottlers from Texas to Minnesota, from Georgia to Massachusetts had banded together in mutual cooperation. With the development of A.B.C.B., the state bodies affiliated themselves, retaining their autonomy . . . but looking to the national association for leadership and counsel. There are organized groups in every state today, although some are not as strong as they should be. Some states employ paid executive secretaries to mind the affairs of their members but in many cases a member bottler handles the job with only his clerical expenses paid. There is organization on the regional and local level as well.[52]

Pyramid Sales Plans

No description of franchising would be complete without reference to pyramid sales plans, even though legitimate franchisors, and indeed some "illegitimate" ones, hasten to disassociate themselves from such plans.

The pyramid sales plan is one in which a parent company sells the right to a territory to an individual who in turn has the right (franchise) to sell the right to operate under him or her. The procedure may be repeated in turn at several descending levels, so the base continually broadens from the pointed peak. Thus the term *pyramid sales plan.*

The procedure was used to amass fortunes in the cosmetics field, especially by Glenn W. Turner with firms he named Koscot Interplanetary and Dare-to-Be-Great. Two other cosmetics firms using this approach were Holiday Magic and Bestline Products.

This pyramid method of operation came under severe legal attacks as "fraudulent," "a chain letter approach," "selling securities without meeting the legal requirements for securities sales," and so on. Too great an emphasis was placed on the sale of "directorships" or "distributorships", in a chain letter manner, with little emphasis on supplying consumers with acceptable products.

The attacks on pyramiders made by authorities were finally successful, and this method of operation disappeared, with severe penalties to the perpetrators. One should, however, caution franchisors, franchisees, and others that pyramidal sales plans are only extreme instances: some so-called legitimate franchisors seem more interested in selling franchises than they do in supplying customers with products and services. Fortunately, however, high-pressure franchise sales plans also seem to be on the wane.

Summary and Conclusions

Franchising is a form of marketing or distribution in which a parent company, the franchisor, grants an individual or firm, the franchisee, the right, or franchise, to do business in a prescribed manner over a certain period of time in a specified place. The right may be quite varied: it may be the right to sell the parent company's products, to use his name, to adopt his methods, to copy his symbols, trademarks, architecture, or it may include all these rights. The time period and geographic area may vary greatly from company to company; and the franchise contract (between franchisor and franchisee) may be quite complex and be completely written out. It may, however, be simple and entirely oral. The franchise relationship is akin to but by no means identical with, the licensing and agency relationships. The French term *concession* is synonymous with the American term franchise.

There were more than 1,100 franchise chains and 380,000 franchised outlets in 1978, with sales of $239 billion. The sizable impact of franchising is further illustrated by the abundance of franchised units that dot towns and cities over the nation.

Franchise systems may be grouped into four broad categories in terms of the levels of the distribution chain which are linked by the franchise arrangements:

Type I: Manufacturer-retailer (automobile dealerships, gasoline service stations)

Type II: Manufacturer-wholesaler (soft drink bottlers)

Type III: Wholesaler-retailer (hardware and drugstore chains, automotive aftermarket stores)

Type IV: Trade name (service sponsor), retailer (fast food chains, business aids; the business format type of franchise)

These types can, of course, be broken down into subgroups.

Type I systems accounted for 79 percent of sales through franchise chains in 1978; but the burgeoning of franchises, characterized as the franchise boom, in the past twenty years has largely been in Type IV systems (McDonald's hamburg chain, Kentucky Fried Chicken, Dunkin' Donuts, Mister Donut, Holiday Inns, and H&R Block (the income tax people), among others. However, in 1978 all Type IV systems combined had only 33 percent of all franchise units and less than 11 percent of all franchise sales.

Illustrative of the growth in fast food chains and motels in the ten-year period from 1961 to 1971 was the 563 percent increase in the number of Holiday Inn units and the 758 percent increase in the number of McDonald's units.

In its modern form franchising began in the United States at the turn of the century in the automotive and soft drink fields. The petroleum industry began to franchise gasoline stations around 1930; and wholesalers (Type III chains), their retail outlets in the mid-1930s. The boom in fast food and other trade name franchising got its impetus in the late 1950s.

Reasons vary for the adoption of franchising by the different types of companies during the respective periods—the 1900s, the 1930s, and the 1950s. In 1900 the United States was emerging from an agricultural economy and heading into an economy featuring industrial production. In the automotive and soft drink fields, marketing chores were relegated to franchisees, who were practically given sales rights for broad areas. Demand for products, particularly automobiles, mounted to astronomical levels, and the sales effort needed was nil.

Later, the franchise method was continued by the automobile manufac-turers in order to absorb the shock of the marketplace: for example, in the financing of inventories of new and used cars and in insulating the manufacturer against consumer claims.

However, the production-oriented economy of the first three decades of the twentieth century changed abruptly around 1930, and men out of work or with marginal businesses began to look for new ways to make a living.

Although Howard Johnson began franchising in 1935, it was not until the 1950s that the fast food and other Type IV chains really began to mushroom, and this uptrend continued throughout the fifties and sixties. Formation of new franchise chains from 1955 to 1960 was double that in the previous five years, and growth continued at a fast pace until it peaked in 1968, with probably more fast food companies being formed in 1968 than in all previous history.

One pattern with respect to the origin of successful fast food chains emerges: An individual with marginal economic resources starts a business that becomes quite successful. A friend or relative who has observed the success expresses the desire to start a similar business. His request for assistance is accepted by the innovator, who promises to help the friend get started and to supply him. The friend's business is successful, and the process is duplicated until the originator (franchisor) decides to embark upon a campaign to sell franchises.

Diverse factors contributed to the speed and success of franchising at various times. For example, the deep economic depression of the thirties, which left many talented men jobless or with marginal businesses, undoubtedly contributed to the origin and growth of gasoline station and wholesaler franchising.

Special situations arose, however, among wholesalers and in the petroleum field, and these led to franchising. Wholesalers banded together in a franchise arrangement in order to compete against fully integrated chains which could advertise national and regional brands. Franchised together, wholesalers, too, could advertise national and regional brands. The petroleum marketers were faced with local price wars, several new taxes, and unprofitable stations—a situation which speeded the franchising of stations to local people. In any event, both "labor" and "management" were anxious to experiment with the franchise method of doing business—with anything that gave some hope of success in the depression ridden 1930s. There was no other way to turn, and the technique led to success.

The early 1950s, although not a period of severe depression, did suffer from the aftereffects of United States involvement in the Korean War. Military men came home jobless, and defense industry engineers and others were laid off. Innovation in business was a possible solution to unemployment, and franchising was a type of innovation. Coupled with these factors was the great mobility of the American public: the continuing move to the suburbs, the increased employment of women away from home, and the tremendous highway construction program.

In the rush to franchising, some firms began to place greater emphasis on the sale of franchises than on the sale of products and services to consumers, and as this emphasis increased during the decade of the sixties, trouble ensued. Not only was there misconduct in the sale, or granting, of franchises; there were also questionable practices in their operation and termination. Committees of the U.S. Senate initiated investigations of franchising, states passed laws, and civil suits brought by franchisees against franchisors mounted.

Several other trends occurred in the late 1960s, during the height of the Type IV franchise boom. Public figures from the sports and entertainment fields lent their names to retail outlets in the fast food, clothing, and other fields; food producers bought fast food chains to get into the restaurant market; trade associations were formed by franchisees and franchisors; miniconglomerates of franchisors were formed; many franchise firms went public by selling stock; and publications increased. Most of these special trends were ill-fated, but others have established their permanence.

Curiously, certain of these events that occurred in franchising paralleled the upsurge in the stock market, and the two phenomena seem to have peaked at about the same time, in 1968 and 1969. International franchising in particular, with the United States as a base, is now surging.

2 Marketing the Product or Service

The Role of Franchising in Marketing

Much of franchising's popular appeal results from the spectacular financial success of several Type IV franchisors and franchisees, who started with little or no capital and amassed fortunes, at least so it seemed.[1] Underlying this success was probably in part the built-in creativity of franchising, on which a government publication recently noted: "The remarkable thing about franchising is that it is probably the only form of business entity that, by its very nature, contributes to the creation of new business units."[2]

Actually, however, franchising's classic role is in the so-called marketing mix. Specifically, franchising is that component of the firm's marketing mix which seeks to bring the product or service to the customer at the right place at the right time, whether that product be an automobile, temporary office help, a hamburger, a bottled soft drink, or a tax service. In academic language, this component of the marketing mix which seeks to distribute the product or service where and when the customer wants it, is called the *place* variable, and technical discussion of the subject comes under the heading channels of distribution.

The parent firm may attempt to achieve the place objective in one or several different ways besides franchising—through company-owned retailers or distributors, through units that are jointly owned by the parent firm and the local entrepreneur whether by stock or by partnership arrangements, or through completely independent retailers or wholesalers who may handle a diversity of brands from a wide selection of companies. In fact, the franchise form of integration is probably relatively infrequent compared with these other types of relationships.

Often overlooked by the eager would-be entrepreneur, or prospective franchisee, as well as by the poorly capitalized and possibly inexperienced embryonic franchisor, are the other components of the marketing mix. Again in the language of marketing textbooks, these elements of the marketing mix are designated the four p's: product, place, promotion, and price.[3]

To be successful, the firm must have a product (or service) whose qualities satisfy at least some people (termed the target market), a product which is available where and when the target group wants it (place), one which has its qualities and availability communicated (promoted) to them, and one which is priced in line with their expectations. If properly conducted, the franchising of retailers or wholesalers to sell the product or service aids in getting it where and when the target customers may want it, that is it aids in achieving the place objective; but if the target group does not know about the product, or if the product is priced out of line with customers' expectations, or if the product qualities themselves just do not satisfy customer desires, the franchising of retailers or distributors to fulfill the place requirements will have been virtually useless. Similar statements, of course, may be applied to other types of distribution or channel arrangements, but the other marketing mix variables can assume critical importance to the prospective franchisee who may spend his entire life savings to acquire the franchise, or even to the poorly capitalized and perhaps overzealous franchisor. If the franchise program does not provide proper balance among all four elements of the market mix, the whole endeavor may fail.

The Product

Definition

A vast array of products and services is distributed through franchised establishments, and many more have fallen by the wayside. At this point it would seem wise to define the term *product*, since in technical circles the term has taken on a somewhat broader meaning than it has in popular thinking. First, let us dispense with the term *service*. Hereafter, services will be considered products. For example, the furnishing of temporary office help, aiding with income tax preparation, cleaning out the plumbing, providing travel services, assisting the individual with weight reduction, and so on will be termed products.

Once we have included services under the term product, the next step is simple: a product is not just a set of physical characteristics such as a patty of fried chopped beef, a bottle of colored and flavored water, a collection of glass, pistons, plastic and wheels. A product is a collection of physical and psychological characteristics, qualities or attributes that satisfy certain motives. A McDonald's hamburg is not just the patty of cooked ground beef on a bun; it is also the McDonald's brand name, the arches, the rapid service, the relatively low cost, and all those other things that go to make up the context within which the hamburg is consumed. For example, to some people, eating at McDonald's is a kind of love affair, as reported by David Sampson, writing in *The New York Times*: "But I like McDonald's because they seem to care a little. Maybe it's all business and they really don't. But they seem to, and even that's rare enough these days!"[4]

With automobiles, of course, the service, the warranties, the sales approach, and a host of other things are part of the product. Many studies have shown that people think of a particular gasoline not only in terms of brand name but also in terms of the convenience of outlets, the acceptance of credit cards, cleanliness of toilets, and many other factors as well as the physical composition of the fluid itself. In fact, most people are probably ignorant of the physical components, although many attempts have been made to sell that extra special ingredient.

It is because of the importance of these other features of the product that franchisors generally insist that the franchisee follow the demonstrably success-ful practices of the franchisor in such meticulous detail, particularly in the Type IV franchises. Franchisee failure to understand the meaning of the term *product*, the importance of the factors that enter into the target group's acceptance or rejection of the product is often the basis of franchisor-franchisee conflict and may ruin the franchise system by clouding the customer's image of the system's product.

Of course, this failure to understand or at least to deal with the features of product success is not limited to franchisees. For example, target groups may not distinguish between products with variations in ingredients, such as the quality of flour in doughnuts, the amount of plain syrup in the soft drink, and the amount of filler in pies, and if the maintenance of overly refined standards is quite costly, there is room for disagreement between the parties affected. On the other hand, hidden elements in the auto or other machinery often contribute to the safety and durability of the product even though target customer groups may not be immediately aware of them. The parent firm must assess the importance of these factors and produce specifications accordingly, even though the local entrepreneur, the franchisee, may be tempted to profit for a short period and then withdraw from the business. Some franchisors have done the same thing, and prospective franchisees must be alert to possible entanglements with such characters.

The Life Cycle and New Products

One phenomenon in marketing that many people fail to understand is that products, like people, have life cycles. Although different products have different life cycles, a common example can be pictured as an S-shaped curve. During its introduction and for an initial period, the product gains acceptance (new customers) slowly. This slow catching-on period is followed by a sharp increase in consumer acceptance, and profits may seem to soar. Then the rate of growth slows and sales level off; for some products they may actually decline as competition intensifies. During one or more stages of the life cycle new products should be introduced to maintain the firm's position.

Most marketing textbooks cover the subject of new products and the life cycle thoroughly, but it is an especially delicate problem in franchising because the franchise arrangement is so difficult to change, for good reason. But store buildings (and they are part of the product) lose their attractiveness, the decor of signs becomes obsolete, peoples' food tastes change, package designs lose their appeal, package sizes must be altered, car designs and performance standards change. Too often, the franchise arrangement is formulated without proper—indeed in many instances without any—regard for life cycle. The prospective franchisee should be cognizant of potential changes; the franchisor should have anticipated them in his corporate planning, if not at first, then early in his corporate existence.

In the early stages of franchising, appreciation of the fact that products have life cycles was seemingly totally absent, and many conflicts ensued when buildings deteriorated and costly renovations had to be made, menus had to be altered, new products came aboard. Franchisees did not see the need for spending the money necessary to implement the indicated changes. In some cases, franchisees felt that the changes should be subsidized by the franchisors. Some franchisors gave up in despair and withdrew from franchising in favor of company-owned establishments, not solely because of the difficulty in making the changes, but nevertheless due to the strong impetus provided by this problem.

One major change indicated because of recent attention to potential energy shortages and high costs has been the trend toward self-service gasoline stations. These have presented many problems with franchisees. Another change (not due to the energy situation) was the elimination of distributors, or wholesalers, in the automobile field. Still another was Coca-Cola's need to introduce so-called flavors a few years ago—a term used in the trade to designate orange, grape, lemon, and other drinks besides Coke itself. Antedating flavors was Coca-Cola's introduction of the large bottle, a new product as defined herein and one whose introduction produced great debates in the Coca-Cola Company. Perhaps as a sideline, one should note that the introduction of new products may require consultation with the government. For example, the Coca-Cola Company, in test marketing its Nu-Maid, an acid-reduced, frozen concentrate orange juice, had to obtain permission from the Food and Drug Administration, originally in 1975 and again in 1978, for an extension of the earlier permit.[5]

The need for product changes and additions has been rapid and broad indeed in the fast food field. For example, McDonald's, Burger King, and others recently introduced breakfasts in at least some test stores (but as *Business Week* noted, they ran right into a jump in commodity prices—for orange juice, for bacon, and for coffee in particular).[6] A spokesman for Burger King gave as their reason for introducing breakfasts in test stores simply the need to optimize their hours of operation.

Changes at Howard Johnson's were headlined thus in a recent article in *The Wall Street Journal:* "Howard Johnson Giving Its Restaurants and Menus New Look in Bid for Rebound."[7] In brief, the new look involves "a trendy new restaurant replete with wicker chairs, chandeliers and eggs benedict . . . ," and it was estimated that the new look would cost the company some $15 million to

$20 million annually for several years. Two years earlier *The Wall Street Journal* had noted that drive-in windows were becoming the rage, with Burger King, Kentucky Fried Chicken, Gino's, and others leading the parade, but following some like Jack-in-the-Box (not a franchise) that had started with them.[8]

McDonald's, of course, has always been very conscious of product and has tested many new menu items, signs, architecture, and methods of preparation. Their "close-to-the-customer" approach providing feedback for needed changes among other things, is illustrated by "store-day" for company executives. It was pictured and described in *Time* magazine as a day in which the executives, including Ray Kroc, the founder, and the president and other top executives waited on customers and thus sampled first-hand what goes on at the point of customer contact.[9] Although McDonald's has not yet marketed chicken nationally, they test marketed it for several years in a limited number of places and worked closely with a meat packing company to develop cooking methods to satisfy the palates of target customers. McDonald's widespread marketing of chicken would introduce strong competition for Kentucky Fried Chicken, but then Wendy's had introduced competition for McDonald's by taking aim at a target group of older customers with "hot and juicy" hamburgers. Product competition is a fact of the marketplace which must be taken into account in planning so that new products will be coming out to occupy a dominant position as long as possible.

New Product Testing

The words *product testing* or *market testing* have appeared frequently in the prior discussion and deliberately so. In the early days of Type IV franchising it was not uncommon for people to come in with what they termed "a hot franchise with great potential," "a chance to get in on the ground floor and make a fortune." Further inquiry often revealed that the product was actually in its incipient stages, a gleam in someone's eyes so to speak, but the budding franchisor was so enthusiastic about the product that his listeners caught the bug and became enthusiastic, too. Long before trial units had been opened franchises were being sold, not only for individual sites but for whole chunks of the nation. Trying to dissuade the franchisor or the franchisee, for that matter, was viewed as unimaginative and indeed almost sinful. The thought of trial testing the concept was just beyond the boundaries of people's thinking.

This overly enthusiastic acceptance of new product ideas was, of course, not confined to franchising. Not so long ago, in fact, many fully integrated large companies embarked upon the marketing of new products without field testing, and it was not until many new products approved and indeed enthusiastically supported by experienced corporate personnel dismally failed that companies began testing new concepts in the field, under actual conditions of purchase and use.

At first it was thought that test marketing in one or two places such as Syracuse, New York, and DesMoines, Iowa (favorite sites for test marketing) was sufficient to indicate whether the product would be accepted. Now as many tests as possible in as many different places as possible, particularly with foods, are considered desirable before a broad-scale marketing program is embarked upon for a new product.

It is difficult to convince many neophytes in franchising, particularly those with a presumed new idea, that they should try out their ideas before selling them. Would-be purchasers of franchises to sell the products are often difficult to restrain from buying the franchise and get started—perhaps because of greed, but seemingly many times out of affliction with the contagious enthusiasm!

A recent lead article in *The Wall Street Journal,* however, should tend to rein in the hyperenthusiasts.[10] The heads read thus: "Success Comes Hard in the Tricky Business of Creating Products. Marketing Experts Help Sift Ideas, Weeding Out 99% and Garnering Big Fees." It is noteworthy that the lead says "Weeding Out 99%". "Booz Allen & Hamilton, a giant management consulting firm, says that it commonly considers 100 ideas before finding one that can succeed in the marketplace."[10] Other companies in this business report similar results. So it is questionable whether the neophyte can bring out a new product that will be successful without even a trial test, but even experienced persons are taken in by broad and untested claims in the franchise field. Although many franchise companies have tried, few have been able to come up with a second successful franchise.

Before proceeding to the next *"p"* in the marketing mix, I would like to emphasize that the franchisee in a successful chain profits by being a member of that chain, by having a product that has demonstrable consumer acceptance, including a brand name which in itself will pull in customers and by having an organization with special capabilities for developing new products with the costs being spread over many units, depending on, of course, the size of the chain. The franchisor, in turn, profits from being able to spread his risks over more units and to add new units speedily at relatively low cost, that is to achieve the *location* objective in his marketing mix. He does not have to have the capital that would be required if he were to expand with company-owned units.

Promotion

Now let us turn to the second *p* in the marketing mix, *promotion*. Promotion is not in any way subordinate to product. The four elements in the market mix interact, and no one is more or less important than the other.

Definition

Promotion is that element of the marketing mix which is concerned with communicating to the prospective customer, or target group of customers, what product is available, its qualities, where and when it is available, and at what price. Promotion may take the form of personal selling, mass selling (or advertising), sales promotion, and public relations, including publicity.

Promotion is a key element in the marketing program of a firm which franchises, and most franchisors require the franchisee to contribute to a national pool for advertising, and some pressure franchisees to participate in sales promotion programs as well. Membership in a chain permits the franchisee to obtain the assistance through the franchisor of specialists such as the giant advertising agencies that he would not have access to as a small entrepreneur.

Personal Selling

Everyone is familiar to some extent at least with personal selling, ranging from the forthright approach of the stereotyped salesperson to the indirect approach of the president-to-president contact for selling the big-ticket items. Franchising covers so many different product lines that all degrees and types of selling may be required in one franchise company or another. Many companies feel that the franchisee should be a sales individual, and some evidence has accumulated that the sales-minded entrepreneur is indeed likely to be more successful than, say, the production-minded small businessman.

In the automotive field personal selling of cars is quite important, at least compared with selling a hamburg across the counter, although the sales approach implied in a pleasant smile, a friendly hello, and an extended hand may encourage the customer to return when he would not otherwise do so, and there are tested sales sentences that evoke surprising results even at the counter for small-ticket merchandise. On the other hand, bigger sales such as catering events with ice cream cakes or Big Macs, obtaining a company president's recommendation that his firm obtain office help from a certain temporary help firm, or selling a contract with a firm to acquire all of its real estate for transferred employees through a certain franchised agency, inducing conventions or meetings to come to the establishment—all of these things require considerable aptitude for selling. Most of this selling is provided by the franchisee, and it is incumbent upon the franchisor to select franchisees with the capabilities required along these lines or at least to train selected franchisees insofar as possible. If the franchises become large enough, as in a hotel, the franchisor must employ someone, a functions manager for example, who can perform the required sales job. Many training firms are available in this field: the American Management Association, the National Restaurant Association, and the American Marketing Association conduct seminars in this and related fields.

Mass Selling, Advertising

Once a product with demonstrable consumer acceptance and a business format have been developed, the next step is to communicate to the target group of customers what is available, where it is sold, when it is there, and at what price. Of course, as soon as the franchisee hoists a well-known sign such as Holiday Inn's, McDonald's, Howard Johnson's, Buick, he has begun to tell his story to the masses. But many potential customers simply do not pass by the units, particularly if the franchisor is just beginning to expand or if, as in the case of specialties such as cleaning home plumbing systems, furnishing temporary office help, or supplying roadside brake service, the target group of customers never sees the signs.

The mass selling of the product is known as advertising, and this may be classified in many ways. One classification is national or regional versus local advertising; another is product contrasted with institutional advertising. One may also classify advertising by the medium in which it appears: television, radio, magazines, newspapers, billboards, telephone directories. Another grouping might be in terms of type of appeals, whether designed to push the product through hard-sell appeals and unique sales propositions or to create an atmosphere conducive to the eventual sale of the product.

Mass selling is a highly specialized function, and it is probably in mass selling that the franchisor can be of greatest assistance to the franchisee. Not only can the large franchisor attract employees with the necessary specialized experience in advertising, but the big franchisor can attract the larger and more effective advertising agencies. Even though the franchisor may delegate responsibility for local advertising to the franchisee or his local association, the franchisor can still fulfill the important role of guiding and counseling the local people with regard to their advertising, for example, with respect to budgets, media, appeals, and frequency. Much of the franchisor's counseling may be in advising the franchisee what trend the company's national advertising will take and how the franchisee or association of franchisees might tie into it locally.

Advertising by Large Franchisors

Most people are aware of the advertising of General Motors cars, of Coca-Cola's soft drinks, of Firestone's general merchandise. These companies are among the earlier types (I, II, III) of franchisors. But the newer franchises (Type IV), particularly the fast food franchisors, have also created an enviable awareness. To do so, they have had to spend tremendous sums of money, and this expenditure is not just a recent thing. For example, according to *Restaurant Business*, "During an average week in 1973, McDonald's placed 2,471 commercials on spot TV, Kentucky Fried Chicken used 1,210 television spots, and Burger King 739."[11] These television expenditures ($60,000 per minute on television) produced sizable jumps in sales.

More than thirty food service franchisors were in *Institutions* magazine's top 100 companies in dollar volume of sales in 1977, and it was estimated that McDonald's Corporation, the leader with more than $3 billions in sales in 1976, had an advertising budget of more than $60 million; Burger King had about

$900 million in sales, with an advertising budget of about $30 million.[1 2] These big figures had to be handled by big advertising agencies, too: McDonald's by Needham, Harper, and Steers; Burger King by J. Walter Thompson Company.

Characteristic of large advertisers is the adoption of a central theme ("Have It Your Way" for Burger King, "You Deserve a Break Today" for McDonald's) and often a character, a spokesman such as Ronald McDonald or Burger King's new Magic Burger King. Such characters have a special appeal to children, although the eminently successful Redi-Kilowatt seemed to have a universal appeal.

The adoption of a theme makes it possible to measure the effect of the advertising simply by asking representative cross sections of target groups to recall who advertises a particular theme. The percentage of people who correctly name the sponsor indicates how well the advertising is penetrating, especially if the measurements are repeated at periodic intervals over the course of the campaign. If a random cross section is sampled, one may also break the results down by age, sex, and so on to determine whether the targeted groups are being reached and with what degree of penetration.

The battle for "the kids' minds" between McDonald's and Burger King, with television programs on Saturday mornings is heating up,[1 3] and the trade press is full of stories about the advertising war between the two fast food franchising giants. Lest one overlook some of the lesser known firms, it should be observed that other Type IV franchisors are notable advertisers, too. For example, Dunkin' Donuts introduced commercials nationally with Mason Reese, the ten-year-old television personality, as a spokesman in 1976. Convenient Food Mart began sponsoring spot television commercials on national game shows in March 1976. Foote, Cone & Belding, one of the nation's largest advertising agencies, introduced the "pizza eating experience" in its first campaign for Pizza Hut, later a giant in the field. Gino's steak and hamburg chains spent about $6 million on advertising through Lewis & Gilman and Weightman in 1977. In 1976 Wrangler Ranch sportswear embarked upon an advertising campaign to convince people that "Wrangler thinks Americans should get what they pay for and when you see the name Wrangler you know you are going to get your money's worth." (As is not unusual in this business, however, Wrangler switched advertising agencies from Altman, Stoller, Weiss to Doyle Dane Bernbach in 1978.)

The preceding discussion will provide the franchisee and beginning franchisor with some indication of the topics that have or will come up in connection with the mass selling, or advertising, of the product. Now let us turn to a more detailed study of how a particular firm goes about advertising.

Case Example in Promotion: Convenient Food Mart

Nature of the Franchise

Convenient Food Mart (CFM) is a franchised chain of neighborhood convenience grocery stores which as a class have more or less supplanted the earlier

Mom-and-Pop stores.[14] Convenient Food Mart stores are two thousand to three thousand square feet in size with ample parking. The stores are open 365 days a year from 7:00 a.m. until midnight. According to the *Franchise Opportunities Handbook*, stores stock complete lines of top-name national brand merchandise normally stocked in a chain supermarket (except fresh meat requiring cutting at store level).[15] In the greater metropolitan Chicago area, stores are franchised directly by the parent company. In other areas CFM franchises regional territories to a subfranchisor under a licensing agreement who, as an independent contractor, in turn franchises stores to individuals. The regional franchisor selects locations, negotiates with investors to build the stores, and takes a long term lease, subleasing to CFM owner operators.

In 1978 there were eight hundred stores throughout the United States. The company had been in business since 1958. From eighteen thousand dollars to twenty-five thousand dollars in capital was needed by the franchisee, with financing, training and managerial assistance provided by the franchisor.

Total Sales

Sales of Convenient Food Mart stores for the year 1977 were $356 million, with an increase expected for 1978. Approximately 90 percent of the company's sales were franchisee sales, with very few of the stores being operated as company-owned units either by the parent company or by subfranchisors.

Advertising Expenditures

Advertising expenditures for the year 1977 were in excess of $3.7 million, or 1 percent of sales. Most of this amount, the media portion, was spent locally by the licensed regional franchisors with the parent company providing the radio and television production, newspaper advertising layouts, reproduction proofs, point-of-purchase kits for special promotions plus coordination of national sales events.

Advertising Agencies

For radio and television, the advertising agency was Fessel, Siegfriedt & Moeller, of Louisville, Kentucky. For print media, the agency was David Johnson & Associates, of Crystal Lake, Illinois.

Media

In general, print media are used: direct mail color circulars, black-and-white newspaper advertisements, and window posters. In addition, radio is used in about 70 percent of the company's marketing area and television in about 50 percent of the area.

Advertising Message

Convenient Food Mart considers their stores a sturdy hybrid, that is a cross between the supermarket and the usual convenience store. Their stores are bigger than most convenience stores; they stock a larger variety of brand name products, and they tend to be more competitive in their pricing; yet they offer the convenience features associated with convenience stores: convenient location, convenient hours, and fast, friendly service.

They would like each store to be known as a place where consumers can get most grocery items they need at almost any time they need them and still receive good value for their money. Convenience, quality, good selection, friendly service and fair price are the recurring themes used in the company's advertising. The selection and fair prices are dramatized in their product promotions, such as breakfast values and cookout time specials.

Sales Promotion Activities, 1977

The parent company provided advertising layouts and merchandising suggestions for twenty-six advertisements during the year 1977. (Advertisements are run every other week with the sale in effect for two weeks.) In addition, elaborate point-of-purchase kits were provided for the following seasonal promotions: Cookout time (summer), back-to-school (fall), Halloween, Christmas holidays, and breakfast values (February). The promotional package included free book covers for distribution at the stores during the Halloween promotion.

Illustrative Advertisements

Figures 2-1, 2-2, and 2-3, are miniature advertising layouts which give a better idea of the type of print advertising that is used locally. The ad miniatures are sent out to the regional subfranchisors approximately four months prior to the ad date. The final advertising art (in eight-column and five-column sizes) is mailed to the subfranchisors four to six weeks prior to the ad date.

Other Cases Summarized

Another company with about twenty-five hundred franchisees and a total gross of about $2.5 billion, spent about $11.4 million on advertising in 1977, that is,

Figure 2-1. Miniature Advertising Layout: Convenient Food Mart

Figure 2-2. Miniature Advertising Layout: Convenient Food Mart

Figure 2-3. Miniature Advertising Layout: Convenient Food Mart

approximately ½ percent of sales. The company does all of its advertising out of its own in-house agency and makes no direct charge to franchisees, but the company owns about 60 percent of its total stores, and they account for about 60 percent of sales; franchise sales were about $1 billion in 1977. The breakdown by media was as follows:

Television	$4.1 million
Radio	3.5 million
Newspapers	0.375 million
Outdoor	0.035 million

Production and miscellaneous expenses accounted for the balance of the advertising budget.

A special jingle runs through all their advertising, and two characters (employees) supply the same distinctive voices on radio. The attitude, or mood, that the advertising attempts to create is that the store is convenient and a fun place to shop. (Advertising of this nature helps not only with the customers but also with employees who consciously or unconsciously make the theme self-fulfilling.) The company spent about a half a million dollars on market research in 1977, designed to measure the registration of advertising with potential customers and their purchase of the products advertised. The research is also aimed at developing a profile of the customers.

Still another company, Midas, describes their promotional activities thus in a paper for prospective franchisees: "Midas has both a national and local media advertising effort to promote specialization, the Midas guarantee, expertise, completeness of inventory and speed of muffler installation by Midas Muffler Shops. In addition, radio, newspaper, and outdoor billboard ads are used to create awareness of a new Midas Muffler Shop in a community. Grand opening promotional materials are available when a new shop opens together with press releases and other promotional suggestions." (This opening promotion is very important, and most franchisors supply material and personnel assistance at this critical juncture in the business.)

Promotional Budgets

Many companies have policies against the release of budgets and strategies, and the larger ones would be difficult to evaluate in any case. (Moreover, trading intimate details with competitors may bring antitrust action.) The prospective franchisee, however, should be aware at least of what the parent company is doing in promotion, for a variety of reasons. Planning by even small franchisors should certainly include budgets for promoting the product. There are many ways in which the budgets can be determined, but the best way seems to be first to set certain objectives in terms of, say, target group awareness of products, when and where available, and at what general price level. The objective may be to achieve targeted gains in product sales through outlets in a given area; or the aim may be to attain a certain share of the market. Advertising expenditures should then be budgeted to achieve those measurable objectives.

Unfortunately, in some companies during the early days of Type IV franchising in particular, franchisees were assessed a certain percentage of gross sales (for instance, 4 percent) for product advertising, and then the money was used by the parent company to promote the sale of franchises. To be sure, as distribution of a product is expanded and word-of-mouth reports on the establishments spread, there is a promotional effect, assuming that the product is a good one and that the people-to-people reports are favorable. But advertising funds obtained to promote products would seem to be diverted to the franchisor's self-serving ends when used to sell franchises. Ultimately, moreover, neglecting the promotion of product is as damaging to the franchise system and the franchisor himself as it is to the franchisees who feel that funds are being misused and that the franchisor is in business to take the money from the sale of franchises and run, much as was done in some pyramid sales plans.

Advertising is a broad and complex topic. The neophyte should seek the counsel of experts when faced with decisions in this important branch of marketing. Textbooks cover the subject in great detail, and there are government publications that may be of some help to the entrepreneur. One is a publication by the Small Business Administration, *Advertising Guidelines for Small Retail Firms.*[16] The retailer might profit from perusing it.

Sales Promotion and Publicity

Two other promotional activities intimately tied to advertising are sales promotion and publicity. Although most franchise advertising is directed toward an increase in sales, the term *sales promotion* has a rather specific technical meaning. It covers point-of-purchase displays, booklets and leaflets, premium offers, direct mailings, things that make the advertising and personal sales activities more effective.

Publicity, on the other hand, relates to an activity of a firm designed to communicate things about the firm or its products to target groups without the use of paid advertising. Usually news releases are planned to complement the advertising events, perhaps publicizing the opening of a new store, the marketing of a new product, the changing of the company's logo or its signs, the firm's lowering of prices, celebrating an anniversary. Publicity is often included under public relations, although public relations activities as such in many firms are confined to fire-fighting activities such as countering adverse reaction to the opening of a fast food unit, reacting to claims of environmental pollution, answering charges of selling foods with poor nutritive value, or calling the public's attention to bad laws proposed and enacted. Both sales promotion and publicity can be very effective. Interestingly, sales promotion seems to be costly, and publicity appears cheap.

Illustrations of sales promotion activities by franchisors are many and varied. In 1975, for example, McDonald's celebrated its twentieth anniversary by selling its hamburgers for their original fifteen-cent price. (By 1975 their price had risen to more than thirty cents.) Sales promotion of this nature has to be backed up by publicity and advertising. In another instance, McDonald's gave away glasses as a premium. Since these were an extra cost for the licensee, his participation was optional, and licensees in certain tourist centers considered it unwise to join in the promotion since they would be giving away glasses to tourists who would merely take their business to their home units far from the site of the giveaways. The home units would be reaping the rewards, and licensees in tourist spots would be footing the bill.

Other premiums are offered in other franchise chains: in one chain, free coupons to important persons invited their trial of a product free as a guest; in another chain, each customer was presented with a piece of cake amidst great fanfare to celebrate the company's birthday. Still another firm offered door prizes; International House of Pancakes started with free iron-on patches and five-foot growth charts for children under twelve; Holiday Inns offered free use of their hotels in sunny climates to those who stayed twenty-five nights or more in their motels. In some motels, dressers in the rooms had prominently displayed pictures of luscious dinners and other items promoting the patronizing of their dining rooms. Dutch Pantry Family Restaurants display folders listing the locations of their restaurants. Howard Johnson's sold ice cream desserts in small baseball helmets that the kids could wash and take along with them. The number and variety of these sales promotion items is endless. There are many firms called specialty advertising companies in the business of supplying premiums and other sales promotion items to merchants. There are also associations such as the Direct Mail Association and the Specialty Advertising Association which bring together people interested in the field. The American Association of Advertising Agencies has just recently prepared a treatise on sales promotion techniques.

One survey that I recently did indicated that sales promotion activities may result in friction between the franchisor and the franchisee. The franchisor may apply some pressure to obtain the participation of franchisees who do not see the value, or profit, in the particular sales promotion, at least to them. Of course, others may object to any sales promotion activity at all since the premiums cost money; ones who object the most may be those whose profits are marginal, and they may be just the ones who need a boost such as might be provided by a sales promotion effort. Other franchisees may favor the sales promotion but object to the high price of the premiums. The parent company, or franchisor, usually favors participation by all members of the system to insure maximum impact; moreover, the price of the premiums which the franchisor may buy and then merchandise to franchisees is lower with a higher volume of purchases. The local or regional franchisee association or advisory board may be of great assistance in supplying group opinion as to the efficacy of the promotion. Franchisee advertising advisory boards operating at the national level may also be of some help in specific situations; the growth of these national advisory boards has been of great help in minimizing franchisor-franchisee friction and suspicion which formerly existed in connection with advertising assessments. The problem does not exist in fully integrated, or company-owned, chains, even though local management may complain about the deals from headquarters. Corporate or regional headquarters rather than local management is responsible for the final decision, depending somewhat on the degree of decentralization of management.

Pricing

The third p in the marketing mix is pricing and in this area the franchisor-franchisee relationship may run headlong into antitrust laws. Franchisees are independent businessmen, and as such it is illegal for them to connive with each other or with the franchisor to set prices. To be sure, automobile manufacturers are required by law to put the familiar price sticker on every new car that goes out as a guide to the consumer, but the local dealer, a franchisee, does not have to sell at that price, and the trade-in gives him wide latitude in what he finally charges. However, if the manufacturer tried to force the dealer to sell at a certain price and the franchisee went along with it, that would be termed "resale price maintenance" and is illegal per se in the United States. (For many years fair trade laws did provide for resale price maintenance but these have been repealed in the United States.) On the other hand, in Germany, for example, vertical price restraints are not illegal as of this writing, but horizontal collusion in setting prices is forbidden.

There are many theories of pricing, and the choice of one is not as simple as it might seem. The generally accepted theory that the charge should be the firm's costs plus a reasonable profit fails to take into account what the customer might pay, how stiff the competition is and will be, and what the costs will be a few months hence, as changing prices every few weeks or months is not a good idea.

The franchisor can help the franchisee determine his costs and point to inefficiencies in his operation that may lead to unduly high costs. The franchisor may furnish operational statements of company-owned units and other franchised units to guide the franchisee not only in operating efficiently but in setting reasonable prices. One reason for the quick success of fast food restaurants has undoubtedly been the reasonable pricing of meals or snacks (in contrast, for example, with the high prices in atmosphere restaurants), and facts of this nature should undoubtedly be a guide for the franchisees. That is, although the inclusion of pricing as an item in the franchise agreement would be illegal in the United States, the pricing of products sold by members of a chain is undoubtedly an important aspect of the customer image of that chain, and it must be taken into consideration by the franchisee. In actual practice, franchisees probably use the prices posted by company-owned units (in the final analysis these are competitors) as guides in setting their own prices, just as they would prices of competitors outside the chain.

Of course, the acid test of the pricing is the bottom line over some period of time, usually a year. If the unit does not operate at a profit, prices must be changed if the unit is operating efficiently. Whether prices can be changed rests on consumer acceptance, and that is why pricing is such a key element in the marketing mix.

Various theories of pricing are treated in marketing textbooks such as McCarthy's *Basic Marketing*[17] and will not be repeated here, but some other things about pricing are peculiar to franchising. The most important of these is simply that both pro forma and actual operating statements often show the net results of the operation for a period (month, year) without allowing the owner-operator and his family a salary, and as a result the statements indicate a much larger return on investment than is actually the case. Considering that the typical small retail business requires the owner to work sixty hours a week and his family to put time in the business, too, an operating statement that does not allow something for this time spent is very misleading as to the actual costs involved and to the return on investment. The alert potential franchisee should note in pro forma operating statements whether such unspecified costs exist and allow for them.

Of course, the operator of any small business, franchised or not, may be misled as to the success or profitability of his business by comparing his year-end net with his investment without including family salaries. As a result, some entrepreneurs who consider themselves financially successful in their businesses might just as well invest in government bonds or other comparatively riskless undertakings and go fishing. Their return on investment would be just as great. However, there are some counterbalancing and somewhat concealed factors, factors that cannot be given a very accurate weight in the operating statement, for example, the charging of automobiles, and even in some enterprises, homes, and other quasi-business costs to operating the business. Many, if not most, small businessmen literally live their businesses so that the practice of charging these normally personal items to the business is not quite the tax evasion that it first may seem. So much for the role of pricing in the marketing mix in the franchise situation.

Place

Channelling, or placing the product where the customer wants it when he or she wants it, is the *place* component in the marketing mix, and that is the whole story of this book. Franchising is a method of expanding in order to channel, or place, the product where the target group wants it at the time the target group wants it. It is a way of maximizing in the shortest time at the least cost the number of people whose demands, or motivations, will be satisfied.

But, to repeat, franchising merely to achieve the place objective will not in itself be sufficient to guarantee successful marketing unless the other three components of the marketing mix, product, promotion, and price, are effectively handled. To be sure, franchising is unique in that it systematically creates new businesses, and the creation of new businesses is in itself good to the American way of thinking. But disregard for product, promotion, and pricing in the pursuit of franchise sales can only lead to failure, and, as a matter of fact, to the pyramidal types of operation which have met with disaster.

The place element of the marketing mix (and franchising specifically) is intimately tied in with real estate problems and will be treated in more detail in the chapter on real estate. As has been indicated in earlier paragraphs, the place element is discussed in academic circles under the heading channels of distribution, and will not be covered at this point in great detail. It suffices to repeat briefly the earlier discussion. A supplier, or parent firm, has a product (including a service and all that surrounds the product as the term is used herein) and asks himself through what channels it will be best to try to reach the target markets. He may answer the question by deciding to distribute through franchised retail outlets, as a thousand or more firms have so decided in the United States alone, or he may decide to combine franchising with company ownership of some units and have dual distribution. In other situations he may decide to own all retail outlets; or he may take his product only so far as the distributor, or wholesaler, as in the Type II (soft drink bottler) franchises, and let the franchised distributors market to retailers. The franchisor may still (and usually does) promote the product to the ultimate consumer so as to assure that target groups know about the product and "pull" it through the channels by their constant requests for it. In the Type III systems the franchisor may act only as a distributor, or wholesaler, and franchise retailers as in the Type I and IV franchises.

Summary

The marketing of products entails a market mix comprising four major components, known as the four *p*'s: product, promotion, price, and place. These four elements must be combined to form an effective marketing program, and although franchising has probably gained its popular appeal because it creates new businesses, its primary role in the marketing mix is helping to achieve the place objective for the product.

As used herein, the term *product* applies to services as well as physical products, and to all the imagery, or purely psychological attributes, associated with the physical characteristics of the product—including the architecture of the store, the packaging of the item, its brand name.

When Type IV franchising started to expand rapidly in the early 1960s, franchises were sometimes offered on the basis of concepts only, without demonstrable product acceptance among target groups of customers. Also, the life cycle of products was ignored so that costs associated with renovations and new product development and testing created franchisor-franchisee friction when these costs had to be allocated. Franchisors found that the franchise contract could be a rigid instrument when new products were to be introduced or costly renovations were to be made. On the other hand, the franchise firm can spread costs of developing new products over many units so that the individual franchisee is not overburdened with these charges.

Another *p* in the marketing mix is promotion, which covers personal selling, mass selling, or advertising, sales promotion, and publicity, or more generally speaking, public relations. Production-minded people may develop an antipathy toward advertising, and franchisees often resent the costs associated with the premiums they are asked to buy for sales promotions. Sometimes franchisors seem to take advantage of franchisees in overcharging for sales promotion premiums and in using product promotion funds to sell franchises, but franchisee councils, advisory boards, and associations can help prevent such problems. It is probably in the field of advertising that the franchisor can be of greatest assistance to franchisees, through national television programs after a critical point has been reached in the size of the chain, by attracting the larger advertising agencies, by employing the necessary specialized personnel, and by guiding franchisees or associations in their advertising at the local level, and by properly tying it in with the national or regional campaigns.

Marketing the product also requires the setting of a price for which it will be sold. The franchisor cannot, in the United States, at least, determine the price at which the franchisee will sell his products, but the franchisor can assist in determining costs and in maintaining operating efficiencies that affect those costs. Franchisor studies can also shed light on what consumers will pay for products, and company-owned units' practices in pricing will have a competitive effect on the franchisee's prices. One factor in franchisee costs that is likely to be ignored is the time that the manager or owner puts in beyond the financial investment that he may have in the operation. The alert prospective franchisee and the ethical franchisor will not interpret the money remaining after costs have been covered to be profit or return on investment if the costs do not include reasonable compensation for the owner's time. Some upward adjustment in pricing may actually be necessary to provide adequate compensation for the owner-operator's work on the job.

Finally we come to the place component of the marketing mix. The franchising of retail or wholesale operations is one way to achieve place objectives. There are other ways as well: through company-owned establishments, through partnerships, through joint ownership of stock, and through distributing to completely independent retailers who may carry an assortment of brands and quality levels. The advantages and disadvantages of franchising will be covered in more detail in the next chapter, and the chapter on real estate will go into more detail with regard to achieving the place objective. But it should be emphasized that the viewing of franchising as one means of achieving place satisfaction in the marketing process does not detract from its uniqueness as a systematic means of creating new businesses.

3

The Advantages and Disadvantages of Franchising to the Franchisor and Franchisee

To the Franchisor

The large company with a product or service to sell has many distribution channels open to the general public, or the market. Which channel or channels should the company select? Franchising is one alternative. Yet the little fellow with an idea, a product, or a service may not have so many options. Franchising, in fact, may be his only choice, unless he wishes to cast his lot with a big company or expand at a slow pace.

Likewise, the person who wants to enter business as an entrepreneur and has sizable funds as well as business experience can choose one of several alternatives. One alternative is an appropriate franchise. On the other hand, the fellow with limited funds and experience may find a particular franchise to be the only thing open to him. There is thus a wide range of circumstances, or conditions, which must be considered in discussing the advantages and disadvantages of franchising.

In evaluating distribution channels open to General Motors, Alfred P. Sloan noted two alternatives, namely: "manufacturer-owned, manager-operated dealerships, or the selling of cars by anyone and everyone, as cigarettes are sold—with the manufacturer maintaining a system of service agencies. . . ." He concludes, "I look askance at either of these changes. I believe that the franchise system, which has long prevailed in the automobile industry, is the best one for manufacturers, dealers and consumers."[1]

Hewitt summarized thus the basic distribution needs of the automobile manufacturers:

In summary, the basic distribution needs of the manufacturers were: (1) some rapid means of acquiring retail outlets requiring a minimum of attention, outlay, and fixed expense; (2) some means of making their cars conveniently available for customer inspection in advance of purchase on a nationwide basis; (3) some means of coping with the repair problem; (4) some means of coping with the off-season storage problem; (5) some means of acquiring a ready market for their goods without having fixed legal commitments for delivery; (6) some means of acquiring cash on delivery or even in advance if possible.[2]

61

These needs which Sloan contended franchising fulfilled so well were·those of manufacturers of big-ticket items, and the needs were and are present in the appliance, as well as in the automotive, field. ·Franchising has in fact been adopted successfully in the appliance field.

Franchising has not been successful in the furniture field, with possibly one or two exceptions; yet in the United States furniture seems to possess many characteristics similar to those of automobiles and appliances. Perhaps the absence of mechanical parts needing service, together with the long-established domination of retail outlets by local entrepreneurs and a low premium on brand name, have militated against the franchise method in the furniture field. On the other hand, franchising of furniture stores has been very successful in Europe, particularly Levitan and Conforama in France, and one would expect it to be in the United States eventually.

The distribution needs facing the U.S. oil companies in the 1920s and early 1930s were quite different from those of automobile manufacturers. The oil companies already had chains of gasoline service stations across the nation, and the companies generally owned the real estate. The stations were unprofitable, to a large extent because of local price wars. Without computers and modern communications devices, it was all but impossible for central management to make appropriate price decisions. Compounding this situation was the local opposition to chain networks which developed in the United States as the Great Depression of the thirties set in; special taxes were imposed on the chains. Moreover, collective bargaining and other labor-favoring measures were instituted.

Franchising was adopted as the solution to these problems, but the problems which motivated franchising in the petroleum industry were unique. The fact that the parent companies already owned the stations permitted them to retain control over the leases and, to that extent, over the franchisees. In other words, the petroleum marketers were able to incorporate certain aspects of franchising which others starting to franchise are now not able to do. Thus, when one considers the relative advantages and disadvantages of franchising, it should be kept in mind that different kinds and levels of franchising can be adopted.

In brief, franchising accomplished the following in the petroleum industry, and these may be construed as advantages of franchising:

1. Franchising permitted franchisees to adjust prices in line with the competitive situation locally and to make other decisions appropriate to the local scene, for example, the franchisee, or "owner" could work whatever hours were required, other family members could be brought in, or the franchisee could do his own work around the station (repair jobs on the station, for example) that he might not do as a hired manager.

2. Franchising made it necessary for labor union organizers to deal with a number of independent stations and entrepreneurs rather than with one central management owning units across the nation.

3. Local taxes such as those imposed on company-owned chains were avoided.
4. And rental income from the stations accrued to the parent companies. This income was not there when the units were company owned.

So these were the advantages of franchising to the petroleum marketers, and they were able to retain considerable control over the units through property ownership. The original franchisees were, in fact, formerly managers for the companies. Thus franchising was for the oil companies a middle ground between completely independent dealerships and chains of fully integrated company units.

When one considers the advantages and disadvantages of franchising to the prospective franchisor, it is necessary to review several things before arriving at conclusions: (1) the current stage in the life cycle of the company considering franchising, (2) the alternatives open to the company, (3) the type and extent of franchising possible, and (4) the type and size of the product or service that will be the nucleus of the franchise. (The prospective franchisee should also consider the alternatives and, in particular, the risk in relation to the expected returns.)

Advantages of Franchised over
Company-Owned Operations

Senior executives from nine companies (eight well-known franchise companies plus one other) spoke at the Boston College Franchising Conferences on the advantages and disadvantages of franchising, and six of the nine executives pointed to the fact that franchising is a way to secure capital.[3] Hewitt also pointed to this virtue of franchising in his study of automobile franchising.[4] Less capital is required by the company that expands through franchising: the franchisees furnish the capital. The franchisor can use his capital for other purposes.

Five of the nine executives pointed to the increased motivation which the franchise system instills in the local manager by evoking the profit incentive and through the binding nature of the investment in the operation.[5]

Various other advantages of franchised over company-owned units were advanced by one or two executives. For example, Robert E. Bennett indicated that economies of scale in purchasing could be achieved much faster by a small company expanding through the franchise route.[6] The cooperative advertising dollar could achieve much more than the dollar spent by an individual unit alone; and the franchising of wholesalers, which received great impetus in the 1930s, was stimulated by the small wholesaler's need for some means of competing against the fully integrated chains.

According to Richard J. Boylan, the franchised unit, because it is locally owned, also arouses less hostility in the community.[7] The franchisee is not considered a link in a foreign chain but a local citizen. He is likely to be more cognizant of and responsive to local ordinances, tax assessments, and realty evaluations.[8] As a local resident known as the owner he can handle local authorities better.[9]

The company manager is interested in the showing on the books each reporting period; whereas the franchisee takes the longer-term view. He expands as the need arises, for example, and makes repairs immediately.[10] Curiously, the franchisee as an owner of a unit commands better the attention of company management. They listen to his suggestions for improving the system,[11] and as partners franchisees contribute to other aspects of the business. They are the grass-roots link to the buying public.[12]

One franchisor noted that franchising enabled him to devote more time to improving the franchise program itself.[13] Rapid expansion through company-owned units requires the development of sizable management structure, a problem which was just too big for one company.[14] Central management capability is just too difficult to build up for a fully integrated chain. One executive noted[15] that company-owned units across the nation require a mountain of paper work—lawyers to organize corporations, bank accounts, a multitude of contracts, personal property financing, annual meetings, the qualifying in all states where operating, and so on. Franchising avoided many of these burdens.

Labor relations is another area in which franchising provides an advantage. The franchisee can handle individual employees as he sees fit, but company-owned units across the nation are an invitation to labor organizers' confronting central management.[16]

If the parent firm's choice is between expansion through franchising and no expansion at all, the franchising route can provide income that otherwise would not be present—income from franchise sales and royalties.[17]

Advantages of Company-Owned over Franchised Units

Six of the nine executives discussing the subject at the Boston College Franchise Conferences stated that company-owned units are more profitable to the parent company than are franchised units.[18] As one authority put the matter, "the money's at the retail site."

The parent company also has more control over the units, according to three of the company executives.[19] With corporate ownership it is simpler to test and evaluate new approaches.[20] Management has greater flexibility with a company-owned chain.[21] They can move in any direction and exploit the market potential with a changed selling strategy if desirable.[22]

Also, in the vertically integrated chain there is better feedback,[23] and cumulative experience can be exploited. This feedback enables the development of management personnel.[24]

Several comments were made with regard to the attitudes and capabilities of company managers and franchisees. Franchisees, of course, must have the money to buy the franchise, and since the amount may be substantial, only the older people qualify. On the other hand, the company may recruit aggressive, imaginative, and ambitious young people as managers.[25] Also, franchised operators are too easily satisfied with a "satisfactory level of income," and taper off when that is reached.[26] Then too, after a year or so they are likely to balk at the payments.[27] On the other hand, they are likely to be too impatient for success, thinking that the franchisor has some sort of magic wand to wave for success.

On the financial side, one executive pointed out that the cost of capital secured from franchisees is exorbitant.[28] The franchisee's initial investment, he maintained, should be recovered by him in two or three years. That means a 33 1/3 percent—50 percent return on investment! This is pretty expensive capital for the franchisor. He could probably get the money easier and much cheaper directly from lending sources.

In addition to the high rate of return on capital which the franchisees might be led to expect, he pays royalties, perhaps a mark-up to the franchisor on the landlord's rental charge, and other charges which theoretically, according to one authority, would make the franchise operation unsound.[29] There are also special types of retail operations probably not suited to franchise operations because the financial requirements are too high for Mom-and-Pop operators but too low for the syndicate investor.[30]

As a final advantage of the company-owned fully integrated chain, one authority pointed out that all services required in the company-owned chain are also needed in the franchise chain—large consumer marketing, market research, computerization, central accounting, plus a franchise sales department.[31] The costs are thus greater in the franchise system than in the company-owned system, and more effective use can be made of these services in the company-owned system.[32]

There are also some legal advantages in the fully integrated operation.[33] The integrated chains do not so often come under antitrust fire, class action suits, and other legal attacks. In the past few years legal entanglements in franchising have become so involved and costly that would-be franchisors have been scared off from this type of system.

In all, however, a combination of company-owned and franchised operations appears to be superior to either alone.[34] The two are supplementary, stimulating growth and strengthening each other.

To the Franchisee

Alternatives Open to Potential Franchisees

Much has been written about the advantages and disadvantages of franchising to the franchisor and to the distribution system in general. But with two or three exceptions,[35] relatively little has been written about the advantages and disadvantages of franchising to the franchisee. It is important for the individual who is considering the acquisition of a franchise to fully understand these advantages and disadvantages—in particular, the merits of acquiring a franchise in comparison with those of other alternatives that may be open to him.

Among the alternatives which may be open to the potential franchisee are the following:

1. The purchase of a going business in the manufacturing, wholesaling, or retailing field from an owner who wants to dispose of the business.
2. Starting a business from scratch in one of these lines, without the aid of a franchisor.
3. Securing a salaried job with a small or large company in one of these lines.
4. Acquiring a franchise from a franchisee.
5. Acquiring a franchise from a franchisor.

Franchising Concentrated in Retailing Recently

Making broad generalizations about whether acquiring a franchise or operating alone is more advantageous to the individual is likely to be hazardous. For example, franchise offerings are pretty much confined to the retail field. If the individual wants to be in manufacturing, the opportunity to obtain a franchise is practically nonexistent; there are, though, a few opportunities for acquiring franchises in wholesaling, but they are quite limited. Currently, franchising is pretty much confined to the retail field, and if one wishes to enter manufacturing or even wholesaling, he practically has to eliminate the franchise route.

Broad Selection in Retail Field. Within the retail field, however, there is a wide variety of business classifications in which franchises are currently being offered, and the person to whom one type of franchised business has no attractions may find another to his liking, a situation which ordinarily just does not exist for nonfranchised businesses.

For example, among the many business classifications in which franchises have recently been offered are fast food or restaurant operations; accounting services; agriculture; art galleries; automotive accessories, parts and products; automotive repair services; auto, trailer, truck rentals; automotive transmission repairs; auto washes, products, and equipment; beauty and slenderizing; building and construction; business services; campgrounds. Rather extensive directories of franchise companies are available for those who wish to make a thorough study of franchise offerings. Among these are the *Franchise Opportunities Handbook*, published annually by the Department of Commerce, and the directory published annually by Pilot Industries in New York. Thursday's *Wall Street Journal* and Sunday's *New York Times* specialize in franchise advertising.

The question, What are the advantages and disadvantages of franchising? should be rephrased thus by the individual contemplating the acquisition of a franchise: What are the advantages and disadvantages to me of this particular franchise over the other ways in which I can operate? The International Franchise Association has published a handbook designed to assist prospective franchisees in evaluating franchise offerings, *Investigate before Investing.*[36] The Department of Commerce's *Franchise Opportunities Handbook* also lists questions that should be asked about the franchise before buying it.

Five Advantages to Franchisee. Generally speaking, franchising has these advantages to the franchisee:

1. Most (but not all) franchisees in the business for a few years are happy with their positions, due in a large measure to the generally satisfactory level of franchisee income and the feeling of independence.
2. In starting a new business, the franchisor usually provides experience, or know-how, gained from starting other businesses successfully. The franchisor usually provides on-the-job and classroom training to the inexperienced franchisee.
3. The franchisor is a continuing source of know-how to the franchisee.
4. The franchisor usually brings to the retail unit an accepted trade name that not only attracts customers but also provides the unit with a niche in the community and easier access to credit, for example.
5. In general, franchisees feel independent; they run their own show.

Four Disadvantages to Franchisee. Following are four disadvantages of franchising to the franchisee:

1. Services provided by the franchisor are an expense item to the franchisee, and in some instances, at least, the services are of dubious value.
2. The rather high level of satisfaction of the majority of franchisees is offset in a significant percentage of franchises by dissatisfaction often resulting from the franchisor's not performing up to initial promises, by marginal incomes, and by a felt lack of prestige in the position.
3. Misleading and fraudulent franchise sales practices victimize some would-be franchisees.
4. The value of the trade name is questionable in certain business classifications. In those in which repeat sales at frequent intervals are sought, customer satisfaction with the product or service soon becomes much more important than the name or banner under which the establishment operates.

Experience of Franchisor in Starting in
Business, Including Initial Training

A major advantage of the franchise over other alternatives is that the franchisee ordinarily acquires the know-how of the franchisor in successfully starting and operating similar businesses. Starting the retail business usually requires

1. Obtaining credit
2. Selecting a site
3. Drawing architectural plans for the building
4. Employing the builder and supervising the construction
5. Selecting (and perhaps designing), purchasing, and installing fixtures and equipment
6. Training on the job and occasionally in the classroom
7. Preparing for and opening the unit for business, including advertising and publicity
8. Operating the unit for the initial break-in period.

If the individual starts the business on his own without a franchisor, he has to do these things himself; whereas, if he buys a going business, most of these items are eliminated, although the buyer should certainly know why the owner wishes to dispose of the business. And the sales price for the going business may be out of line with earnings. Initial training may just not be available to the person who acquires a nonfranchised business.

On the other hand, there are many degrees and types of assistance that are actually provided by franchisors or that are really needed. For example, many franchises do not require free-standing buildings: remodeled storefronts are sufficient, and in some instances, the business can even be operated out of the franchisee's home or a building otherwise vacant most of the time.

However, the value of the assistance provided by newly organized franchisor firms may be dubious; franchisor personnel, particularly in new ventures, may know little more about the requirements of starting a business than does the would-be entrepreneur himself. In other instances, the franchisor may be too busy with other things—such as selling franchises—to provide sufficient help to the neophyte, and would-be entrepreneurs with a business education at the undergraduate or graduate level may be able to do about as well after observing and possibly working for a short period as an employee in one or two establishments.

Moreover, many suppliers, particularly large companies in the restaurant field, provide a great deal of help gratis, so to speak, to induce the entrepreneur to buy from them; and consultants are often available at a fee for those who wish to go it alone. It is difficult to assess whether the fees charged, explicitly or implicitly, by the franchisor are greater than what the cost would be for providing one's own services before and during opening; but the meager evidence available seems to indicate that failure rates of new franchisees appear to be much less than those for persons starting on their own.

Experience of Franchisor in Operating
the Establishment

A second major advantage of acquiring a franchise over starting or purchasing a going business which is not a member of a chain is the franchisor's continuing assistance to the franchisee after the unit opens. This assistance may range from the franchisor's providing a sympathetic ear to the providing of monthly and even daily merchandizing aids such as those furnished in the highly successful Baskin-Robbins chain for the sale of ice cream; from introducing the franchisee to sources of credit, to sources of supply, to the handling of "teenage hangout problems." Cooperative purchasing for most or all franchisees by the franchisor may also reduce cost of supplies and guarantee a source of supply, although possible violation of the federal antitrust laws is a hazard here.

It is easy for the entrepreneur to overlook or disregard the value of these types of aids, but no one appreciates their value more than the most successful businessman or professional person. For that matter, such individuals may pay an outside consultant just to come in occasionally and to suggest whatever he deems appropriate.

Also, well-established and large franchisors have the resources to employ specialists in the different aspects of the business: in advertising, accounting, purchasing, operations, merchandising, and indeed, the research of food technology and the market. On the negative side, perhaps, is that assistance costs money, and the franchisee who has operated his establishment successfully for a few years may fret at what he considers an exorbitant continuing payment to the franchisor, a payment subtracted from his own profits. Then too, this payment may continue without any visible continuing services whatsoever–at least to the franchisee paying the bill! And he may feel, perhaps justifiably, that the central or even regional office experts are much more attuned to the national picture and their own profits than they are to the realities of his local situation.

After a few years of operating the business and performing all the functions necessary to it, the entrepreneur, at least the successful one, does indeed become an expert in the many functions necessary to the success of the small business. In fact, this opportunity to learn and perform almost daily these diverse functions is probably one main attraction of small business entrepreneurship, whether it be franchised[37] or wholly independent, as opposed, for example, to employment in a large firm or the government.

An Accepted Trade Name

The well-known and accepted trade name of the franchisor may be the most valuable asset which the franchisor brings to the franchisee. Not many consumers, for example, are unfamiliar with the name Howard Johnson's, Holiday Inns, Kentucky Fried Chicken (Colonel Sanders), Hertz, Avis, Budget Rent-A-Car, U-Haul, Chevrolet, Ford, Plymouth. Put one of these names on a big sign over a store, and the unit already has customers (and probably an easier path to credit).

The traveler–a tired, hot tourist with a carload of screaming fighting children, and perhaps a "snappy" spouse–knows that a Howard Johnson's sign means a standard menu, uniform prices, and no need for a jacket. But the standardization of the architecture, menus, procedures, operating policies, and so on requires constant vigilance, inspection, and policing by the franchisor. A sloppy establishment operating under the franchisor's banner in one place may, for the patrons of that place, conjure up similar images elsewhere. This policing may be distasteful to some franchisees and a disadvantage of franchising to them.

There is a wide variation in the amount of policing that franchisors do, and the franchisee may be paying for a service that he is not getting; in many cases, the trade or brand name may not be a particularly valuable asset. In fact, the assessment of the value of trade and brand names is a difficult matter. Surely, if the retail outlet sells to local customers only, the value of a national name is questionable except perhaps for purposes of introducing the unit. If the products or services sold are items that are purchased and used at frequent intervals by the same customer, he will soon choose them on the basis of taste, family appeal, price, regardless of the brand name. Of course, national advertising may be a help in bringing in new customers locally and possibly even for holding some customers, but the franchisee may be paying for something (the trade name, the advertising) which is of little value to him.

In the late 1960s and early 1970s the wave of "celebrity franchising" swept the country: celebrities were linked with franchise chains or systems in diverse fields. Undoubtedly the names of these sports stars and entertainers attracted great attention to the franchises with which they were associated—initially, perhaps a great advantage. But for various reasons, probably largely because of inexperience of the operations people in the franchised businesses, many of the units either failed or never opened, and a wave of unfavorable opinion toward them (and, indeed, franchising in general) ensued.

Thus, even though the celebrated names were proven commodities, the managements themselves were not, and the enterprises often resulted in catastrophes. The magnetism of the celebrity names called attention to a more serious situation than would have been the case without the attraction. Thus an advantage, particularly a widely known name, can emphasize the disadvantage (inept management, poor product, or poor service, for example). An old adage in advertising applies to this situation: The quickest way to kill a bad product is to advertise it widely!

Empirical Studies of Franchising

It is a relatively simple matter to theorize about the advantages and disadvantages of franchising to the franchisee or the franchisor, for that matter, and to do so with some validity if the theorizing ensues from expertise acquired over the years through observation and labor in the field. Such theorizing may, however, lead to erroneous conclusions, but there have been five empirical studies of franchising which bear on the advantages and disadvantages of franchising to the franchisee. These are studies by Vaughn,[38] Ozanne and Hunt,[39] McGuire,[40] and Walker.[41] (Plus a study by Vaughn, reported for the first time here.)

The Vaughn 1969-1970 Study

Vaughn (1969-1970) made personal telephone interviews with top executives in 116 franchisor firms from a total of 136 franchisor firms in six types of fast food chains which existed in 1968—chicken, hamburger/hotdogs, pizza, roast beef, assorted sandwich, and seafood establishments.

An indication of the cost of franchisor services to the franchisee in these fast food chains in the 1969-1970 period may be obtained from the following findings of the Vaughn study:

1. Ninety-two percent of the franchisors reported that they charged a continuing royalty fee. Average: 3.0 percent-4.8 percent of gross sales.
2. Eighty-nine percent of the franchisors charged a franchise fee. Average: $5,950-$11,540.
3. Seventy-three percent of the franchisors obtained revenues from renting or leasing the land or building. Average fee not reported.
4. Seventy percent of the franchisors obtained revenue from an advertising assessment. Average: 1.3 percent-2.6 percent of gross sales.
5. Sixty percent of the franchisors obtained revenues from sale or lease of equipment. Average fee not reported.
6. Forty-seven percent of the franchisors obtained revenues from the sale of food products. Average fee not reported.
7. Thirty-nine percent of the franchisors obtained revenues from the sale of paper products. Average fee not reported.[42]

Thus the initial and continuing services and other things provided by the franchisor are not without cost to the franchisee. On the other hand, 97 percent of the franchisors in the Vaughn 1969-1970 study reported that fewer than 5 percent of their franchisees failed, and 92 percent reported that fewer than 10 percent of their franchisees were even moderately unsuccessful.[43] Although these reports came from franchisors, whose thinking might understandably be biased, they do provide some empirical evidence for the value of the franchisor activities.

The Vaughn 1975 Study

Face-to-face personal interviews were made with the owners of 224 small retail businesses in eighteen Greater Boston suburban communities in late spring 1975 by thirty-five upperclassmen and graduate students in courses in franchising under my direction. Interviewers followed a four-page questionnaire with four types of proprietors, three franchised types and one independent group, namely: gasoline station proprietors, automobile dealers, owners of other types of franchises, and a matched group of independents.

An attempt was made to determine the reasons for the respondents' starting or acquiring their businesses. The usual pattern that emerged was for the proprietor to have worked in the business and finally to have acquired it. However, automobile dealerships seemed to pass down through the family somewhat more often, and in nonautomotive franchises the proprietor was generally looking around for a business and settled on the current one, apparently relying on franchisor training and assistance during the initial stages, at least, to offset his lack of experience with the particular operation.

Although proprietors generally reported that they had to rely on themselves to solve their problems, operators of franchised units most often named their franchisor, or parent firm, among outside sources, as being of greatest assistance to them in solving their problems. Among nonfranchised units, suppliers and banks were named the most often as outside sources of greatest help. Suppliers and banks—and accountants and lawyers in certain types of franchises—were also listed near the top by franchisees.

According to the franchisees, franchisor help had extended across the board to the many specific things necessary to starting and operating the business. But assistance by accountants, banks, and lawyers was largely limited to their professional areas. However, franchisor assistance was most often provided in the areas of product or service promotion, franchisee training, and the providing of operations manuals and sales kits.

Franchisees were asked what two sources of franchisor help were of greatest value. Franchisor advertising was most often listed as being of greatest value by two (gas stations and others) of the three franchisee groups. Automobile dealers, however, listed the product first; advertising was second with them. Franchisees also frequently listed franchisor company name and training as being of greatest help to them.

Conversely, the single most frequent complaint of franchisees against franchisors was poor or inadequate supervision, which was named by one in every three nonautomotive franchisees but hardly at all by the automotive franchisees. Automobile dealers and gasoline service station operators more often pointed to overly aggressive sales policy and the high price of gasoline. About one in seven of the franchisees pointed to too many controls.

The nonautomotive franchisees were asked whether their royalty payments were too high, too low, or about right. Of those who made royalty payments, sixteen replied too much and thirteen about right; none replied too little.

Many franchises are not structured around a royalty payment as such; the franchisor (for example, practically always in gasoline stations and automobile dealerships) obtains his revenues from sale of product. As discussed earlier, petroleum marketers also obtain revenues from station rentals.

Median sales figures reported for gasoline stations were $190,000 per year; for automobile dealerships, over $500,000 per year; for other franchises, $300,000 per year; and for independent proprietors, $170,000 per year.

More than half (52 percent) of the gasoline station proprietors reported annual personal incomes of $25,000 or more; and more than three-fourths (81 percent) of the automobile dealers reported $25,000 or more per year. The *median* incomes for other franchisees as reported were $20,000-$25,000 per year, and for independent proprietors, $15,000-$20,000 per year. (Incomes of more than $25,000 per year were not broken down in the questionnaire, and precise medians could not be computed for groups with more than 50 percent of their members reporting more than this amount.)

These income figures appear high, but all four groups reported they worked sixty to sixty-nine (median) per week, and spouses and children also worked in the business in a significant percentage of cases.

Despite some complaints about the franchise, an overwhelming percentage (80 percent or more) of the franchisees reported they would buy the franchise again. Reasons for wanting to buy the franchise again were largely the *result* of the excellent income, although the reasons did cover a broad spectrum.

The Ozanne and Hunt Study

Ozanne and Hunt (1969-1970), conducted a study of franchising at the University of Wisconsin; the study was sponsored by the Small Business Administration. They surveyed by mail 800 franchisors in the fast food, convenience grocery, and laundry and dry cleaning fields and received mail replies from 146 firms, or 18.3 percent of the universe; concomittantly, mail surveys were made of 3,927 franchisees, of whom 986, or 25.1 percent, replied.

In brief, their findings pertinent to the matter of advantages and disadvantages of franchising to the franchisee are as follows:

1. The median family income for fast food franchises in 1969 was $16,000. . . . Over 10% of the franchisees were existing at a semi-poverty level of less than $5,000 in 1969 and, at the other extreme, 18% made more than $30,000. . . .
2. Data from 67 systems show that 72.5% of the franchises earned less than the "minimum expected." . . .
3. Fast food franchisees work long hours. The median franchisee worked sixty hours per week. For a married franchisee with two children living at home, it would not be unusual for the family to work over 120 hours per week in the franchised business—60 by the franchisee, 35 by the spouse, 25.5 by the children. . . .
4. Over half the franchisees believe they have "almost complete responsibility

for" five of the seven areas: hours of operation, bookkeeping, local advertising, pricing, and number of employees. Even in the other two areas (menus, standards of cleanliness) franchisees perceived themselves as having significant control. . . .

5. Eighty percent of all franchisors charge a royalty. . . . Royalty payments range from a low of 1.0% to a high of 18.0% of gross sales. The median royalty fee is 4.0% of gross sales.[44]

Although responses from franchisees of convenience grocery stores in the Ozanne-Hunt survey were too few to provide reliable indications, results from franchisors would suggest that franchisor controls in this field are much tighter than they are in the fast food field.

Summarizing briefly then, the Ozanne-Hunt study would indicate these to be advantages of franchising to the franchisee:

1. The family income for fast food franchisees is high: Median $16,000 in 1969.
2. Franchisees feel very strongly that they are independent.

These might be considered disadvantages of franchising to the franchisee based upon the Ozanne-Hunt study:

1. The franchisor's sales pitch is likely to be misleadingly favorable to the franchise (leading to false expectations and dissatisfactions with the franchise).
2. Fast food franchisees in particular work long long hours. (As most proprietors in the food field probably do and in other fields, whether franchised or not.)
3. The median royalty payment by franchisees to franchisors was 4 percent of gross sales, a percentage which is not negligible since it is before profit.

The McGuire Conference Board Study

In 1971 the Conference Board published a report on franchising; it was the result of a survey by staff member E. Patrick McGuire, who based it on mail questionnaire returns from 189 franchisor companies and 437 franchisees.[45] The returns represent mailings to approximately one thousand franchise companies and more than six thousand franchisees. Additionally, telephone interviews were made.

The median franchisor estimated that his franchisees averaged a yearly net profit of $15,000-$20,000.[46] This estimate is in line with that of the franchisees in the Ozanne-Hunt study and would appear to be rather high for the period in question, and an advantage of franchising to the franchisee. "On the other hand," McGuire states, "A number of franchisees are operating on perilously close profit margins"—certainly a disadvantage to them.[47]

Almost half of the franchisees in the McGuire study (actually 45.2 percent)[48] reported their net income to be less than the franchisor's initial projection, as contrasted with only a fourth (24.5 percent) who reported income above the franchisor's original projection.

"Cooperative advertising support, or the payment of a promotional allowance, though very much welcomed by most franchisees, is for some a source of friction."[49]

More than half (51.3 percent) of the franchisors in the McGuire study reported that the annual failure rate among their companies' total outlets was less than 1 percent, and 59.6 percent of the fast food and beverage franchisors so reported.[50] Perhaps subject to less unconscious (or conscious) bias on the part of the franchisor is the overwhelming preponderance (81.6 percent) of franchisors in the McGuire study who reported an annual franchisee turnover rate of less than 10 percent. (Among gasoline service stations this rate may be 25 percent-30 percent.)[51]

The Walker Study

Walker's doctoral dissertation at the University of Colorado (1971) was a mail questionnaire survey of 1,146 franchisees in five chains: rental centers, employment agencies, home-and-auto stores, automotive maintenance and repair shops, and limited-menu restaurants. Usable questionnaires were returned by 319 franchisees. Certain advantages of franchising to the franchisee may be inferred from the following results of the survey:

1. . . . More than three-quarters of franchisees were generally satisfied with present position, while less than one-tenth were considerably dissatisfied. . . .
2. . . . most franchisees considered themselves independent businessmen rather than employees or semi-independent businessmen—at least to the point of having sufficient decision-making authority and operational freedom. . . .
3. The social and autonomy needs were satisfactorily gratified for most franchisees; the esteem, self-actualization, and security needs were deficient for most. . . .[52]

In nontechnical language, these statements mean simply that

1. Franchisees generally like their positions—at least those who replied in the Walker study.

2. Franchisees responding in this survey considered themselves independent.
3. However, franchisee respondents in this survey did not feel secure, nor did they feel they were highly regarded by others—the latter possibly because they were so autonomous that they could not compare themselves with others as to the amount of prestige and esteem connected with their positions.

Franchisee satisfactions tended to be derived from "excellent income and/or profits, and being own boss."[53]

The most common sources of dissatisfaction were poor financial return, lack of support from the franchisor, and prospects' being oversold. Apparently, franchisees' satisfaction with their franchises is heavily dependent on the materialization of expected improvements over the last positions which they held and the realization of promised rewards.

A weakness in inferring the advantages and disadvantages of franchising from these findings, as well as those of the other three studies is the lack of comparative data from nonfranchised businessmen and even from salaried employees of large and small firms. Nevertheless, the results do tend to confirm the contention that franchisees feel independent, they do well financially, and they are satisfied with their position. Unique to franchising, however, would be the feeling on the part of some franchisees that financial returns are not what they were promised and that franchisor support is inadequate. On the other hand, poor financial return, pointed to by some franchisees, might equally well apply to employment for wages and to proprietorship in nonfranchised establishments!

With respect to methodology of the studies it should also be noted that there were larger percentages of nonrespondents than respondents in the Ozanne-Hunt, McGuire, and Walker mail surveys, and no results are available for the nonrespondents. The Vaughn study was a personal interview telephone census of all known firms in the six categories of fast food operations which were investigated, and respondent cooperation was very high: completed interviews were obtained with more than 80 percent of the predesignated firms.

Conclusions

Broad generalizations about the advantages and disadvantages of franchising to the franchisee are hazardous, and the individual should ask himself, "What are the advantages and disadvantages of this particular franchise to me, as opposed to other alternatives?" Among the alternatives are securing a salaried job with a small or large firm, buying a going business, and starting a business from scratch on one's own. *Franchising Today 1969* (as well as certain other sources) contains guides for investigating and evaluating a franchise.

Generally, franchises currently being offered are pretty much confined to the retail field, but there is a broad selection of business classifications in retailing. Results of surveys (Vaughn, Ozanne and Hunt, McGuire, and Walker) now available would indicate that franchisees are generally satisfied, primarily because of their good income and feelings of independence.

Some franchisees, however, apparently fewer than 10 percent, are dissatisfied largely because these franchisees feel that franchisors do not live up to their promises, franchisees' incomes are marginal, and their prestige is questionable. Misleading and downright fraudulent sales practices have soured and even bilked some would-be franchisees.

The franchisor provides the new franchisee, with assistance in the many functions required in opening the new business and in the continuing operation of the business. He may bring to the business an accepted name, which attracts customers and provides a ready-made niche in the community for the new business, leading, among other things, to credit sources which might not otherwise be available.

The franchisor services, however, cost the franchisee money, and some franchisees become unhappy with the results. Among the payments by the franchisee may be franchise fees, royalty payments, advertising assessments, and mark-up on real estate, equipment, products, and services. The franchisor name may be of questionable value in some instances—when, for example, celebrity names are used without effective back-up.

A problem in evaluating the relative merits of franchising versus the alternatives is the lack of comparative empirical data for nonfranchised businesses and even for salaried jobs. Undoubtedly, most of the negative features of franchising are present in the alternatives, and many of franchising's advantages are lacking in these alternatives. In the nonfranchised business, however, the entrepreneur is not faced with exaggerations in regard to the profits and franchisor assistance which are to be forthcoming.

4 Starting and Developing a Franchise Operation as a Franchisor

Over the years a great many firms both large and small as well as individuals have sought to learn how to start and develop a franchise operation as a franchisor. Many large companies impressed with the great success of franchise chains in the late 1960s began to explore franchising. Thirty years before, gasoline marketers with vast chains of gasoline stations turned to franchising after encountering losses on their company-owned gasoline stations and objections to out-of-state companies.

The problem involved in starting and developing a viable franchise operation can, of course, be greatly different, as between a fellow with an idea to franchise and the firm that wishes to convert its company-owned to franchised units, or, perhaps, to start from scratch in opening a retail chain.

Most successful franchisors have been the entrepreneurs who started small with one or more profitable units and then expanded through franchising. In fact, some of the more successful franchise chains were actually pulled into franchising by would-be entrepreneurs who observed the success of the units and wanted to enjoy some of the success for themselves.

In a sense this whole book is about the successful starting and development of a franchise program, and topics are covered in other chapters which contribute directly to this mission. This chapter, however, is directed to the initial planning of the program, leaving such topics as marketing the product, recruitment and selection of franchisees, training of franchisees, financing, real estate, franchisor-franchisee relations, and international franchising to other chapters.

It is a long road from an initial idea or even the first retail outlet or two to the fully developed and viable franchise chain. There is no magic wand which can be waved to assure or even hasten success, and a lot of plain old-fashioned luck is seemingly needed along the route. Probably the earlier franchisors more or less felt their way, discovering new problems and achieving new solutions as they proceeded to expand through franchising, for it is only in the last few years that a formalized body of literature has grown up in franchising. Now, however, some of the necessary steps in expanding through franchising are well known and recorded. It should be emphasized that largely because of the various laws on termination of franchises, it is difficult to reverse the decision to franchise once it has been made and implemented.

Fortunate are those who have enough foresight when starting the franchise to anticipate the life cycle of their product or service and plan ahead with sufficient acumen to maintain their competitive advantage. For example, the big chains of gasoline stations seem to be heading toward obsolescence, and real estate problems are assuming major proportions. One trend in the petroleum field is toward self-service stations attached, particularly in the southeastern United States, to convenience grocery stores. In other instances the gasoline units have been converted either partially or wholly into lawn mower or bicycle shops. In other cases the chain's trade name has been converted into a brand name for diet foods. Simple things such as the need for remodeling the facilities at certain intervals, if anticipated and written into the agreements, will greatly enhance the viability of the chain.

In the restaurant field, several years ago two researchers at Arthur D. Little drew up a chart which they labeled "Potential Life Cycle of a Fast Food Franchisor."[1] The chart (figure 4-1) has proved to be a good model, as I have indicated in my 1976 article:

> This hypothetical firm starts as a one-product stand, then expands the menu and introduces inside seating. Services are added; the image is modified. The firm's second stage is a limited service, limited menu restaurant, and the firm integrates into food manufacturing. Cocktails and dining rooms are added, and the firm becomes a full-service restaurant. (It is at this stage that lodging facilities become a logical extension of the services already offered, and diversification into this area sometimes develops.) As the decor is improved and amenities added, the operation takes on the image and prestige of a full-service restaurant.

> When the firm reaches this last stage of maturity, a new generation of one-product stands is spawned, and the life cycle begins anew.

> This paradigm, of course, has not been followed precisely by most firms—and the tempo of change has varied from firm to firm—but the trend to menu expansion, increased seating capacity, and so on is already well along in many companies.[2]

The franchising firm which is started with some attempt to project the life cycle of the product or service is in a better position than one oblivious to some of the elemental facts having to do with business enterprises.

Starting the Franchise System

Seltz's Seventeen Basic Requirements for Entering Franchising

Speaking at the 1970 Franchise Management Conference held at Boston College, David D. Seltz, a franchise consultant with many years experience, listed the

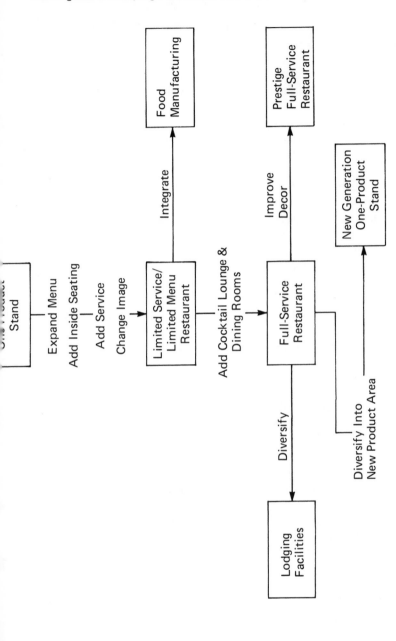

Source: John Angeline and William Hale, *Potential Life-Cycle of a Fast Food Franchisor* (Arthur D. Little, Inc., 1970). Reprinted by permission.

Figure 4-1. Potential Life Cycle of a Fast Food Franchisor

following seventeen basic requirements for judging one's qualifications as a potential franchisor:

1. Do you have an adequate organization for franchising?
2. Is the business established long enough so that its success is adequately tested?
3. Is the business financially solid?
4. Is it geared for production on an expanded scale?
5. Is it adequately manned?
6. Does the product or service which is to be part of the program have an enduring customer appeal, in terms, for example, of distinctive packaging or structure?
7. Does it have merchandising possibilities?
8. Does the product or service have repeat sale potentialities?
9. Does it have a good profit margin?
10. Is it the kind of product or service which the inexperienced franchisee can be taught to handle?
11. Is it the kind of product or service that can be marketed nationwide?
12. Is installation a part of the product sale, and if so, can it be farmed out?
13. Is freight a factor?
14. Does the potential franchisor have a viable franchising plan, with contacts in business, banking, and government lending circles?
15. What are your objectives in entering franchising, and are they long-range or short-range?
16. Are the franchise fees equitable to the franchisee and to the franchisor?
17. Is training programmed suitably for the new franchisee?[3]

The potential franchisor who has read this list is well aware of the complexities involved in doing business by franchising. Too often potential franchisors, from the fellow with an untried idea to the big company executive with an envious regard for the success stories, fail to appreciate that franchising is no key to guaranteed success. Hard work, experience, marketable products and services, and organization are necessary for success.

Dillman and Grant Emphasize
Franchisor Requirements

The one thing the potential franchisee can and should expect from the franchisor is know-how, and too often the would-be franchisor is hardly more experienced than the neophyte franchisee. Not only did Seltz emphasize this and similar points at the conferences, but others did so as well. For example, Dallas consultant George Dillman emphasized that the franchisor must bring to the venture: (1) his own expertise, (2) a packaged operation, (3) a sound credit standing, (4) a staff qualified in advertising and promotion, personnel training, purchasing, sources of supply for equipment and inventory, systems and procedures, and control.[4]

According to John Grant, a top executive with Denny's Restaurants, one of the most important decisions that the franchisor must make is, "Who does what, the franchisor or the franchisee?"[5] Henderson enumerated six problems in delivering the franchise:

1. Deciding on when and how to concentrate expansion.
2. Determining how to find, screen, and sign up prospective franchisees.
3. Deciding on tight or relaxed operating policies.
4. Creating prototypes.
5. Deciding on the price of the product.
6. Determining what regulations must be lived with.[6]

The Pilot Operation

John Grant stated:

> I take the conservative approach that any franchise which has a ghost of a chance of succeeding today must be based not on an unproven and untested idea but rather on several pilot operations which have worked out well.[7]

Grant added further:

> Determine the business you want to be in and open your pilot operations—at least two or three and, if possible, in different geographic and marketing areas. You should plan well the first operation, considering the all-important characteristics of your real estate location, the building to be erected or redesigned on the property, the fixturization of the premises to accommodate the kind of operation or service you will be offering, effective signing for the business, advertising, training of your employees, accounting, marketing, promotion, financing of all this, and a host of other rather elementary items.[8]

Starting the pilot operations is, of course, like starting any retail business, except that the planning should include the option to expand through franchising, or, perhaps, through other routes as well, such as joint ventures, branch units, or nonintegrated independent dealerships. Although I realize that the individual determined to be an entrepreneur abhors reading of any kind, here is a short list of books on starting one's own business, since this subject will not be reviewed in detail here except insofar as franchising presents special problems: *How To Start Your Own Business,* edited by William Putt;[9] *Entrepreneurship and Venture Management,* by Baumback and Mancuso;[10] Mancuso's *The Entrepreneur's Handbook;*[11] and *The Female Entrepreneur, A Pilot Study,*[12] by James W. Schreier.

Bailey's Sophisticated Approach to Franchising

Franklin Wyman, Jr., president and treasurer of Bailey's of Boston, describes one very sophisticated approach to starting and developing a franchise operation.[13] The company selected a Bailey's location (retail outlet for selling bulk ice cream, sundaes, sandwiches) that most nearly corresponded to the profile of ideal and sold the assets to a separate corporation, holding a management contract as well as a franchise agreement. The unit was then operated as a franchise, with franchise fees and all the other things associated with a franchise.

What did the two-year operation of Bailey's pilot franchise reveal to the company? First, it was clearly demonstrated that Bailey's could sell a franchise, collect the franchise fees, and provide a generous profit to the investor if the location was of the ideal type. Second, it was soon discovered that the systems, procedures, and accounting practices were inadequate and required revision. Third, Bailey's also came to the conclusion that the major stockholder in a franchise corporation must be thoroughly experienced in the food business and preferably this major stockholder should be the manager. Fourth, certain services performed were initially overlooked and had not been included in the costs. Fifth, any franchise sold must be for an ideal location.[14]

Wyman does not catalog the elements of an ideal location, and, of course, many elements that apply to an ice cream store would not apply to other types of businesses, but the point is that the pilot operation is essential in demonstrating the profitability of the type of unit being franchised. It is also essential for discovering and correcting the many errors in procedures, for only an actual test will show which procedures may be inadequate, and sometimes grossly so.

However, Bailey's seemingly ideal pilot franchise did not prosper, and the company reacquired the unit and gave up the idea of expanding through the franchise route. It is not clear why Bailey's franchised unit did not prosper, but the franchise had been sold to a group of investors and not to an owner-operator, a procedure which usually turns out to be unsuccessful in the franchise field. Bickering between principals over different objectives and between them and management either collectively or individually often produces an impossible situation. Curiously, this Bailey unit turned out to be one of the company's most successful units under company ownership and management. As it often is, timing of the introduction of the outlet in relation to market demand was probably an important factor in this abortive attempt at franchising.

Steps in Developing the Franchise

Most people experienced in franchising emphasize the utter necessity for developing one territory solidly with company-owned units and for using figures and procedures derived from these. Only then, do they say, proceed to expand by first franchising these units and then going to other areas.[15] Wyman noted that Bailey's used four existing locations and gleaned from each the characteristics which would, if combined, produce the ideal size and location for a Bailey's store.[16] The company then analyzed operating statements and determined which store accounts contributed most significantly to net profit. Next, it prepared two contracts, one a franchise agreement and the other a management contract. (The latter, of course, reflects a situation somewhat unique to Bailey's.)

Notice that even before the pilot operation, however, it is necessary to develop and organize concepts, visualize the attractions of the prospective franchise, and decide on where to grow.[17]

Master Franchises Covering Large Area

From time to time franchisors have not been able to resist the temptation to grant master franchises, covering, for example, an entire state or region. The master franchisee then builds his own units in the area, or he may subfranchise. This procedure has not worked too well with many firms, one example being A&W Root Beer. Smart contended:

1. All franchisees were not properly coached by the master franchisee.
2. Controls slipped away from the parent company, A&W.
3. Field services were neglected by the responsible master franchisee.
4. New units were getting off to a weak start.
5. The parent company lost its rapport with the subfranchisee and the general public.[18]

As a result, A&W Root Beer changed to unit franchising only. On the other hand, franchising of broad areas is desirable and often seemingly necessary in the international field, and Wendy's has apparently used this approach most recently with success in the domestic field.

Blueprint of Proposed Franchise Program

Once the concepts have been generated and organized, the pilot operations have been underway for a year or two, and decisions have been arrived at for areas of expansion, it is necessary to develop a blueprint of the projected program.[19] This blueprint should depict the following:

1. The prospective franchisee, who he is and how and where he may be found
2. The franchise package, things that the franchisor will supply the franchisee
   a. Opening program
   b. Sales presentation
   c. Operating manual
   d. Advertisements (mats) and direct mail program
   e. Promotional kit
   f. Public relations kit
   g. Flow and control forms
   h. Record keeping system
3. The franchise sales program
   a. Publicity kit
   b. Recruitment advertisements
   c. Exhibit booths, posters for shows
   d. Materials for seminars
4. Breakdown of costs and revenues to the
   a. Franchisor
   b. Franchisee
5. Market criteria
   a. How big
   b. Type of area per franchise
6. The franchise agreement

George Dillman, who has been consulted in the development of numerous franchise programs, enumerates several other steps that should be taken in starting a franchise program.[20] Many of these, of course, are taken for granted, or implied, in Seltz's steps. The franchisor, Dillman states, should incorporate, register to do business in at least two states, and formulate his capital structure with a board of directors and officers and one- to three-year pro forma profit and cash flow projections. The franchisor should arrange for short-term financing and establish a plan for funding prototype units, equipment, and inventory. He should also develop plans for eventual public offering. He should develop criteria for site selection and approval mechanisms as well as for leasing requirements.

The franchisor must detail merchandise characteristics, sources of supply, costs and margins, inventory requirements, warehousing, and supply systems. Another important step is to develop a list of trade and service marks, search the legal archives to ascertain their proprietary status, and register them if available. Over the long term it will be necessary to plan and ascertain the cost of a name-holding corporation and design, register, and copyright the marks. It is also necessary at this juncture to prepare contracts and agreements for licensing and equipment purchase and to secure primary sources of supply.

The franchisor, Dillman points out, should formulate the architectural concept, design the detailed plans, and arrange for bids. Sign concepts must be formulated and decisions made as to ownership or base and charges. Also, stationery must be designed and literature prepared. Employee specifications including job profiles must be developed, and everything possible be prepared in writing.

Rothenberg's Fast Food Magazine
PERT Chart

In 1968 *Fast Food Magazine* published a "PERT Chart for Establishing a Franchise Network," authored by Aaron Rothenberg, a West Coast franchise consultant.[21] PERT is the acronym for Progress Evaluation and Review Technique, a technique developed primarily during the post-World War II years by the U.S. Navy for managing the development of atomic submarines. The management method has subsequently been applied to other programs and, in this case, specifically to the development of a franchised fast food restaurant chain. Although the time periods allotted to various operations may be unrealistic, since every development program differs from others to a great extent, the Rothenberg PERT chart does portray the vast complexity of developing a viable franchise program.

Although most successful franchisor operations start from the successful operation of two or three retail units, the chart starts with the "idea" and depicts the steps from the initial establishment of objectives to the grand opening of the unit. The chart proceeds through the development of the concept, determination of the franchisability of the concept, estimating of program costs and franchisee earnings and profit projections, recruitment of franchisees, and signing of the franchise agreement with the franchisee.

Intermediate steps include, among many others, the formulation of requirements of the franchisee, the employment of architects, the development and implementation of a franchisee recruitment or sales program, and, of course, the formulation of menus, supply flows, and training programs.

The development program, of course, may not be the same in other fields, nor will it necessarily be the same from firm to firm in the restaurant field. Some chains already established as company-owned networks may want to expand through the franchise route for one or more of the advantages which have already been catalogued for franchising. The problems of such chains are quite different from those of the little fellow who has two or three units and friends across town wanting to climb on his bandwagon with similar units. The would-be franchisor starting with an idea only is indeed different, although certainly not unique, and should be made aware of the high mortality rate of new products and ideas in companies already financially and organizationally equipped to market them.

The Franchise Package

The term *franchise package* occurs frequently in discussions of the franchise program, and reflects, according to franchise consultant David Seltz "the substance behind the franchise program, commensurate value that the franchisee receives for the money he pays, franchisee's realistic chances for success, and motivations of the franchisor in offering franchises."[22]

Contents of the franchise package are not the same from the two points of view, that of the franchisor and of the franchisee. From the point of view of the franchisor the franchise package should contain estimates for the following costs, amortized per franchisee:

1. Recruitment advertising costs
2. Recruitment sales expense
3. Promotional tools costs
4. Schooling and training costs
5. Administrative expenses
6. Equipment and inventory costs—as supplied to the franchisee in the initial package
7. Costs of supplementary personal services that franchisor offers, for example, site selection, lease negotiation, field training.[23]

More or less in Seltz's words, the franchisee must obtain the following from the franchise package:

1. Specific material commitments designed to enable the franchisee to learn the business better or to increase roles (preproven as effective within the franchisor's own showcase operation). Among these are
   a. Direct mail (to help franchisees generate sales on a local level
   b. Operations manual
   c. Door-opener promotional projects
   d. Media advertisement
   e. Sales manual
   f. Site selection guide
   g. Publicity kit
   h. Public relations helps
   i. Grand opening promotion kit
   j. Sales brochures
   k. Sales presentation books

l.   Contest and incentive programs (for both franchisees and customers)
m.   Salesman recruitment program
n.   National "name image" advertising and publicity
o.   Forms, systems enabling better work flow
p.   Record-keeping and accounting systems for better cost and profit control

2.   Physical assistance commitments
a.   Home office schooling of franchisees
b.   Field and in-territory training of franchisees (to help place them in a winning momentum)
c.   Regional and national get-togethers of franchisees (sponsored and supervised by the franchisor) including regional self help clinics
d.   Continuing training and field visits by franchisor executives to franchisee's territory
e.   Miscellaneous factors including site selection, lease negotiation, construction assistance, and financing helps

3.   Equipment factors considered part of the franchise package. These include pertinent machinery, designs, fixtures or other getting set-up items given to the franchisee as part of his initial franchise package. For example,
a.   for the sale of sauna baths—a model sauna for franchisee's office or home
b.   for sale of closed-circuit television—an actual model for franchisee's demonstration
c.   for the sale of a food drive-in—actual furnishings, or in some instances, a turnkey operation
d.   for the sale of an automatic transmission shop—basic repair machinery plus office furnishings

4.   Merchandise factors given as part of the franchisee's package providing the equivalent of a starting inventory. In most instances, it is endeavored, via such inventories, to reimburse the franchisee over a period of years—based on his meeting designated performance quotas—for whole or part of his franchise fee.[24]

The franchisor may, depending on the nature of the franchise, provide a products inventory on which the franchise may draw as sales are made, and in some instances a schedule of bonuses may be provided to enable franchisees to earn discounts.

Organization of the Franchisor Firm

The franchisor firm organization chart may be very complex as in the automotive companies, petroleum marketers, or large motel chains; or the chart may be quite simple, as, for example, in a chain just getting started (the early days of Colonel Sanders' Kentucky Fried Chicken, Mister Donut, or even International House of Pancakes).

For a firm to expand effectively through the franchise route, however, it is necessary to have a franchise sales manager. Actually, most other positions in the franchise firm are analogous to those in any retail organization with multiple outlets.

It cannot be overemphasized, moreover, that the firm expanding through franchising and embarking on a marketing program to sell franchises must have organizational support for its advertising and sales effort. Too many firms just waste time and money in heavy advertising for franchisees without the capability for handling inquiries. McGuire, in his chapter on franchisor operations in The Conference Board Report describes four key organizational positions and presents several tables of organization.[25] He notes that in addition to the director of franchising, three other positions assume key roles in franchising organizations. These other positions are director of real estate operations, director of training, and field supervisor. These latter, of course, reflect the fact that most franchisors are in the retail field.

Franchisor Sources of Revenue (and Franchisee Costs)

Of particular importance to the franchisor is the matter of how and where he will obtain revenues sufficient to cover expenses involved in providing (1) materials and services he promises the franchisee; (2) the administrative expenses of the organization that must be developed; (3) the promotional and operating expenses necessary to secure and set up franchisees; and (4) a profit large enough to justify the risks which the franchisor and other financial backers take in entering into franchising. An argument, of course, in favor of franchising is that capital requirements of the franchisor need not be large initially. But too often the costs of the services promised are not clearly realized by would-be franchisors, with the result that the operation goes down the drain.

The franchisee, of course, must have a similarly clear picture of what his revenues and expenses will be, but these are usually straightforward. Revenues come from the sale of a relatively small number of standard products or services with definite price tags, and expenses are pretty clearly the cost of labor and materials required to furnish the product or services. The projected operating statement covering these costs and revenues based initially on precisely detailed expenses with one or more pilot units and amended later as new experience is acquired is furnished by the franchisor.

Vaughn in a 1969 survey of 136 fast food franchisors in six categories ascertained the sources of revenues of those firms.[26] The results are shown in table 4-1. Royalty and franchise fees were in practically all companies surveyed sources of revenue for the franchisor (and items of cost to the franchisee). The royalty fee is generally a continuing payment by the franchisee to the franchisor of a certain percentage of gross sales; the franchise fee is usually a one-time lump-sum payment by the franchisee to the franchisor when the franchise is acquired. (There are, of course, many types of installment payments and of collection periods.)

It should also be carefully noted that significant percentages of franchisors obtained revenues from other sources such as the rental or lease of property, advertising efforts, the rental or sale of equipment, and the sale of products. In fact, a third of the profit of one of the biggest fast food franchisors customarily comes from the rental of the land and building to the franchisee. It should be pointed out, however, that requirements for purchase of products tied to the acquisition of the franchisor trade name have been declared illegal in the United States, and sales of product to the franchisee by the franchisor should avoid the legal pitfalls which surround such transactions.

The magnitude of three categories of charges to franchisees by franchisors in 1969 are shown in table 4-2. These figures have changed in an upward direction since the survey, but they provide an indication of the general magnitude of these charges by franchisors. Whether they are excessive or not can only be determined after a careful assessment of the costs of operating the franchisor firm and a determination of other sources of revenue available to the franchisor. One should also emphasize that other sources of income to the franchisor may be subject to question. For example, the franchisor's selling of products to franchisees may encounter legal problems in the antitrust field if the conditions

Table 4-1
Franchisor Sources of Revenue, Six Categories of Fast Food Franchises, Frequency of Ways in Which Revenues Obtained
(in percents)

Source of Revenue	Percent of Franchisors Obtaining Revenue
Royalty fees	92
Franchisee fees	89
Rent/lease of land/building	73
Advertisement assessment	70
Sale/lease of equipment	60
Sale of food products	47
Sale of paper products	39
Other	38
Number of firms (base for percent)	116

Source: Charles L. Vaughn, *The Vaughn Report on Franchising of Fast Food Restaurants: Six Categories of Franchises* (Lynbrook, N.Y.: Farnsworth Publishing Company, 1970), p. 10.

Table 4-2
Franchisor Sources of Revenue, Six Categories of Fast
Food Franchises

| | Three Average Fees | | |
Principal Product	Franchise Fee ($)	Royalty Fee (%)[a]	Advertising Assessment (%)[a]
Chicken	6,560	3.5	2.3
Hamburgers, hot dogs	11,500	3.0	2.2
Pizza	5,950	4.0	2.6
Roast beef	9,180	3.4	1.4
Sandwich shops	10,250	3.9	1.3
Seafood	10,275	4.8	1.9

Source: Charles L. Vaughn, *The Vaughn Report on Franchising of Fast Food Restaurants: Six Categories of Franchises* (Lynbrook, N.Y.: Farnsworth Publishing Company, 1970), p. 10.

[a]Of gross sales.

are not carefully worked out—at least in the United States. Even the sale of products by franchisor agents may cause problems. It should also be emphasized that tables 4-1 and 4-2 present figures from fast food operations and that figures from other types of franchises will undoubtedly be quite different. As table 4-2 shows, figures vary considerably even from one type of fast food firm to another. Also, the Vaughn study of ten years ago certainly needs updating.

Those who wish to start and develop a restaurant business will find suggestions in Dyer's book, *So You Want to Start a Restaurant.*[27] Chapter headings are: "The Plan Is the Thing," "Where Will You Find Your Customer?" "What Will the Customer of the Future Demand?" "Why Do People Eat Out?" "Menu Planning," "Determining Building Requirements," "Designing Your Facility," "Kitchen Design," "Staffing and the Manager," "Hiring Personnel," "Receiving and Training Personnel," "Getting the Most Out of Your People," "Comparative Analysis of Well-Known Food Service Operations," "Changing American Values: What of the Future?" The chapter headings, of course, are indicative of what the beginning entrepreneur in the restaurant field should consider, whether or not he studies the particular book or even wishes to franchise.

The Franchise Agreement

Many legal problems arise during the birth and development of the franchise, and various legal documents are desirable if not absolutely necessary. Of paramount importance is the franchise agreement, or contract, which should spell out the respective obligations of the franchisor and the franchisee much as they were described before. No doubt much litigation and public controversy surrounding franchising in recent years is due to the inadequacy of franchise contracts.

In drawing up the franchise contract the lawyer, in the United States at least, must be sensitive to several bodies of laws: the federal and state antitrust laws, the state laws directly pertinent to franchising, the Federal Trade Commission Trade Regulation Rule on Franchising, and, of course, the multitudinous laws applicable to any business venture. At this point, we are primarily concerned with those laws and regulations which are most directly applicable to franchising. The franchise contract brings these laws and regulations into focus, although they may operate quite apart from the franchise contract itself.

The laws and regulations which surround franchising today stem in a large measure from problems arising between franchisor and franchisee. Aware of the general nature of these problems, the Boston College Franchise Center as early as 1968 appointed a committee to study unfair and deceptive practices in franchising, and the eminent New York antitrust attorney, Jerrold G. Van Cise, volunteered to chair the committee. The committee's report, published in 1969, described in detail three major types of misconduct in franchising: (1) unfair practices in the granting of the franchise, (2) unfair practices in the operation of the franchise, and (3) unfair practices in the termination of the franchise.[28]

Since that time many legislative bodies at the state and federal levels and the Federal Trade Commission have held hearings on these problems, and the courts have received their share of cases to adjudicate. For example, in 1972 Lewis G. Rudnick, associate general counsel of the International Franchise Association, wrote in the *National Franchise Directory* that there were " . . . perhaps 50 class action suits pending in the federal courts against franchisors in which franchisees are seeking treble damages for alleged violations of the federal antitrust laws and permanent modifications of their franchise relationships."[29] Several individuals and franchisee associations have also been quite articulate in calling the public's attention to unethical practices, chief among them being Harold Brown, the Boston attorney, whose books, articles, and speeches have been aimed at franchisor misconduct.

State Laws on Franchising

According to *Continental Franchise Review,* by 1973 thirteen states and Puerto Rico had passed a hodgepodge of laws regarding franchise sales or the relationship between franchisor and franchisee. These were Arkansas, California, Connecticut, Delaware, Florida, Georgia, Minnesota, Nevada, New Jersey, Rhode Island, Virginia, Puerto Rico, Wisconsin, and Washington. An additional ten states had laws pending: Arizona, Hawaii, Illinois, Massachusetts, Michigan, New York, North Dakota, Oklahoma, Pennsylvania, and South Dakota.[30] No such laws existed prior to 1970.

By 1976 twenty states had passed laws bearing in some way on Type IV franchises, according to synopses of state laws appearing in Glickman.[31] Of these laws, eleven seemed to have been patterned after the California Franchise Investment Law of 1970, which requires full disclosure to the franchisee by the franchisor. Moreover, by 1976 all but six states had passed laws pertinent to at least some type of franchising, usually the Type I systems, and specifically to the termination of an automobile dealership by the parent company, or franchisor. Many of the laws, however, dealt with gasoline service stations (another of the Type I franchises) and some with farm implement dealerships or beer distributorships (the last of which, incidentally, are not included in the Commerce Department's statistics).

Uniform Franchise Offering Circular

Recognizing the legal and financial burden placed on franchisors as a result of the differing state laws on franchising, the Midwest Securities Commissioners Association attempted to formulate a uniform prospectus to serve as a guide for offering franchises and registering under the state laws. In 1975 the association came up with a second version of a uniform franchise offering circular that is more or less accepted by fourteen states. This circular covers twenty-three topics: the franchisor's name and that of any predecessors within the past fifteen years; the identity and business experience of persons affiliated with the franchisor; any litigation in which he might be involved; his history of bankruptcy; the franchisee's initial franchise fee or other initial payment; other fees; the franchisee's initial investment; obligations of the franchisee to purchase or lease from designated sources; obligations of the franchisee to purchase or lease in accordance with specifications or from approved suppliers; financing arrangements; obligations of the franchisor; exclusive area or territory; trademarks, service marks, trade names, logotypes, and commercial symbols; patents and copyrights; obligations of the franchisee to participate in the actual operation of the franchise business; restrictions on goods and services offered by the franchisee; renewal, termination, repurchase, modification, and assignment of the franchise agreement and related information; actual, average, projected, or forecasted franchisee sales, profits or earnings in the event the franchisor discloses these to franchisees; information regarding franchises of the franchisor; financial statements; contracts; and acknowledgment of receipt by the prospective franchisee.

Federal Trade Commission Rule on Franchising

Late in 1978 the Federal Trade Commission promulgated a trade regulation rule on franchising, with an effective date of 21 July 1979. It is entitled "Disclosure Requirements and Prohibitions Concerning Franchising and Business Opportunity Ventures." The rule requires a franchisor to disclose material facts about his business and about the franchise relationship to prospective franchisees. The rule also prohibits misrepresentations concerning actual or potential sales, income, or profits.

The FTC's rule requires that franchisors and franchise brokers furnish prospective franchisees with a disclosure statement at least ten days prior to the execution of the contract or the payment of money. The disclosure will include information on twenty subjects including:

Business experience of the franchisor and its key management personnel

Litigation and bankruptcy history of the franchisor and its key management personnel

Financial information on the franchisor

Costs, both initial and recurring, which the franchisee will be required to pay

Statistical information on the number of franchises and company-owned outlets

Termination, cancellation, and renewal provisions of the franchise agreement

Number of franchisees terminated during the past year and the reasons for their termination

Training offered by the franchisor

Restrictions imposed by the franchisor on the manner in which the franchisee may operate his business, including restrictions on such things as the types of goods which can be sold, suppliers that can be used and the geographic area in which the franchise may operate

In addition, the rule prohibits franchisors and franchise brokers from making general representations about actual or potential sales, income, or profits unless:

There is a reasonable basis for the representation.

The representation is based on information which has been prepared in accordance with generally accepted accounting principles.

The franchisor has material to substantiate claims made and makes such information available to a prospective franchisee and to the commission upon reasonable demand.

The rule imposes additional restrictions on earnings representations made directly to a prospective franchisee. It further requires that franchisors provide prospective franchisees with an additional disclosure document covering such representations.

A trade regulation rule, when issued on a final basis as this rule was, carries the full force of law. Firms that violate a rule are liable for civil penalties of up to $10,000 per violation.

In addition to promulgating the final rule, the FTC has issued proposed interpretative guides to the rule. These guides are designed to assist those covered by the rule in understanding their compliance obligations and in preparing their disclosure statements. The FTC's more detailed summary of the rule together with eleven frequently asked questions and their answers appear in Appendix D.

As the reader will note, many elements of the rule are similar to those in the Uniform Franchise Offering Circular, and, in fact, the commission will permit franchisors to use the UFOC format in lieu of the disclosure document provided by the rule, as shown in the FTC summary appearing in Appendix D.

The disclosures required by the rule as well as those in the UFOC are items of information that the prospective franchisee should seek in order to evaluate the franchise or franchises that he is considering buying. Moreover, the sound franchisor will want to furnish this information to his prospects whether or not it is required by law, although it should be noted that six lawsuits against the commission seeking to void the rule had been brought within a month after its promulgation—a situation due no doubt to special problems in complying with the rule. It should be added that the rule does not have any grandfather clauses, nor does it provide exceptions for large companies. Undoubtedly, many changes albeit minor ones will accrue as the rule is implemented and further hearings take place.

The prospective franchisee, however, should exercise great prudence in interpreting the information once it has been provided: even the most ethical and profitable franchise for the ordinary prospect may not be the right one for the particular individual who is evaluating it. Also, even though on the surface some items are valuable, it may be very difficult for the average individual or even the experts to evaluate them. Further, it should be noted that states which have adopted the uniform circular may require other information as well. In fact, the practicing attorney should obtain whatever requirements are imposed directly from the state or states in which the franchisor wishes to operate.

The Ray O. Burch Study

It would appear that some of the criticism of franchising has been overdone, as illustrated by an analysis conducted in 1972 by Ray O. Burch, vice-president of marketing for the Schwinn Bicycle Company and president for 1973-1974 of International Franchise Association. Burch analyzed twenty-one hundred pages of alleged complaint material against franchising (246 separate complaints about franchising) in the files of the Federal Trade Commission.[32] Although referred to as franchise complaints, only 55 were actually so. For example, 14 were rack jobber complaints, 42 were complaints about phony distributorships, 14 were miscellaneous business complaints, and 8 were complaints about pyramid schemes. Most of the complaints pertained to fraudulent sales schemes prosecutable under many and diverse laws; the schemes are hardly classifiable. Undoubtedly, many other criticisms of franchising could be dissipated with similar thorough scrutiny of the complaints.

Guiding Principles in Formulating the
Franchise Contract

After reviewing the three major areas of misconduct by franchisors, Van Cise prepared a dissertation on the principles that underlie the so-called ideal franchise contract.[33] The article is reprinted in Appendix A.

In brief, the three general principles that should serve to guide the draftsman in preparing a suitable franchise agreement are the following: (1) the contract should be frank; (2) its provisions should be fair; and (3) its contents should be enforceable. Following the enumeration of these principles, Van Cise discusses general provisions of the contract and start-up, operating, and termination provisions, as recorded in Appendix A.

The prospective franchisee should bear in mind that the contract in most instances is drawn up by the franchisor's lawyers; and working for the franchisor, these lawyers must be committed to protecting and advancing the franchisor's interests, however objective the lawyer might wish to be. For that reason alone, the prospective franchisee should engage an experienced lawyer to protect his interests, at least to the extent of pointing out problem areas in which franchisor and franchisee interests may not be precisely congruent. Generally, however, the interests of the two parties will be parallel, since franchisors and franchisees are, in a sense, partners, but the unhappy fact is simply that some franchisors (and indeed franchisees) have not realized this fact.

Specific Contractual Provisions

Proceeding on an empirical basis and from a somewhat different viewpoint, Udell analyzed 172 contracts to ascertain the frequency of occurrence of 167 relatively standardized contractual provisions.[34] These are the ten provisions that appeared in at least 70 percent of the contracts:

1. Franchise fee paid to the franchisor (for privilege of doing business under franchisor banner).
2. Royalty payments by franchisee to franchisor (generally based on percentage of gross sales).
3. Payments for equipment purchased on the installment plan.
4. Length of contract term.
5. Incorporation of franchisee permitted.
6. Periodic reports to franchisor required of franchisee.
7. Franchisor's right to inspect.
8. Standards of cleanliness.
9. Franchisor approval of sale of the franchise.
10. Franchisor termination.

Many other provisions appeared in at least half the contracts. These provisions relate to the following: the amount of local advertising by the franchisee; franchisee's option to renew the contract; exclusive territory; prohibition against franchisor's disclosure of confidential information about franchisee; statement that franchisee is not agent or employee but independent contractor; franchisor held harmless for acts of franchisee; no waiver of default on contract if franchisor does not enforce provisions; contract is legal even if a particular provision is declared illegal; franchisee must comply with local laws; trademark, trade names, and copyrights owned by franchisor; specification of franchisee's days open and for hours open; product line; alteration approval; use of franchisor's bookkeeping system required; franchisee completion of formal training required; franchise maintenance required; franchisee must meet franchisor standards of quality in product or service; franchisee must operate franchise at level (standard) acceptable to franchisor; franchisee must meet franchisor standards of quality in product or service; franchisee must coinsure the franchisor; franchisee must carry property and product liability insurance; franchisee must buy paper goods from franchisor; franchisee may or must buy operating supplies from the franchisor;[35] franchisee may buy equipment from the franchisor; franchisee may or must buy or lease signs from the franchisor; franchisee must obtain franchisor's approval of suppliers (vendors); franchisee is required to install and maintain signs; franchisee must obtain franchisor's approval of advertising; and franchisee must not compete with franchisor in a similar business.

Udell's detailed report is reproduced in Appendix B. Whereas the Van Cise article (Appendix A) covers the general principles underlying the franchise contract, Udell's report (Appendix B) depicts what was actually being done in practice. These provisions on the whole are directed at protecting the interest of the franchise system, or the franchisor, and only obliquely those of the franchisee.

It should be added that the firms Udell surveyed were rather often in the fast food field, and at least two provisions are clearly illegal in view of current interpretations of the law.

Reproduced in Appendix C is an illustration of a franchise agreement. It is the Chicken Delight contract, revised under the supervision of M. Laurence Popofsky, attorney with the San Francisco law firm, Heller, Ehrman, White, and McAuliffe, which defended Chicken Delight in the famous class action suit brought by franchisees. This revision eliminates the earlier illegal provisions (except possibly for one, which is footnoted on the copy of Appendix C). This contract might serve as a concrete "model" in the fast food field, but laws and court interpretations are changing so fast that the "model contract" of today may bring about litigation tomorrow.

Other Legal Problems

There are many legal problems which one faces when entering business, and these seem to be complicated in the franchise field. A treatment of these problems in a rather detailed manner may be found in Glickman.[36] She covers some twenty different topics ranging from the state laws on franchising to consumer credit, taxation, and franchisee's employees.

5 Recruiting and Selecting Franchisees

Two Basic Marketing Problems in Franchising

There are two basic marketing problems in franchising. The first problem is to develop a product or service that has appeal to the ultimate consumer, the general public in most instances. The second problem is, once the product or service has been developed, to convince the prospective middleman, or franchisee, that the product or service can be sold at a profit, in other words, that the franchised product can be marketed. Although the two problems are intertwined, this chapter is confined to the second problem; the problem of marketing the product or service was treated in chapter 2.

Enterprising individuals and even companies too often sell franchises before they have any evidence of consumer acceptance of the product. Franchises to sell a product or service may be sold without any evidence that the product is in fact saleable. Whether such practices are employed through ignorance of sound business procedure or through intent to defraud, the result for the unsuspecting victim can be just as disastrous.

Of course, the franchising system of distribution is not the only system that suffers from the attempted selling of nonmarketable products. Hardly any executive suite from Park Avenue to Sunset Boulevard is without at least one top man who has not at one time or another in his career with the vertically integrated firm been burned in trying to sell untested (and, yes, even tested) new products which have turned out to be unsellable.

In franchising, however, the problem is somewhat more serious than it is in the well-financed, vertically integrated firm. By and large, franchises are sold to individuals with relatively little capital. Franchisees may put their last cent into the franchise without full appreciation of the risks involved. It is in the recruiting and screening of franchisees that ethical problems in business are brought into sharp focus.

This is the way in which Robert C. Townsend, then chairman of the board, Avis Rent-A-Car, expressed the problem years ago in his speech at the Boston College 1965 Management Conference on Franchising:

> Your industry, franchising, as I see it, breaks down into two parts, those who are selling franchises and those who are selling donuts or motel rooms or custard or rent-a-car service or something, but there is a big difference between selling pieces of paper which entitle you to do

something and offering the service itself, and I really do not think there is much future for those of you who are just selling pieces of paper to other people.[1]

Mr. Townsend went on to add a remark that brings into focus the public relations problem which franchising has had for many a year and which does not seem to abate:

> I came up here [to Boston College]. I talked to my good friend, the chairman of the executive committee [of Avis Rent-A-Car], Don Petrie and he said, "They are a fascinating bunch, fascinating." He said, "You will find somebody there if you talk to enough people who will sell you a franchise to live in Locust Valley."
>
> ... there is a lunatic fringe in our industry who are selling pieces of paper to unsuspecting people, who think that all they have to do is own that piece of paper and they will get rich.
>
> ... My message to you is, if you are going to be a pure franchise operation, for heaven's sake, own two or three operations so you can find out what the batter is like that goes in to make pralines that you are selling along the roadside. Don't go into a pure franchise business. It is an Alice in Wonderland field and you tend to get unhooked from the business of selling things to people. . . .[1]

These apparently simple principles are ignored by many people who offer franchises. Sophisticated and unsophisticated alike seem to forget that the first thing in a sound franchise operation is a marketable product or service, and by "marketable" is meant marketable at a profit both to the franchisor and to the franchisee.

Rather than "selling pieces of paper," the sound franchisor offers the prospective franchisee a carefully designed franchise package. As indicated in the previous chapter, this franchise package "should be based on specific 'values' given to the franchisee in relation to his investment. . . ." According to David Seltz these values are reflected in (1) the substance behind the franchise program, (2) commensurate value that the franchisee receives for the money he pays, the (3) franchisee's realistic chances for success, and (4) motivations of the franchisor in offering franchises.

Broad Spectrum of Recruitment Methods

Since the spectrum of franchise operations is broad, the problems and methods of recruitment and selection differ greatly from firm to firm. That is to say:

1. Franchise operations range from those with initial cash requirements of a few thousand dollars, or even nothing for that matter, to those requiring hundreds of thousands of dollars.

2. Franchising cuts across many industries.
3. Although in recent years the word *franchising* is associated more closely with retailing operations, this method of distribution is also used at the wholesaling and manufacturing levels.
4. Franchises may be offered covering broad geographic areas, small geographic areas, or individual retail outlets.

The most frequently offered franchise today is that covering the individual retail outlet. But even among similar firms in similar industries, the problems and methods of recruitment and selection may differ greatly because one franchisor is relatively old and has a large number of franchisees already, and another firm is relatively a newcomer with fewer franchisees.

Faced with this great diversity of problems and methods, the best course to follow in initiating a discussion of recruitment and selection is to develop case studies. One problem that should be constantly in mind in recruiting franchisees is the overwhelming prestige of employment in big business even though the financial and other opportunities in the small business may far surpass those in the big company.

By far the most common practice today is that in which the franchisor recruits directly the individual franchisee, the retail operator. To be sure, in larger franchise operations, this recruitment may be made through area supervisors, but these supervisors are generally employees of the franchisor. Nevertheless, approaches to recruitment differ according to the goals of the franchisor. In some companies the objective has been to expand nationally at the earliest possible time, and in others, regional expansion is the goal, at least for the near term.

Once the franchise package has been formulated and a track record has been established, the problem is to establish the goals for recruiting. Will the franchisor expand nationally or regionally? Will the franchisor spot franchisees over the nation to serve as nuclei for expansion? What type of individual will be sought? Just what are the company's objectives in franchising?

Obtaining Leads to Prospective Franchisees

Leads for franchise salesmen to follow are obtained in a variety of ways:

1. Through advertising in newspapers: *The New York Times, The Wall Street Journal,* area and city dailies, and even weekly newspapers. Occasionally, a major franchisor will take a Sunday supplement in a newspaper such as the *Boston Herald,* with the aim of obtaining applications from prospective franchisees, as well as accomplishing various other public relations objectives such as building a sound corporate image.
2. Through display and classified advertising in national magazines of general scope, such as *Time* and *Newsweek,* but more often in magazines devoted

specifically to franchising. Advertising in *Army Times* and *Air Force Times* has also proved quite effective for some firms; trade and other specialized publications, such as *Golf Digest*, may also serve a useful purpose.

3. Through seminars on franchising held in hotels and motels, and occasionally on college campuses across the nation. Sometimes these seminars are held at the franchisor's national or regional headquarters.

4. Through exhibiting at various trade, or "Own Your Own Business" shows, such as those held annually in New York and occasionally in Boston, Chicago, Detroit, Toronto, Los Angeles, and a host of other places.

5. Through direct mail to lists of various types of persons—in the case of large operations such as the motels, to real estate developers for example.

6. Through reply (inquiry) cards placed conspicuously at franchisee sites. The franchisees are usually given bonuses ($100-$500) for productive leads. Many franchisors consider this method of obtaining leads to be by far the most productive.

7. Through public relations or publicity activities generally, and specifically in towns and cities where the franchisor wishes to obtain franchisees.

Recruitment advertising for franchisees has continued at a fast pace over the years. As the example discussed in chapter 1 illustrated, one recent issue of *The Wall Street Journal* carried forty-five new business offering advertisements. Although not all the offerings would qualify technically as franchises, they can be considered such for all practical purposes. Another example of the active search for franchisees was shown by the illustration from a recent issue of *The New York Times* (Sunday, 27 November 1977), which had thirty-six franchisee recruitment advertisements. Moreover, public relations people have also been quite active. For example, the *Boston Herald* recently had a long feature story on Weight Watchers and Diet Workshop, two franchisors in the weight reduction field. A full-page advertisement in *The Wall Street Journal* the same day for Midas also mentioned the Midas franchising program. Howard Johnson's took a two-page spread in the 6 April 1978 issue of *The Wall Street Journal* that offered information on becoming a restaurant or lodging licensee. The 16 January 1978 issue of the *Journal* carried a two-page advertisement for Holiday Inn franchises, "The number one hotel franchise in the world."

As indicated earlier, a total of 244 columnar inches of space were devoted to advertisements for franchisees in *The Wall Street Journal's* November 17 issue. That number contained a page and a half of display advertising. Types of franchises offered covered diverse fields, as shown in table 5-1.

An analysis of the attractions used to recuit franchisees and topics covered in these advertisements revealed an average of 4.9 separate appeals, or topics, per advertisement, in some sixteen categories of claims plus a group of miscellaneous sales propositions. The most frequent benefit to prospective franchisees concerned the assistance which the franchisor said he provided the franchisee: thirty-five of the forty-five advertisements made at least some reference to this

Table 5-1
Recent "New Business Offerings" in *The Wall Street Journal*
(Eastern Edition, Thursday, 17 November 1977)

Kinds of New Businesses Advertising for Recruits	*Number of Advertisements*
Automotive aftermarket (Truck attachment installation, transmission repair, rust proofing, collision body-repair service, muffler installation)	9
Employment (personnel) service (Personnel recruitment, executive search, temporary help service, motivation training)	7
Fast food shops (restaurants) (Subway sandwiches, pizza parlors, ice cream stores, hot dogs, donuts)	5
Quick copy establishments	3
Business counseling services	2
Carpet cleaning shops	2
Product distributorships (Mopeds 2, others 3)	5
Miscellaneous (Rental service, furniture restoration, giant-screen television, personal grooming, flower sales, home nursing service, bookstore, security devices, leisure craft, yellow page advertising, computer store, lawn care)	12
Total advertisements	45

assistance. Help in financing, mentioned in ten of the forty-five advertisements, and training were the most frequent types of assistance named. Coupled with reference to assistance was mention of the investment or cash required; thirty-four advertisements specified the investment or cash involved, ranging from none at all to $125,000. The median investment (or cash) required to secure the new business was about $18,000. Other topics covered in at least some of the advertisements were the great market potential of the product(s); high profitability of the units; franchisee qualifications; fast growth of the franchisor; experience of the franchisor, evidenced, for example, by his many years in the business; the franchisor's large organization; the personal satisfaction which the business afforded the franchisee; the prestige provided by the franchisor; the opportunity for the person to be in business for himself; the areas available; the product that the franchisee offers (a rather complete description); the protected territory; the fact that company executives or the company itself own units; the need to act fast; and a small number of miscellaneous items. Table 5-2 shows the topics covered in the various advertisements with the

Table 5-2

Appeals Used (Topics Covered) to Attract Recruits to New Business Offerings (Forty-five Advertisements, Eastern Edition, *The Wall Street Journal,* **17 November 1977)**

Appeal (Topic)	Frequency	
	Number	Percent
Assistance provided by franchisor Training, financing (10)[a]; television backup, turnkey operation	35	78
Investment (or cash) required No franchise-distribution fee (4); inventory only: $5,000; $6,495; $7,500; $9,500 (2); $10,000 (2); $12,500; $14,500; $15,000; $15,000-$30,000; $18,000; $20,000-$35,000; $22,500; $25,000 (2); $25,000-$50,000; $28,500; $29,400; $30,000; $45,000; $45,000-$55,000 (2); $48,000; $50,000; $56,000; $60,000-$65,000; $125,000	34	76
Market potential great, product sells self, exploding field, fast growing market, industry large, new product (7)	27	60
Very profitable, success proven, high gross, chance of a lifetime	27	60
Qualifications required in franchisees (Includes ten who said experience unnecessary) Strong desire "to be on his own"; sales and management background; reliable; sound of character; $3,500 to invest; sophisticated, professional businessman	18	40
Fast-growing franchisor, expanding fast	13	29
Experienced company (franchisor), in field a long time, proven record In field twenty years, leader in field twelve years, "long time—sixteen years, proven procedures," "we know our stuff"	13	29
Big organization, big company, nationwide, international, many established franchisees	11	24
Business personally satisfying Pleasant, exciting, limited amount of work, efficient, clean	7	16
Highly respected company (franchisor), prestigious, leader in field	7	16
Be in business for self (franchisee)	7	16
Areas (territories) available	6	13
Description of product that franchisee will offer	4	9
Exclusive (protected) territory	3	7

Table 5-2 continued

Appeal (Topic)	Frequency	
	Number	Percent
Company (or executive) owns stores itself	2	4
Don't delay, "someone in your territory may call first"	2	4
Miscellaneous	5	11
Total number of advertisements (base for percentages)	45	b
Number of appeals (topics covered per advertisement)	4.9	

aNumbers in parentheses are numbers of mentions for item.
bPercents add to more than 100 because of multiple mentions in advertisements.

number of mentions for each topic, or appeal. So much for the various ways in which franchisees may be recruited, with special reference to the use of print media advertisements.

Minorities

Many people, particularly high officials in the U.S. Departments of Labor and Commerce, see franchising as a means of drawing minorities, and especially blacks, into the mainstream of American business. In fact, the *Franchise Opportunities Handbook,* prepared by the U.S. Department of Commerce, is funded by the Office of Minority Business Enterprise and "identifies franchisors who do not discriminate on the basis of race, color, or national origin in the availability, terms, or conditions of their franchise."

In the 1966-1968 period, the U.S. Department of Labor, stimulated initially by the U.S. Department of Commerce, entered into two successive and sizable contracts with Boston College to recruit and train disadvantaged youths aged sixteen to twenty-one years in franchised establishments with the aim of interesting the youths in later acquiring franchised businesses.

Since minorities are often reluctant to leave the security of their fellow minority group members, it was found that special recruitment procedures had to be used to secure participation from such groups. In the Franchise Industry Training Projects (FIT) operated through Boston College, more than two hundred social agencies were contacted to enlist their help in securing trainees, for example, Neighborhood Youth Centers, Community Action Centers, churches, city schools, Boys' Clubs, special ghetto area organizations, courts, health departments, YMCA's, and settlement houses.[2]

The franchisor planning to operate in central city areas might well contact such agencies, as well as special minority media such as *Ebony Magazine* and *Black Enterprisor*. For example, a successful employment agency type of franchise which furnishes live-in domestic help locates its units near ghetto areas and makes contacts with potential employees through nearby social agencies even though its primary customers reside in the affluent suburbs. The problem of securing customers is much less serious than that of securing help.

According to the U.S. Department of Commerce survey minority participation in franchising continues to expand steadily.[3] In 1976, 393 franchisors had 4,301 franchises owned by minority businessmen: 1,894 owned by blacks; 1,502 by persons with Spanish surnames; 770 by Orientals; and 135 by American Indians. In 1974 there were only 3,072 franchises owned by minority businessmen. Of the 1976 total 1,359 minority-owned franchises were in automotive products; 746 in fast foods; 592 in food retailing other than convenience stores; 508 in convenience stores; and 223 in construction, home improvement, maintenance, and cleaning services.

Indications of the Relative Effectiveness of Different Approaches: Four Case Studies

Some indications of the effectiveness of the different approaches may be obtained from case examples of certain firms which were represented at the Annual Management Conferences on Franchising held at Boston College.

Four of these case examples from rather diverse fields of franchising illustrate some of the different problems in recruiting effectively. Three other examples will be touched on when we discuss the selection process, since they provide insights into specific situations. To avoid distractions due to the company names these will be altered in the following presentation.

Recruitment by Charger Enterprises, Inc.

The first case is that of Charger Enterprises, Inc. The most important consideration with the Charger company was not the obtaining of leads as such but the obtaining of qualified leads. To this end the company considered all media possibilities: newspaper, direct mail, radio, television, publicity, consumer distributed material, and, of course, the franchisees themselves.

The next most important thing was the cost. What kind of audience would be reached through various media—those who earn $4,000 or those who earn $40,000? The type of copy has to be considered. Some franchisor advertisers do not give the people the facts. Some say that the franchisee can make $10,000-a-year profit with an initial investment of only $10,000. This is a pretty good return for the investment, but the fact is that perhaps by the time the individual gets his unit installed, whether it be a hamburger stand or some other franchise, the franchisee may have $40,000 invested, and his return might not be $10,000 a year. For example, an 8 or 10 percent return (as contrasted with the 100 percent return promised) on one's money is also perhaps pretty good when money rates are not unusually high. Why disillusion people? The copy must show what their investment is and give them realistic figures to expect.

The next decision to be made was whether to go into national magazines or stick to a market-by-market coverage. What would the media schedule be? The Charger company found the national media to be the best, and it decided to use both display and classified advertisements. But testing and coding of advertisements is very important. If the company were to enter a new medium, the company should not go into it with a four-hundred- or two-hundred-line ad. The company should take a one-inch ad and place it in the medium—whether it be *Playboy*, *True*, *Business Week*—and test its pull before deciding to go into a six-inch or half-page advertisement. That is, the advertisement should be coded so that consequent inquiries can be traced back to their source. Emphasis on the processing of inquiries cannot be overdone, for every inquiry is valuable and must be treated as such.

Charger counted its inquiries and checked carefully on the quality, handling, and cost per inquiry. An inquiry often came in with many pertinent questions. If the questions were not answered properly and were answered with a general form letter, a costly mistake could have been made.

The number of second responses resulting from an inquiry is also important. One may receive six thousand initial inquiries, but the kind of responses received when the firm answers the six thousand inquiries is very important. How many times do the inquirers reply to a firm's first response to the inquirer? Charger kept precise records on second responses.

The method of follow-up and the consistency of response are very important. Does a steady stream of inquiries result, or do the inquiries come in at one time and then stop?

Charger Enterprises, Inc., also paid close attention to conversions (sales of franchises) and particularly the number of inquiries needed to produce a sale and from what media. Qualified leads are the important thing, not just leads of any kind.

With Charger Enterprises, the two most successful media were *The Wall Street Journal* and *Business Week*.

A Convenience Grocery Store Company

This convenience grocery store company is the franchisor of grocery stores of a Mom-and-Pop type, open from early morning until late at night seven days a week. Recruitment is entirely different from what it was with Charger Enterprises, Inc.

The practice of this convenience grocery store company was to select the site, build the store, and then select the franchisee to operate it. The typical franchisee of these Mom-and-Pop stores just did not read *The Wall Street Journal*. He also would not be found in the hiring hall because he was not unemployed. He was not found on college campuses because he was too old. Moreover, if advertisements read like help wanted ads, they would not get the right type of person. He would then be looking for a job, not necessarily an opportunity to exercise his right to be in business for himself.

Although not from the same company, a little study by Convenient Food Mart (CFM), Chicago, in regard to the characteristics of its operators revealed some interesting findings about its franchisees. Recruitment attempts by CFM should, of course, be directed toward securing more of the same types of people for franchisees, since they were definitely successful. Quoting from CFM's house organ:

Profile of a CFM Operator. During September of 1974, questionnaires were mailed from the Chicago Regional Development Department to approximately 535 Convenient Food Mart stores. The purpose was to obtain a profile of a CFM Operator. Of those questionnaires sent out, 151 CFM Operators (28.2%) responded. The following information is representative of the cross section compiled from those responses.

Personal. Of the 151 respondents, 140 are married while the remaining 11 are single, separated, divorced and widowed.

The average age of a CFM Operator is 39.8 years.

Three CFM Operators are below the age of 20 years.

One CFM Operator is above the age of 61 years.

The average number of children is 2.7.

Educational. Of the 151 respondents, 85 CFM Operators (56.3%) have a High School Education, while 41 CFM Operators (27.1%) have a Degree and 10 have education beyond a College Degree. Twenty-five CFM Operators (16.6%) have had special courses beyond High School, including Trade Courses, some College or any other advanced specialty training.

Previous Experience. What kind of background did a CFM Operator have prior to obtaining his store? Eighty-nine CFM Operators (58.9%) had some experience in the food industry. Twelve professional occupations were listed by the respondents with a high concentration in the fields of Law and Engineering.

The remaining list included such diversified vocations as Barber, Language Teacher, Resort Owner, and one respondent who was associated with the C.I.A.

Community Relations. The average CFM Operator participates in 1.3 community organizations such as Kiwanis Club and Little League.[4]

Mom-and-Pop Grocery Store Company found that the effective place to advertise for new franchisees was in the business opportunity publications and trade journals pertaining to the grocery business and through fliers and handouts at franchised stores. Most new leads came from present owners. The owners came in contact with thousands of different people (who are their customers) and in casual conversation with them, their enthusiasm cannot help but show. This enthusiasm is worth many column inches of advertising copy.

Mom-and-Pop store owners were provided with ample literature giving some of the facts and opportunities open to interested people. The packet of literature was very simple and to the point and stressed the theme, "You, too, can be an owner." When the interested party called the company representative, the latter made an appointment for a group meeting where several couples were in attendance.

The initial meeting is very important. Most people are afraid to jump from the known to the unknown and the atmosphere is much better if there are several people around planning the jump. Numbers breed confidence and in open discussion the general feeling of fear is alleviated if they can see what others think of the same thing.

At this initial meeting, time should be spent in emphasizing that the franchisor is behind them 100 percent and that the franchisor will be there to help when they need it. The sincere prospects are a little doubtful of their ability to do a good job. This really is their reason for seeking a franchise and not going it alone. Therefore, the foundation of cooperation and proper attitude toward franchising as a whole must be laid at this time if a successful and permanent franchisee is to be obtained.

In the case of this particular franchise company, films and literature were shown the prospects, pointing to the opportunity for profit and security, with an emphasis on generalities in this first group session. The company tried to make two points clear: that there is an opportunity with them, and that the franchisor would stand by to help the franchisees do a good job.

More literature was distributed to the prospects at the first session, including an application blank, and they were urged to complete the application.

This description reemphasizes that different types of operation require different approaches to recruitment, and, as indicated, this fact is no better illustrated than by a comparison between the Mom-and-Pop Grocery Store Company and Charger Enterprises.

Recruitment by a Major Rental Chain

Now let us turn to a third type of operation: a major product rental chain. Daily rental centers require a few unusual considerations. The hours in the rental business are long; for example, in summertime, from 7 A.M. to 9 P.M. are not unusual hours. It is a seven-day a week business in most communities, with, in many cases, as much as 60 percent of a week's business written on Saturday and

Sunday. A man looking for a 9-to-5, forty-hour-week livelihood would not last six months. A man with religious convictions prohibiting him from conducting business on Saturday or Sunday would not make a satisfactory profit. One not really dedicated to doing things for others would become a raving lunatic in his first year. One incapable of coping with endless detail would lose his way quickly.

To secure franchisees with these and other qualities necessary for success in the general rental business, the rental company resorted to mass advertising, with these two criteria uppermost: the average income level of a media's readership was matched to the financial involvement required of the franchisee; and advertising copy contained clearly stated qualifying requirements, particularly of a financial nature.

To ignore these two criteria would result in prohibitive cost per qualified prospect, dissipation of manpower capabilities, and a waste in every direction.

A study of franchisor follow-through practices served the purpose of compelling the company to revise its answer package to eliminate a lot of window dressing and to present its story in a clear, comprehensive, complete fashion including realistic, supportable earnings and expense data.

Recruiting Practices of a Major Motel

A major motel franchise operation (which differs considerably from others in that a sizable initial cash investment of more than half a million dollars is required) recruits through the hotel industry, real estate developers, publicity, word-of-mouth about particular locations, and direct solicitation by mail to potential investors. Motels, unlike many franchised operations, are likely to be investor- (absentee) owned and not operator-owned businesses.

**Indirect Recruitment: The Franchise
Broker and the Itinerant Salesman**

The follow-up of leads and even the generating of leads have been delegated to itinerant commissioned franchise salesmen and to resident franchise brokers by some if not many franchisor firms. New franchisors most often engage in this practice. Obviously, giving the itinerant salesman free rein suffers from all the limitations in control and possible misrepresentation inherent in the sales operation built upon compensation by commission alone. The salesmen may generate the "fat commissions" and the company the "fat problems."

Conceptually, at least, the national franchise sales organization operating through resident local brokers would appear to have great merit, particularly for the franchisor just starting out. Although the broker is not to be confused with the franchise consultant, the broker can theoretically provide guidance in the development of the franchise package and in modifying it to gain greater acceptance among prospective franchisees and ultimate consumers.

Several firms have operated nationally as franchise brokers, but they generally have not done well financially. Although the basic concept would appear to be sound, in practice it has suffered many shortcomings. One of these was the fact that resident brokers were usually franchisees themselves, and they were not equipped with the personality, temperament, and entrepreneurial outlook to assume a dynamic role in the complex operation required. Where national representation was desired by the franchisor, he was limited by the capabilities of the local franchisees of the national concern. If the franchisee broker was capable, results were good. If the franchisee broker for some reason did not have the capabilities required, his representation of the franchisor was correspondingly limited.

The resident broker did have one advantage, however, over the itinerant salesman. He had to live with his sale, and suffer its consequences or continue to profit from its merits. The situation, of course, was akin to that in many other types of business operations in which the activities of local wholesalers may be compared with those of itinerant commission salesmen. To prevent the obvious problems, the suggestion was made that salesmen and brokers be provided with so many franchise packages and leads that the sorting-out process would mean adequate matching of franchisee and franchise package and suitable compensation for all.

The Screening and Selection Process in Five Companies

In practice, of course, the requirements, or qualifications, of prospective franchisees should be carefully formulated before recruitment begins, but since recruitment precedes selection, the recruitment problem could legitimately be discussed first. Now let us turn to the screening and selection process.

The Melvin J. Evans Company gave "endless tests to prospective franchisees" in connection with its activities on behalf of Mister Donut of America, and Evans characterized the personality of the successful franchisee thus:

1. He is anxious to step out of what may have been a rut and become a businessman in his own right. In other words, he has just a little more push and vitality than the other individuals—a little more drive, that is,
2. He is also interested in increasing his income. Many times this phase of the operation may have ballooned in his mind to a point where it is almost out of proportion.
3. He is apt to be opinionated and anxious to work on his own and, therefore, may be somewhat difficult to bring into a new pattern.

4. Sometimes the capabilities of the prospects are not as great as their ambition.
5. Frequently they are men with considerable instability in their personalities. In other words they are not emotionally mature.[5]

However, as Evans points out, the subject is so complex with so many ramifications that it is difficult to characterize the successful franchisee in a few words. Nor would the characteristics of successful Mister Donut franchisees necessarily be the same as those of successful franchisees in other networks.

One of the best indications of the capabilities of a person is his actual performance on the job during an initial period blocked off for test and training purposes. Many franchisors do not sign the final franchise agreement until the prospective franchisee has satisfactorily completed at least the initial period of training, during which the franchisee experiences the various phases of operation in which he is to engage, and the franchisor has the opportunity to observe his performance. At the end of this trial period, the franchisee's deposit may be refunded in part or in full at the request of either signee of the agreement. In operations in which considerable technical skill must be acquired, the initial trial period is particularly important. Pretrial indicators are generally of little value.

The range of problems and practices is so great, however, that generalizations are of dubious value. For this reason, the case example approach will be resorted to on the following pages.

Building Materials Company

Here is a list of franchisee characteristics required by a building materials company, according to its president.

1. Prior business experience is mandatory. The franchisor found that the firm could teach only the technical information franchisees required, yet a franchisee could not succeed without being a good businessman. The firm also found that this business experience automatically helped the selection process because a good businessman could do a better job of "selecting" the franchisor and was more apt to select a field in which he was certain to succeed.
2. All of the company's franchisees must have sales experience or sales ability because this also is a requirement for success and yet is something that time does not permit the franchisor to teach.
3. The firm's franchisees must have money. The franchisor frequently helped a franchisee with his finances but insisted that it was not in the banking business.

To the casual observer, it would appear that this franchisor did very little screening. However, the company screened by recruiting in the right places. Why? The company found early in the game that it was too late to be truly objective when an application with a $10,000 check arrived on the sales manager's desk. Also, the firm found it was better off to overrecruit so that its field representatives could have several qualified prospects from which to select.

Credit Checking Service

This company supplied a credit management service, including credit reporting and collection services to retail business and professional men. The service was marketed through franchise holders. There were no company outlets.

Upon receipt of an application for a franchise, the company proceeded as follows:

1. His references were contacted to check the applicant's character.
2. He was interviewed personally by telephone or face-to-face to ascertain how he sounded and acted. Two to four company principals judged the applicant independently.
3. The company paid the applicant's travel expenses for a personal visit to the New York offices for evaluation and personal selling of the franchise.

The company was interested in the answers to seven questions regarding the franchisee:

1. His personality
2. Health
3. Willingness to work
4. Ability to work unsupervised
5. His family's attitude toward the business (part of the business is collections, and this is a dirty word in many circles)
6. Will a member of the family be working with him?
7. Does the applicant understand that it takes time and hard work to build his business?

Manpower, Inc.

Since Manpower's success and practices are public knowledge, its actual name will be used. Manpower, Inc. is an international firm supplying temporary office help. In 1965 the company had some 363 offices on five continents and no more than one office per city.[6] Of those outside the United States, some 60 were located in twenty-three foreign countries serving fifty-one cities.

Personal trips to these countries were required as a part of the recruitment procedure. Language barriers were, of course, a problem of major proportions. Quoting Motte:

> Our name alone, Manpower, is untranslatable in some foreign languages. Recently I placed some ads in a foreign country, Nigeria. You may wonder why we want to go there, but we do. One gentleman in all seriousness wrote back and said in a very disjointed way, "I would like to have your catalogue." We thought "Fine," and read on. He said, "I would like to become a better man." He was translating "Manpower" as a way to become more powerful as a man. He wanted a catalogue of our "talismans," as he called it, our good luck charms. He wanted to buy one.[7]

As is apparent, problems of describing the franchise are magnified in foreign countries. Manpower requires the prospective franchisee to visit offices in the United States as a part of the selection and training process.

Reliance may be placed on Dun & Bradstreet credit checks, but these are slow in coming, and as a result, resort must be made to banks and other credit report services—special investigations by people who do this kind of work. Manpower insists that any future franchisee or interested one visit an existing franchise office.

> We want him to spend some time to learn what the business is all about, to learn all about it before he commits himself to us. We only want him if he wants us. . . . We also have our prospective franchisees visit the home office. . . . We pay the transportation costs for the trip to Milwaukee. Since he has to come back again for training at his own expense, we only pay for one of the trips, and then only if he is signed. He knows this before he comes. It is part of his investment. It is unlikely he will make the trip even with that offer unless he is truly interested and ready to go ahead. In the United States we found the best media for us to use to attract qualified recruits is, again, display advertising in local newspapers, and we use this, I would say, fifty percent of the time and other types such as personal business appeals the remainder of the time.[8]

Mom-and-Pop Convenience Grocery Store Company

The Mom-and-Pop Stores made a study of its existing franchise owners and came up with the following profile of the most successful people:

1. Optimum age: 43½ years
2. Married
3. One or more teenagers who help in the business
4. Wife has worked at some job other than being a housewife
5. Since the business is retail grocery stores, experience in a grocery store at some time (This situation was true in 60 percent of the cases.)
6. Saved initial down payment from hard work—not being set up in business by a rich uncle
7. A person genuinely interested in being in business for himself, and not just an unemployed person looking for a job

In connection with recruiting, it was necessary that the qualifications of the prospective franchisee be kept in mind in the choice of media, appeals, and so on.

The applicant for the franchise completed the application blank, and headquarters personnel carefully studied it to determine the following points:

1. *The applicant's management plan:* "If they state that the wife is going to help and there are some real young children, we have to deduct a few points," says a corporate officer. "We take a real close look at how they plan to operate their unit and what outside help they feel they need." In fact, the applicant is requested to write a fifty-word statement on his management plan. If he seems to want to run an absentee ownership store and use only hired help, the company tends to bow out because the secret to the success of this type of franchise rests in the owner participation concept.
2. *Where do they live?* Will it be necessary for them to make a long and costly move or commute?
3. *Personal history:* Have they had any scrapes with the law that would keep them from obtaining local licenses required?
4. *Employment history:* Have they worked in a clock punching type of work, or has it been one where they could exercise some independent thinking? Have they jumped from job to job?
5. *Previous independent business:* Some special checks should be made in the area of his last business.
6. *Bank and credit references*
7. *Earnings:* "We are most interested in what they have been earning annually and also what they think they should earn the first year and after three years. Every new business takes a while to develop and we want to be sure our prospect is aware of this. If they say, '$100,000 a year net earnings,' we then know that what we have to offer won't do and it is much better to

clear the air before you start. It doesn't mean you have lost them as a prospect—it does mean, however, that you must re-educate them."

8. *Financial status:* "We make a close study of their financial statement. If their liabilities are too great and their monthly obligations keep them strapped, we hesitate to let them take on more, especially if they are doing so on borrowed money. If their capital comes as a gift or loan from their relatives, we also become concerned. A slow start tends to disrupt an entire family and you'll very well end up with a casualty. We are in a position of being their business advisors and we ought not shirk our duty—or pay later—dearly."

9. *Health record:* "We scrutinize very closely their health record. Going into business for yourself does present a strain, especially in our type, so special note should be made of cardiac problems. If the wife is going to be an important factor in the franchise and she indicates varicose veins, they are going to be in trouble, because our people are required to stand up a lot."

As an executive in the company stated it, "If, after all of this, we still feel that they will be a good franchisee, we invite them [husband and wife] in for a private discussion to talk about the details. This is done by the same individual who talked to them in the group. We do not want them to feel that we are bringing in the 'shock troops' to make a 'sale.' We talk about the possible areas available, their estimated potential, etc. Then we go through the contract word by word. No attempt is made to have them sign at this time. We urge them to see their attorney, their accountant, their banker, and other franchise owners, and to visit their area and make a careful study in the light of what we have learned about it from our real estate people."

The company had Rohrer, Hibler, and Replogle, an outstanding firm in the field of psychological assessments, develop a battery of selection tests for company use. The battery was used initially in selection, but the long testing procedure tended to scare away the franchise applicants. Although the battery of tests was used later in counseling and placement, it was soon discontinued in the selection process.

"We Rent Everything" Company

The selection procedures in "We Rent Everything" Company were discussed in connection with recruitment, but will be reviewed here. In essence, the company's selection process made use of what might be termed the concept of successive hurdles—in broad terms, age, financial responsibility, and experience. Of these three major criteria, probably that of financial responsibility was predominant. "If the prospect does not have the dollars required, it makes little difference how outstanding his qualifications are."

In daily rental centers there are also some special qualifications that must be met by the prospective franchisee:

1. The franchisee must be willing to work long hours, in summer from 7 A.M. to 9 P.M. seven days a week.
2. Since Saturday and Sunday are apt to be peak days, a man with religious convictions preventing him from conducting business on these days would not make a satisfactory return in the business.
3. One not really dedicated to doing things for others would not make a satisfactory franchisee.
4. One incapable of coping with endless detail would lose his way quickly.
5. One not adept at personal selling will be less satisfied with his results in the rental business.

Summary

The two basic marketing problems in franchising are distinct but interdependent. Sound marketing of the franchise, or the recruitment and selection of franchisees, must be based on demonstrably profitable opportunities for the prospective franchisee to market products or services.

Approaches to problems of recruitment and selection are as varied as the franchise operations themselves. Among other factors pertinent to a successful approach are (1) the objectives of the franchisor firm, (2) the age of the firm, (3) the initial capital and ultimate investment required of the franchise, and (4) the personal and related qualifications the franchisee must have.

An important consideration in the evaluation of the approach is the obtaining of qualified leads. National advertising, particularly in the business opportunities sections of such media as *The Wall Street Journal,* appears to be the most productive source of leads to prospective franchisees. With established franchisor firms, referrals by current franchisees are a most valuable source of leads to new dealers. With some franchisor firms, potentially successful franchisees just do not read *The Wall Street Journal* and similar publications.

The handling of inquiries is of paramount importance. At some point in the recruitment process, and preferable early, face-to-face contact is desirable between franchisor and prospective recruit. In foreign operations, this contact is an absolute must. Presentations should be simple, with the facts being given in a clear and straightforward manner. Realistic, supportable earnings and expense data should be provided. At least one visit by the prospect to another franchise operation is most desirable. Items in the uniform disclosure statement, discussed in an earlier chapter, should be covered in some detail at an opportune time with the prospective franchisee, and hopefully his lawyer.

Even before recruitment begins, however, a list of qualifications desired in franchisees should be formulated. This list might be designed as a series of successive hurdles. The first hurdle is, of course, the capital requirement. Does the prospect have the required capital? Inclusion of this item in the recruitment advertisement itself may eliminate many nonqualified readers who are apt to respond. A second requirement is a management plan for the operation. Does the applicant have a management plan which fits the operation? If not, can his plan be modified through education? Third, can the prospect be trained in the elements of the operation? In operations requiring skill levels above average, this question assumes great importance. One of the best approaches to the answering of this question is to place the prospect in training for a trial period with the stipulation that the franchisee's deposit will be returned and negotiations terminated at the request of either party.

From these approaches more or less applicable in most concerns, the franchisor company can proceed to the special requirements of its own operation, in terms, for example, of age, health, willingness to work long hours, family assistance, interest in selling, and business experience. Probably the best way in which to evaluate these is through the personal interview, conducted not by the salesman with the check for the deposit on the table, but by a reasonably impartial individual not involved in the agreement.

Implicit in all sound recruitment and selection procedures is some assessment of risk to the franchisor and to the prospective franchisee—communicated clearly and in an unbiased manner. Too often this risk has been surrounded with imagery that connotes opportunity without hazard. The franchise system does generally reduce the risks to the individual starting a business, but the risk varies widely, depending not only on the type of franchise operation involved but also on the type of individual applying for the franchise. Franchising is seen by many as an excellent medium for bringing minority groups into the mainstream of American business, and the validity of this view is demonstrated by the increasing numbers of blacks. Hispanics, and other minorities who are opening and operating franchises successfully.

6 Training Franchisees

Two major types or levels of training are involved in franchising. First, the training of franchisees, and second, the training of franchisee employees. Training, of course, goes hand in glove with recruitment and selection: if only potential successes are recruited, selection will not be a problem; if only trained personnel are selected, the training problem will be nonexistent. Initial training is necessary only to fill the gaps in skills and knowledge of newly selected personnel, and the selection methods should, if possible, reveal strengths and weaknesses of the prospects so that training can be tailored accordingly.

Barrett has pointed out that an organization has three functions: to deliver its product or service, to conserve its resources, and to change itself.[1] A business organization is unique in that its objective is to accomplish these objectives at a profit. The function of training is to enhance or increase the efficiency with which these functions are performed. The franchisee in a large measure purchases the franchise to obtain the training necessary to accomplish these purposes most efficiently with maximum profit. Looking at the problem another way, "Training is simply one among many ways to improve productivity."[2]

"Training," according to Barrett, "involves three basic goals: to improve skills, to modify values and knowledge, or to impart information."[3] A skill is something one cannot master simply by reading about it; it requires practice. Values are a composite of personal values, prejudices, attitudes, and beliefs. Information imparted to trainees includes facts, assumptions, or opinions, plus trade gossip and grapevine data.

The training of franchisees is directed toward all three goals: the improvement of skills, the modification of values and knowledge, and the imparting of information. The training of franchisee personnel—clerks, countergirls, doughnut makers, pump hands—is very heavily in the area of skills.

Franchisees are generally retail unit managers, although in recent years franchisors have tended to grant successful unit operators additional units as they become available, and in such cases the franchisee is thoroughly familiar with unit operations when he obtains the second outlet. Training can be minimal, although some attention should be given to certain new elements introduced by the addition of a second, third, and fourth unit. As a matter of fact, as the numbers increase, the problems take on the characteristics of those associated with absentee ownership or corporate management. The owner of multiple units becomes a miniature franchisor, and he is called a franchisor in some franchise companies.

Franchise training, of course, is a special type of training, but certain general criteria must be met by all programs, enumerated by Stevens as follows: (1) The training program must be easily administered. (2) The program must be self-paced and individualized. (3) It must be economical. (4) It must be continuous.[4] The training program must be easily administered because the average firm does not have the managerial resources, or at least will not allocate them for training. Since trainees are ordinarily a diverse group with great variations in ability and experience, the training program must be designed so that individuals can proceed at their own pace.

Three important components of the training system are (1) a task analysis, which identifies the elements of the program and matches them with the abilities and experiences of the students; (2) the medium or media to be used—a teaching machine or purely paper or some combination, with instructors, as well; and (3) validation of the program—that it teaches what it sets out to teach. Stevens advocated programmed instruction as a solution to the training program in the franchise field:

> Programmed instruction provides the student with information in logical sequences that allow him to progress through the training at his own maximum rate. This means that the bright student with good preparation will be exposed to considerably less material than the slow student with minimum preparation. . . . the program will motivate the student to continue and will constantly test the student's progress and mastery of the subject through examinations built into the program.[5]

Sources of Training Materials

Since so many new franchise chains in recent years are in the fast food field it should be noted that the National Restaurant Association (NRA) has developed numerous training aids in the restaurant business. For example, NRA developed at a cost of $80,000 a color film showing career opportunities for teenagers in the food industry. The Proctor & Gamble Company cosponsored the production. Another illustration are three films on sanitary practices in the food industry.

Companies which participated in Boston College's Franchise Industry Training programs developed special training materials for clerks, doughnut makers, and so on.[6]

A book by John W. Stokes titled *How to Manage a Restaurant* will also give the reader a better understanding of the food service field.[7] The book covers a wide range of topics, from planning the menu through principles of design and layout, kitchen equipment and layout, to sanitation, safety, fire protection, laws and regulations affecting restaurants and food services, computers and systems analysis, and alcoholic beverages. Also, the large national accounting firm,

Laventhal Krekstein Horwath & Horwath, monitors operational results of restaurants and has consolidated the information in booklet form for its clientele.

Dun & Bradstreet has published a bibliography pertinent to going into and managing small businesses in diverse fields.[8] Specific businesses covered range from air conditioning through motels, record shops, and restaurants to variety stores. Illustrative of the individual businesses covered in the part of the bibliography headed "Specific Businesses" are the following titles: nursery business, electronic & appliance specialist, handicrafts and home businesses, bakery production and marketing, American hairdresser-salon owner, and how to run a paperback bookshop. There are approximately six hundred fifty titles in the section of the bibliography on specific businesses. In addition, another significant part of the bibliography covers general subjects such as advertising and selling, credit and collections, financing, keeping accounts, and so on.

Also, the Bank of America, San Francisco, publishes the *Small Business Reporter* under three headings, "Business Profiles," "Business Operations," and "Professional Management." These cover formats, investment requirements, and so forth, of specific businesses from apparel manufacturing to shoe stores; business operations such as advertising and finance; and the business side of other professions.

Five Training Programs Illustrated

The following are brief illustrations of five training programs, four involving franchisees and one for supermarket managers. Company names have been changed to avoid identification of individuals and programs. One company is a major bicycle manufacturer that changed its distribution method to a franchise system with retail units selling directly to the general public rather than to intermediaries. Although possessing many characteristics of the Type IV (trade-name sponsor) franchise system, it is essentially a Type I (manufacturer-retailer) franchise system.

The second training program described briefly is that of a major petroleum marketer, and indeed another illustration of training in the Type I franchise system. As with the first system franchisees (or dealers) use the name of the company for their units, and for that reason the system has many characteristics of Type IV systems.

Both the bicycle and gasoline franchise systems require relatively small franchise investments by the franchisees. The third illustration is that of a major motel chain—a Type IV system to be sure, but one in which franchisees must invest sizable sums of money. It is a franchise system, differing from most such systems, in which absentee ownership is common. Following these is an illustration, albeit brief, of the training program of a trade name franchisor in the rental field. In conclusion, the training program for managers of a company-owned (nonfranchised) supermarket chain is discussed briefly.

It should be emphasized that these training programs were not chosen for description because they are necessarily typical. Franchisor training programs vary so widely in breadth, depth, and objectives that it would be virtually impossible to say what program is typical. Nor would it be entirely correct to depict the programs of McDonald's (Hamburger University), Holiday Inns, and the automotive and soft drink companies at their formalized schools and conclude that these training schools reflect general practices in the industry. What is done here is to describe certain programs which highlight rather common training problems and their solutions.

Major Bicycle Manufacturer

Background. This large unnamed manufacturer of bicycles originally sold bicycles through department stores, tire stores, hardware stores, toy stores, and so on, and over a period of years had accumulated fifteen thousand accounts. Analysis of records indicated that 27 percent of the accounts sold 94 percent of the company's bicycles. Yet shopping tests showed that even many of the high volume dealers could not answer customers' questions about the product, did not know how to service bicycles properly, and had little interest in learning. As a result of these analyses and surveys, the company decided to convert their distribution set-up to a franchise system. It began by weeding out the worst accounts, thus reducing the number to three thousand sales and service dealers.

Franchised dealers were more highly motivated to learn the intricacies of the bicycle than department store clerks, and turnover of dealers was considerably less than that of sales employees. Later the franchised dealers were found to maintain higher standards than sales clerk employees did, were more courteous, and learned more readily some of the more complicated bicycles. Most importantly, however, was the fact that sales volume doubled as a result of conversion to a franchised system with ensuing benefits in receptivity to training and lowered turnover.

Formulating Training Objectives. One of the first tasks in establishing the training program was the formulation of training objectives to assure that the training was a sound investment for the franchisor, the franchisee, and the customer. The following three objectives were formulated to meet this requirement:

1. To qualify the franchisee as a true expert in the product and service he offers.
2. To indoctrinate the franchisee with a sincere desire to render outstanding

service to his customers and to the public in a manner which will enhance the good will of the franchisor's trademark and promote its further growth through customer satisfaction.

3. To assure the success, the well-being and the future security of each franchisee and his employees.

These objectives might apply to any franchise system.

Organizing the Training Program. There were four basic steps which the company took to organize their training program, and these are steps which any franchise system (and for that matter, any business system) must take in organizing the training program:

1. Research, planning, and budgeting.
   a. Defining what needs to be taught.
   b. Planning the means by which the material can and will be taught.
   c. Preparing the budget and tailoring the training program to fit that budget.
2. Staffing, training, and managing, including the employing of a training consultant to oversee the various steps, particularly the first step involving research, planning, and budgeting.
3. Field supervision and continuous training.
4. Evaluating results in terms of dealer reaction and month-by-month sales reports.

Types of Training. The company developed two major types of training programs, as follows:

1. The Dealer Service Training School, with classes year around. In the service school, dealers were taught bicycle repair and service methods (and the dealers were actually doing the work). In essence, the teacher says, "Here's how you do it. Now you try it." The schools carried benches, tools, and an ample supply of bicycles, hubs, brakes, and derailleurs. The dealer assembled and disassembled until he passed the test. Initially there was no contractual requirement that the dealer pass the factory training service test, but this requirement was eventually added to the agreement.
2. The Cyclery Sales and Management School, lasting three days with a maximum of forty dealers per class. The dealer was taught
   a. Salesmanship
   b. Proper design and operation of a modern bicycle store
   c. Site evaluation
   d. Store layout and design
   e. Merchandising

f.   Advertising and promotion

g.   Display

h.   Service management and business methods

(The company stocked and sold fixtures and equipment, tools, signs, and store supplies on a nonprofit basis, and the dealer trainees could inspect and order these while at the factory school. The company also provided a free advisory service to new dealers and to those being relocated. In addition, the company provided catalogs, manuals, brochures, specification sheets, bulletins, and a regular house organ; dealer meetings were also held at yearly intervals.)

Training Methods. In the service schools and meetings, "learning by doing" was emphasized. These steps were taken:

1. The instructor explained and demonstrated the operation of a component to the class—for instance, a coaster brake or three-speed hub. He showed how to disassemble it and diagnose the causes of the faulty operation. The instructor showed how the repair was made and the unit reassembled, adjusted, and tested.
2. Each trainee repeated the process at his own bench and the instructor graded each student-dealer.
3. If the dealer achieved a passing grade on the three-day training course, he received a Company Factory Trained Service Certificate. If the grade was not passing, the dealer could repeat.

In the sales and management training schools, sales techniques, service-after-the-sale, product knowledge, business know-how, and operational improvement were emphasized.

The following were stressed in the development of sales techniques:

1. Physical demonstrations of the special quality construction features which made the company's bicycles different from other bicycles—for example, the double-thickness tubular rims, which were lighter in weight and five times stronger than ordinary single-thickness rims.
2. How to use the bicycle parts on the demonstration board.
3. How to point out the differences between the company's solid forged steel front forks and the hollow tubular forks used in other bicycles.
4. Welded-on versus bolted-on kickstands.
5. How to demonstrate stronger construction by standing on the chainguard and sitting on the rear fender.

To impress these points upon dealers, soundslide films, manuals, and actual practice in the sales school classes were utilized.

The six steps of the sale and the approach to service-after-the-sale were emphasized, with courtesy in customer contacts (using Dartnell soundslide films) being stressed. Courtesy in handling complaints and adjustments under the company's guarantee was given particular attention.

Since it was necessary to convert the company from a wholesale outlook to a retail outlook, the trainers and training supervisors themselves were initially placed in retail stores. It was soon discovered that salesmanship was much easier in beautiful stores with beautiful displays and a "quality" atmosphere (for example, with carpeted bicycle showrooms), and such features were emphasized. However, product knowledge, applications, and new products were continuously stressed.

In training for operational improvement and modern business management, the company soon learned that dealers must first be persuaded they need it. The second step was to overcome resistance to change. Then the third phase, or actual training in sound and efficient business management, could begin.

Joint sales calls were a feature of the sales training. The neophyte dealer went out with an experienced dealer until he felt qualified to operate alone. Also, plant visits and calls on distribution centers with qualified tour guides were an integral part of the training program.

So much for franchised dealer training by this major bicycle manufacturer.

Large Petroleum Marketer

Background. As is probably well-known, franchisees in the petroleum business are referred to as *dealers*; and in these days of dealer mortality, changes are so rapid that the procedures of one day may be problematic the next. The training program of one major petroleum marketer, however, is such a model program that it is reviewed here in detail.

Dealers are the marketer's first-line salesmen, the men who represent the company to the buying public and the men who actually sell the company's products. The problem of dealer turnover is so important that this description covers what the company was doing to develop and keep better dealers, who contribute so greatly to the company's success or failure in the marketplace.

The trend in recent years, dictated by the motorist customer, is toward "one-stop service," including complete car care, not only the purchase of petroleum products but also tires, batteries, accessories, safety check, brake service, wheel alignment, motor tune-up, and even lawn mower repairs. Many companies are experimenting with the possibilities of merchandising other lines, ranging from groceries to chemical fertilizers. Additional services tried have extended from laundry pick-up stations to car rentals, and experiments are continuing. The so-called filling station has thus rapidly been replaced with first-class marketing establishments.

The businessmen operating service stations today gross more per annum than proprietors of restaurants, drug stores, garages, and most other neighborhood establishments. These trends demand that these businesses be operated by independent businessmen who are extremely well qualified, capable, and knowledgeable in all aspects of today's modern service station operations. Hence, the company decided that its antiquated training program would need considerable revision to meet current needs.

Two Major Objectives of Gas Station Training Programs. The first step in redesigning the company's existing training program was a planning meeting, with attendees composed of sales managers, dealer salesmen, lessee dealers, the manager of sales training, and a newly employed sales consultant. The consultant served as the catalyst for discussion, and the approach was strictly unstructured with emphasis on new approaches. The various diverse groups were brought into the session to assure cooperation in the implementation of the program once it was designed.

As a result of the planning meeting, and subsequent discussions, it was possible to formulate two primary objectives: to provide training that would increase profits for both dealers and the company and to increase sales volume through service stations.

Two Major Components of Training Program. To achieve these objectives two major components of the training program were defined:

I. *Policies*
   A. All new lessee dealers would be required to attend a two-week dealer school prior to taking over a service station.
   B. New, independent dealers would be required also to take on-the-job training at a going service station.
   C. Follow-up training and counseling would be provided both new and old dealers, according to need.
   D. Field training meetings would be held with both dealers and their employees.
   E. Subjects covered would be determined by the specific needs of the group.
II. *Dealer Training Program*
   A. Methods, techniques, and training materials
      1. Lectures (no reading of scripts)
      2. Visualization of all types
      3. Total involvement of students
         a. Assignments
         b. Case discussions
         c. Illustrations

   d. Demonstrations

   e. Role playing

   f. Workshops

  4. Classrooms with tables rearranged in U's to create a council or group meeting atmosphere

  5. Teaching from prepared outlines

  6. Teaching materials, aids

   a. Films

   b. Flannel boards

   c. Passout booklets

B. Course content

  1. Merchandising, including product information

  2. Selling in the service station

  3. Sales promotion and advertising

  4. Personnel

  5. Housekeeping

   a. Maintenance

   b. Safety

  6. Public relations

  7. Management

  8. Customer appeal

  9. Money management (including records)

   a. Credit

   b. Taxes

   c. Insurance

C. Teaching sites

  1. Baltimore

  2. Boston

  3. Cleveland

  4. Chicago

  5. Kansas City

  6. Miami

  7. Shreveport

  8. St. Paul

(A trailer equipped as a classroom was used for teaching certain groups.)

D. On-the-job training stations, standards for selection. (The company selected more than 150 outstanding lessee dealers and their stations as sites for on-the-job training.)

  1. Station appearance

  2. Dealers and employees in uniform

  3. Customer relations

  4. Driveaway service

      5. Merchandizing methods

      6. Sales promotion activities

      7. Clean restrooms

      8. Complete lube room and service-bay service

      9. Use of money management profit-guide record system

    10. Dealer's proper handling of his personal credit accounts

    11. Financial stability of dealer

    12. Sales equal or exceeding potential set for station

    13. Loyalty to the company

(Prospective dealers following their classroom training were immediately placed in these stations at company expense and given a one-week, on-the-job course.)

E. Field training meetings (Dealer counselors periodically held meetings on selected subjects in the field as requested by sales representatives, dealers, or distributors.)

F. Selection, training, and evaluation of instructors

    1. Instructors were young men selected from the ranks of dealer salesmen. They worked with 140 dealers in their stations.

    2. They were given special adult education instruction and were thoroughly familiarized with all training aids, materials, records, and so forth. Before beginning teaching they were required to conduct training sessions under the supervision of the manager of sales training.

    3. Evaluation of instructors was by division managers, division sales managers, and the manager of sales training.

G. Dealer evaluation (This, of course, was the most important step in training.)

    1. Evaluation of dealer by instructor on completion of dealer school. Some points stressed:

      a. Personal appearance

      b. Attitude

      c. Enthusiasm

      d. Initiative

      e. Salesmanship ability

      f. Product knowledge

      g. Apparent leadership qualities

      h. Proficiency in record keeping

    2. Evaluation of trainees by dealer counselors in their stations. Reports from dealer counselors on trainees in their stations pinpoint areas of training still needed by the trainee. The sales representative was responsible for seeing that such training was accomplished.

Fancy Motor Inns, Inc.

The training of personnel and the supervision of franchised Fancy Motor Inns were perhaps more important to Fancy motels than they were to many other franchise operations. This was because the operation of the typical Fancy Motor Inn was complex and involved and because the manner in which the licensed property represented the company was of extremely vital importance to the network. That is, the company had a great many motor inns which it owned and operated itself. These represented assets in the hundreds of millions of dollars, and naturally the performance of franchised properties affected the company's public image and had an important bearing on the success of the parent company as a whole. Therefore, the operation of franchise properties received a great deal of attention.

Training and supervision could not be totally divorced from the subjects of selection and motivation. General managers of Fancy Motor Inns were selected from among individuals who had substantial experience in the field. They may have been general managers or executive assistant managers, or they may have developed through Fancy's own trainee program. They were not newcomers to the industry and probably had a minimum of three or four years in executive capacities.

Basically, Fancy Motels had two types of training: on-the-job training and seminar-type classes. On-the-job training was essential to become familiar with the company's method of operation. In the case of an experienced person, lengthy on-the-job training was not necessary. In the case of a person coming from within the company, this had, of course, been accomplished over the years.

On-the-job training for personnel of franchised Fancy Motor Inns consisted of placing the individual in an existing operation so that he might gain practical experience in each operating department. At the same time, he was given homework consisting of various manuals covering the many phases of operations, which he was required to study during the training period.

The company's seminar-type classes were designed to familiarize general managers with all phases of the operation. In these classes all operating manuals and marketing manuals were reviewed in detail, and a substantial amount of group participation was involved. These classes were kept to fifteen or twenty people, and lasted about three days.

One of the greatest aids to effective training, and supervision for that matter, was the effective motivation of the people involved. Effective motivation came from requiring group participation. The individual attending classes had an opportunity to enter into group discussions of various phases of operation with recognized experts in the field. He had the opportunity to contribute his ideas and these ideas were taken seriously. It is a fact that a number of suggestions contributed were actually put into practice. Fancy Motels attempted to put on a show for these people. Fancy wished them to meet senior staff people, such as the vice-president of engineering, vice-president of food and beverage, the director of advertising and public relations, the reservations director, the senior vice-president of operations, the senior vice-president of staff administration, and many others. Training followed a closely controlled curriculum, but it also included social occasions, and sessions ended with a cocktail party and dinner. The company attempted to establish a personal relationship with each participant and to get him to feel that he was one of the family.

Of course, from within Fancy Motels, the company was occasionally able to supply to licensed properties thoroughly trained company men, and, in these instances, it was not ordinarily necessary for them to attend such classes.

The company trainee program started with the selection of top students at the important hotel schools. The individual was put through a course of on-the-job training in all major departments, a procedure which might last two or three years, and a continual system of follow-up and evaluation was in effect.

Cover-All Rental System

The one single factor more than any other which motivates a man to consider affiliation as a franchisee is his desire to have someone assist him in making correct decisions and provide him with the know-how vital to his new role as a business owner. In the franchising industry the supervisor must be adequately trained to enable him to provide this kind of guidance. The supervisor must be fully informed about his company, his franchise program, and the total details of the business involved. He must be able to train as well as sell. He must be an authority, not an expert.

Three Important Training Aids. Cover-All Rental System used three very important training aids, not generally recognized as such: the job description, the policy manual, and the procedure manual.

The job description was a must in training and included four elements: (1) a clear statement of the next level up—the supervisor must know to whom he reports; (2) a clear statement of the next level down—the supervisor must know whom or what he supervises; (3) a detailed list of responsibilities; and (4) a specific statement of authority.

These four elements gave the supervisor a sense of how he fits into the organization and a clear knowledge of what was expected of him as well as the authority he carried to execute his responsibilities.

Second, the policy manual was a road map. It provided a source to which all could turn to determine the correct route to attainment of the company's goals.

Third, the procedure manual covered twenty-nine steps involving seven departments.

Perhaps problems of Cover-All Rental, Inc., were somewhat more complex than is the case in many franchise systems. One may give a thumbnail sketch of the company's activity in this fashion:

> The company finds a man interested in going into business for himself, convinces him the rental business is good; if he meets company standards, the company assists him in finding the right location, helps negotiate the right kind of lease, selects the inventory of rental equipment he will stock, finances up to 75 percent of his initial equipment cost, guarantees the rentability of his inventory, provides him with insurance, puts him through a preopening training school, handles his advertising for him during his launch period, does his bookkeeping for him, and provides him with continuing management, merchandizing, and money assistance.

The supervisor in the company would have to be at least ten different kinds of specialists: a salesman, an authority on the rental business, a real estate negotiator and market analyst, an equipment expert (and there are three hundred different kinds of equipment in the average rental center), an insurance expert, an advertising consultant, a management consultant, a merchandizing expert, a financial advisor, and a credit manager. The company did not find this combination in many men. This man had to be developed. How was this accomplished? How long did it take? In the Cover-All organization the bulk of training was accomplished in two weeks.

Supervisors Trained in Test Stores. At the outset, Cover-All Rental System was not concerned about sales ability. The supervisor was hired with that background. The first goal was to teach the franchisee all he could absorb about the industry. The company conducted a full-week training course for its franchisees at least once each month. This school was conducted in a permanent test store and training facility in the central office area. Each new supervisor was also enrolled in this course.

During this training course each facet of the rental business was covered. In addition, every item of equipment normally found in a rental center was thoroughly studied. When a franchisee graduated from the school, which spans five full days and three late-evening sessions, he was prepared to open his own rental center and to build a profitable business. The supervisor, therefore, should leave the school with a sound basic knowledge of the business he was to supervise.

The supervisor proceeded to learn a much broader knowledge of the business than the franchisee. The training school was conducted in part by members of the management team. For example, the treasurer conducted a session on financing and proper use of the financing plans available to the franchisee. The advertising manager conducted a session on the use of advertising, promotional aids, and publicity to build business and profits. The supervisor was afforded the extra exposure to each member of the staff. Through these sessions he was able to develop a solid foundation of knowledge in each of the specialized fields. He would be equipped in at least seven of the ten fields of required activity.

Supervisor Put in Field with Superior. The next step in training was to put the supervisor in the field, but not alone. Many a good supervisor had been reduced, as one executive put it, "to a frustrated gibbering parrot by tossing him out to the wolves" without close initial guidance. So Cover-All Rental started him out working with another supervisor or with the franchise manager, or even with the vice-president in charge of marketing—a week with this experienced person followed by a week on his own, and then another week with perhaps a different senior person to broaden his exposure to experience or double check his ability to go it alone.

Once judged capable of going it alone, the supervisor was not finished with training. He was really just starting. At this point, he had graduated temporarily, at least to the school of experience.

Why all this emphasis on and investment in training a supervisor? This led to another question. Could the franchisor really make a better investment in his short- or long-range success? The franchisor's success depended on the success of his franchisees. Their success depended on sound, continuing guidance. The quality of guidance the franchisee got depended a great deal upon the ability of the area supervisor. Was it not logical, therefore, to believe that a dollar invested in training a supervisor today would return many times over in stronger, more profitable franchisees?

The franchise agreement imposed on Cover-All Rental the responsibility of keeping the company's franchisee advised of new methods and procedures developed for the conduct of his business. Many agreements carried a similar requirement. Here was a fixed requirement for further training of the supervisor. One could not turn him out and let him run. His potential contribution to the firm's profits was too great.

This continuing training did not have to be formal, but it would have to be conscious. There would have to be a realization of the vital need for it. There would have to be a recognized effort to carry on such activity. It would not have to be expensive, but it would have to be organized.

Periodic supervisor meetings were one solution, but they were expensive both in terms of time and dollars and, for these reasons, generally too far apart to get the job done. So every morning, first thing in the morning of the training program, the company chose by chance, by a drawing, one individual, and he was directed to the front of the group. For three minutes he expounded on what happened the day before. If in the estimation of his fellow classmates he did a passable job, he was given a silver dollar award.

What this did was to motivate each attendee the night before to review because it just might be that he would be the person chosen to go up front, and he would not want to stand up there for three minutes with nothing to say. This little technique to get them to review what they had been through the day before was well worth the dollar it cost.

The company found that the time to evaluate the program was not the last day of the training program because franchisees were at the peak of enthusiasm. If the training had done a job motivating franchisees, they would not be more enthusiastic. But a month later, perhaps five years later, would be the time to really get the evaluation. The follow-up training was something that the company neglected for a while, but the company soon came to realize that training had to be a continuous effort. Accordingly, regional meetings, association meetings, conventions, and, in fact, every subsequent meeting came to be regarded as and converted into follow-up training.

Supermarket Managers of a Major Chain

A major advantage that a company-owned supermarket chain has is the ability to make long-range training plans involving present employees.

There are training programs which start the first day on the job. These early programs deal with how to perform specific functions. They are aimed at making the new employee productive quickly and at providing him with a sense of accomplishment and job satisfaction at the outset. This major supermarket chain conducted its on-the-job training in selected departments managed by specially selected and trained department heads.

The first step in manager development was to prepare the trainee to be a department manager. Most of his technical training was conducted on the job. A department manager's leadership program concentrates on fundamentals such as "work organization and how to teach a job."

Candidates for store manager were selected from the ranks of department managers. The background of each candidate was analyzed, and a program training set up for him to fill in the gaps in his experience. Many men needed meat department or produce department training. Others required more emphasis on grocery department or store administration.

Another area of store manager training was orientation to the rest of the company. This would give him necessary background to handle his relationships with the accounting, warehousing, maintenance, personnel departments, and others as well. Finally, the company had sophisticated programs of management development for store managers and supervision.

Once the manager-trainee was running his own store, his main source of information, guidance, and inspiration was his boss, the zone manager. The store manager also had guidance in technical areas from his meat merchandiser, produce merchandiser, grocery merchandiser, and front end trainer. He could also call upon the services of a field personnel manager.

Store managers attended sales meetings, special training sessions when new methods were instituted, received company mail several times a week, and had a complete library of operating and policy manuals at their disposal in each store.

Through this course of training, the company tried to make the supermarket store manager a real member of its management team, well oriented to his organization and his function in it, and continually informed of all activities that influenced him.

Some Other Illustrations

McDonald's Hamburger University

Although training programs change over the years, McDonald's curriculum at "Hamburger University" (Elk Grove Village, Illinois) is oriented toward the operation of a McDonald's store, with three major areas of thrust: operation of equipment; quality control; and a less important group banded together—marketing, manpower development, and human relations. Special emphasis is placed on what McDonald's calls QSC (quality, service, cleanliness) in the teaching of subjects such as buns, carbonation, and beverages.

Kentucky Fried Chicken University

Kentucky Fried Chicken University, located in a Kentucky Fried Chicken Take-Home unit, functions both as a regular take-home operation and as a training school. The five-day course, which is required of all new franchisees, features the day-to-day operation of the unit, from the morning opening to the evening closing and covers topics such as preparation of the gravy, potatoes, and salads, cooking chicken, maintenance of the equipment, cleanliness, and rudiments of accounting, salesmanship, advertising, purchasing, and eating. Written tests and discussion periods are introduced at appropriate times. In all, seventeen hours are devoted to the classroom, fifteen hours in the kitchen, and five hours in inspecting other Kentucky Fried Chicken operations.

A&W's Program

A&W has a similar program with topics such as thermal mixology (coffee and hot chocolate), goo-ology (preparation of dressings), and fryocracy (french frying).

Convenient Food Mart

Convenient Food Mart (Chicago) conducts Train-the-Trainer Conferences, with emphasis on the importance of each region being represented at the conferences. The first of these conferences was held in 1976, coinciding with the introduction of a new store operations training program for owner-operators and a new store owner's manual of operations. It was expected that each regional representative would gain enough from the program to implement a training program for owner-operators of 288 hours, with 240 hours of on-the-job training and 48 hours of classroom. Topics such as these from the operations manual are included in these programs: marketing strategy, personnel selection and training, inventory control, pricing procedures, display and turnover requirements, building and equipment maintenance, service procedures, gross profit development, produce merchandising, and a host of other topics. The results of these conferences are reflected in the trainers' teaching of new franchisees, or owner-operators of the Convenient Food Mart units.

Holiday Inn University

Holiday Inn's major training facility, called Holiday Inn University, is located at Olive Branch, Mississippi, not far from the company's international headquarters at Memphis, Tennessee, and offers a comprehensive professional management development program utilizing the most advanced training techniques such as video cassettes, films, and so on. The program is designed for individuals with a degree in hotel-restaurant or business administration. The course is made up of a number of tasks of which every candidate has to prove mastery prior to successful completion of the program; he learns to perform the tasks at his own pace. Tasks to be mastered include food preparation, kitchen equipment maintenance, table service, cash register operation, bartending, management control systems, market analysis, menu design, profit and loss statements, sales and employer relations. Because of its international operations, Holiday Inns conducts worldwide field education.

Midas Muffler's Four-Week Course

In the Midas System (popularly known as Midas Mufflers), each new franchisee is required to attend a four-week training program on how to operate a Midas Shop with the greatest profit potential. Such topics as the following are covered: The Midas Policy Manual; organization procedures for finance, insurance and personnel; how to set up the shop for greatest efficiency; sales techniques, including telephone sales, special promotions, advertising, and the Midas guarantee; use of Midas catalogs; and inventory control and ordering procedures. Two weeks of the course are held at the Muffler Institute of Technology, near Chicago; the remaining two weeks are spent training on the job. Several sound-film cartridges are available to franchisees, and local in-field seminars for franchisees and their employees are held from time to time.

Training and Development Organizations

The foregoing are only a few of the many possible illustrations. In some franchise companies, the parent firm employs outside consultants, or trainers, to cover special topics with franchisees, and in fact in some cases to design and implement the entire program. The multitude of such firms that are available is attested to by the fact that the *Training and Development Organizations Directory*, published by Gale Research Company, provides "current data on 985 individuals and institutions which have thousands of tested training programs ready for use . . . and can tailor special seminars, workshops, and conferences to meet virtually any need of business, industry, and government."[9]

Summary

Training is not unique to franchising, although it is of particular significance in franchising, because that is what the new recruit often pays for, at least in part, with his initial deposit. Just as in company-owned branches, training in franchised establishments must be effective to maintain the uniformity of product and service that the customer expects from retail establishment to retail establishment across the nation, and indeed today, around the world. Often in franchising, the new owner may come from a type of activity, the military, truck driving, and so forth, which is quite different from that in which he will now engage as a franchisee, and for that reason the training must be as detailed as it can possibly be made, with the assumption that he (the franchisee) knows nothing. Illustration of the content, duration, and thrust of several programs are covered in the body of the chapter.

7

Financing the Franchise Operation

To implement a franchise program the franchisor needs money. To get his unit or units under way, the franchisee needs money. Franchising is often described as a means of raising capital by the franchisor, and this description is usually accurate, but franchisors do in fact advance money to franchisees or cosign papers for franchisees so that they can more readily borrow money. In such instances franchising becomes a means by which franchisees also raise money.

Too often neophytes to franchising look upon the selling of franchises as a means for a franchisor to obtain money without resulting expenses, although in a skeletal franchise system, hardly any expenses need be incurred by the franchisor. Certainly, however, the acquisition of real estate, the setting up of a recruiting organization, the formulation of a selection and training program with personnel to implement it, field supervision, and advertising and public relations efforts will involve sizable costs. In fact, some companies even go so far as to eschew franchising because they contend they would have to furnish their retailers with as many services under a franchise arrangement as they would with a fully owned company chain, and superimposed upon the costs for these services are those for selling franchises. If the potential franchisor does not project these costs fairly accurately, at least, serious consequences may result.

On a miniature scale, the franchisee needs funds for similar purposes—that is, for the initial franchise fee; for real estate, at least for the first month's rent; for equipment; for working capital; and for various other start-up expenses.

Sources of Capital for the Franchisor

There are several common types of financing open to franchisors, depending upon the status of the franchise system and its immediate needs. Among these are short-term financing, intermediate-term financing, long-term senior financing, current assets financing, financing through small business investment companies or other venture capital sources, government sources, and sale of equity to the general public.

Short-Term Commercial Bank Loans

Short-term loans are generally unsecured lines of credit intended to meet the borrower's seasonal cash requirements. The borrower will be required to provide adequate proof of his ability to pay off the loan from his earnings, a reduction in inventory, or other internal means.

For example, with an unsecured line of short-term bank credit, the franchisor has access to sufficient funds to accumulate a block of real estate sites and construct and equip his units and then arrange a blanket mortgage or sale and leaseback with institutional lender.[1] The franchisor has ready cash helpful in acquiring an attractive site on advantageous terms without delay. He can "warehouse" sites, perhaps as many as ten, a procedure which is more attractive to the institutional lender than holding single units both with respect to processing costs and to risk.

Revolving credit may be used in the same way as a short-term line of credit, and is a specified number of dollars under contractual arrangement for a period of three to four years. The borrower knows he can count on cash availability for a several-year period, without recall by the bank, and the funds are not treated as a current liability. The big advantage of revolving credit is that the borrower can take down the funds in small bites rather than in one full swoop, thus saving interest expense. Thus, revolving credit is similar to a line of credit in that it allows the franchisor to warehouse his long-term capital requirements without short-term bank business.

Intermediate-Term Financing

Phil Fine, the noted financial attorney, characterizes intermediate-term financing "as financing for not less than three years and not more than five years."[2] It generally requires monthly or quarterly amortization, and, according to Fine, is invariably secured by security interest in real estate, chattels, or other assets, which have a value substantially in excess of the principal amount of the loan.

In making the loan, Fine goes on to say, the loan officer will seek information and impose terms in areas such as the following:

1. the intended use of the proceeds of the loan
2. the available security, for example, chattels
3. the desired terms of the loan
   a. interest rate
   b. schedule of payment of principal and interest
   c. prepayment schedule
4. borrower's covenants as to
   a. maintenance of minimum capital requirements
   b. limitations on dividends and stock acquisitions
   c. limitations on borrowing other than from lender

d.   maintenance of assets free and clear of liens
e.   limitations on loans to and guarantees of the obligations of others
f.   prohibitions against acquisitions, mergers, or consolidation with other corporations and sale or loss of all or substantially all of the borrower's assets
g.   requirements to furnish the lender with periodic interim financial statements, annual audited financial statements, and other information

Long-Term Financing

Long-term financing is generally for a term of from ten to twenty years.[3] Three types of long-term financing are available: (1) unsecured term loans, (2) mortgage loans, and (3) lease arrangements. Insurance companies and pension funds supply such funds at interest rates higher than those of high-grade bonds. The term loan differs from the mortgage loan in that the former is repaid out of savings. Which one to use depends upon the tax savings, the effect upon the borrower's financial rating, and relative costs.

Current Assets Financing

This is usually short- to intermediate-term, often of the revolving credit type, and is secured by a lien on receivables, inventories, and in some cases, equipment. The sources for such financing are commercial lending institutions—commercial finance companies—but the costs are quite high.

Financing Through Small Business Investment
Companies (SBICs) or Other Venture Capital Sources

SBICs are professionally managed banking institutions seeking "equity kickers" concurrent with attractive interest rates. The availability of professional management counseling which they provide, Fine reports, is substantial.[4] He adds, "Generally, SBIC financing is not available for start-up situations, but is available to help management rise from one economic growth plateau to another." The National Association of Small Business Investment Companies, Washington, D.C., has available an SBIC list that includes a breakdown of the types of industries in which they desire to invest their funds. Very few, if any, SBICs are interested in financing franchisee operations, but other venture capital sources are available.

Government Financing

Fine lists six general types of government financing:

1. Commercial, industrial and financial loans
    Small Business Administration
    Treasury Department
    Federal Reserve System
    Federal Home Loan Bank
    Maritime Administration
    Area Redevelopment Administration
        (Later, the Office of Economic Assistance of the U.S. Department
        of Commerce)
2. Agricultural loans
    Farm Credit Administration
    Rural Electrification Administration
    Farmers Home Administration
    Commodity Credit Corporation
3. Housing and community development loans
    Office of Transportation
    Community Facilities Administration
    Public Housing Administration
    Urban Renewal Administration
    Federal Housing Administration
4. Veterans loans
    Veterans Administration
5. Natural resources loans
    Department of Interior
    Bureau of Reclamation
    Bureau of Commercial Fisheries
        (Later, the National Marine Fisheries Service)
    Bureau of Indian Affairs
6. International loans
    Export-Import Bank of Washington
    Agency for International Development[5]

Going Public

The franchisor (and large franchisees occasionally) may go public in five ways:
by selling a minority equity position in the company, by acquiring a majority
position in a company already publicly owned, by merging with a public
company or by being acquired by them, by selling out for cash or debt, by

making a public offering of stock.[6] Lendman enumerates seven advantages of going public as follows:

1. Cash is provided for investment or financing.
2. There is an increase in net worth.
3. Subsequent borrowing is facilitated.
4. Stock option plans are made possible.
5. It helps in attracting franchisees.
6. Subsequently, stock (with a high price: earnings ratio) aids in acquisitions.
7. There is greater liquidity.[7]

As with many other innovations in franchising, the Howard Johnson Company probably initiated this practice in Type IV franchising. Quoting Lendman: "The stock market probably counts the market cycle of the franchise industry from the date Howard Johnson went public. This offering probably more than any other made the public aware of franchising."[8] That was in 1961.

" 'Going public' is like building a 'House of Glass,' " Jack Massey, then chairman of the board of Kentucky Fried Chicken Corporation, exclaimed in a speech at Boston College, and these were some of the questions Kentucky Fried Chicken asked itself before finalizing the decision to go public:

1. Are the costs of this method of financing prohibitive?
2. Are we large enough for a public stock offering?
3. Does Kentucky Fried Chicken Corporation have sufficient appeal to insure success of a stock offering?
4. Could we operate effectively with outside directors?
5. Would we obtain the "right" price for the stock sold?[9]

The company should plan from the very beginning if it expects to go public eventually. When the step is taken, the days of "hiding" earnings will be over, and a great deal of executive time will be spent in dealing with the public, answering questions of financial analysts, completing reports for the Securities Exchange Commission, and so on.

Preparations for going public will include the following:

1. A three-year operating history with certified, or audited, figures.
2. A stock option plan.
3. A profit sharing or pension fund before offering since stockholder approval will be needed after.
4. Adjustments of executive salaries and benefits to eliminate apartments and yachts, for example, and loans to officers and stockholders.
5. Revision in the Board of Directors to eliminate family members, for example.

6. Arrangements for suitable Registrar and Transfer Agent.
7. Appropriate scrutiny and modification of the company's public image.[10]

A vice-president of finance should be added to the company if he is not already billeted. The selection of the underwriter is very important, and legal matters must be given detailed attention. The company is inviting litigation unless all corporate procedures, contractual agreements, executive compensation plans, and other such matters are legally valid. Going public is, of course, irrevocable except with considerable difficulty.

The costs in going public can easily exceed $110,000. The following are factors in this cost: Public relations efforts, legal fees, auditing expenses, printing expenses, and underwriting expenses (8 percent-10 percent of proceeds).[11]

Snelling provides detailed reasons for Snelling and Snelling's going public and the specific means whereby they did so.[12] They went public, according to Snelling, for the following fourteen reasons:

1. To create a public market for Snelling and Snelling stock.
2. For personal estate planning of principals.
   a.   To provide valuation.
   b.   To assure liquidity.
3. To diversify investment of principals.
4. To afford the company the opportunity to acquire other businesses.
5. To afford the company the opportunity to acquire present franchisees.
6. To provide the necessary funds for expansion of existing divisions of the company.
7. To allow franchise holders of Snelling and Snelling to hold some of the stock.
8. To encourage use of the company's services and facilities by customers.
9. To raise the industry's stature in the eyes of the public.
10. To force sophistication upon the company.
11. To provide stock option possibilities to key employees.
12. To provide the company an opportunity to use stock options in hiring new key employees.
13. To attract higher caliber personnel.
14. To obtain publicity.

And Snelling and Snelling found the following steps necessary in going public:

1. Selection of stock broker
2. Pricing of stock
3. Drafting Letter of Intent
4. Placing of stock with funds

5. Selection of attorneys
6. Selection of public accountants
7. Selection of printers

These steps, of course, are those that enter as factors in the process of going public by any company.

Over the years franchise company stocks have become so attractive that many brokerage houses and investment survey firms follow them in great detail. Alex Brown & Sons, a brokerage house based in Baltimore, Maryland, follows the food service company stocks intently, and in 1977 the firm announced the introduction of *Food and Food Service Monthly* containing comments on industry trends, updated information on leading companies in the field, statistical compilations, and other valuable information. The well known *Value Line Investment Survey* covers the food service and lodging and automotive fields explicitly and many other franchise sectors as part of broader groups.

Financing Sources: What They Will Want to Know

Now let us return to financing through banks and other commercial lenders. It is important for the franchisor, the seeker of funds, to have some idea of what will be required of him to obtain money, and Doty, vice-president of the First National Bank of Chicago, furnished the following (paraphrased) checklist of things about which the lender will want information.

1. *Management.* The challenges of a growing firm will require transition from a "comparatively free-wheeling entrepreneurial style of a first generation management team to the more structured, disciplined approach of analytical, professional managers."
2. *Dominant national or regional presence.* Marked by a large share of a particular market segment, be it chicken, hamburgers, or rental cars.
3. *The competence level of franchisees.* Despite selection, training, and work simplification procedures, franchise systems require well-qualified franchisees, and abuses can creep in where commissioned sales agents are employed. Most often, however, banks depend heavily upon the franchisor without ever seeing the franchisees.
4. *Health of relationship between franchisor and his franchisees.* The plethora of class action suits documents franchisors' neglect of franchisees, and lenders will be cautious lest they run into budding situations of this nature.
5. *Economic potential of a franchisor's store locations.* Not only will the choice of particular sites be reviewed, but the likelihood of locations in the wrong parts of the country will be evaluated. Bigger mistakes are made in the appraisal and acquisition of sites, however, than in the choice of particular spots.

6. *Extent of overexpansion if any.* One example of overexpansion may be premature diversification into new franchise concepts. (Not a single food franchisor has successfully launched a second major chain concept, Doty contended.)

7. *Financial discipline on the part of franchisor.* Examples of lack of such discipline are

    a. Acceptance of notes in part payment of franchisee fees—a widespread malady.

    b. Tolerance of an imbalance between recurring and nonrecurring revenue sources. A franchise company's earnings have to be generated independently of such nonrecurring sources as franchise and equipment sales.

    c. Failure to periodically review and eliminate unnecessary items of corporate overhead which inevitably creep in.

    d. Inadequate cost controls and accounting systems.

    e. Willingness to pursue real estate development programs and commence construction without advance long-term financing commitments in hand.

    f. Overextension of lease-financing liabilities in the belief that they do not represent debt.

    g. Inadequate audit procedures to verify the basis of franchise royalty payments.

    h. Failure to utilize a return on investment capital approach to analyzing further expansion.

    i. Miscellaneous accounting malpractices to be described later.

8. *Franchisor's financing according to the mix of debt and equity.* Limitations on debt capacity in franchising are expressed in capital structure ratios and coverage ratios related to fixed charges and anticipated cash flow. Long-term debt to equity ratio in excess of 1:1 is becoming top heavy and bank borrowing may be restricted. Lease financing with an off-balance sheet maneuver can mask excessive debt. If aggregate lease obligations are capitalized on a long-term debt basis, as is proper, the debt: equity ratio can jump to a high point.

9. *Coverage ratio* (the franchisor's bill-paying ability). "A ratio of 1:1 would indicate that a franchisor was generating just enough recurring income to meet his minimum fixed commitments, with no margin for a decline, even temporarily, in royalties or other revenues, an increase in costs, or other financial contingency. The stronger franchisors show a rent and interest coverage ratio generally in excess of 3:1. Others, unbelievably, don't even have a 1:1 coverage, indicating an overly rapid expansion," Doty commented. (First National Bank of Chicago insisted upon a minimum coverage of 2:1 in its loans to franchisors.)

10. *Effect on income of alternative methods of raising funds.* The higher the debt the greater the volatility of earnings as a result of capital structure leverage.[13]

Doty highlighted questionable accounting practices (item 7(i)) which the alert lender will pick up. This is a quotation from Doty's 1971 analysis:

> My friends in the accounting profession, by their passive approval of aggressive accounting techniques, did little to enforce satisfactory financial discipline in franchising and so fostered the misleading financial reporting during the late 1960's which contributed mightily to the recent confidence crisis on Wall Street. The most dramatic case, involving initial franchise fees, was lack of such (financial) discipline.

Thomas L. Holton, partner in a major nationwide accounting firm, listed these accounting methods "that raised doubt as to the fairness of presentation of their financial statements":

1. Initial franchise fees were recognized as revenue at the time the franchise agreement was signed, even though the franchisor was committed to providing substantial services to the franchisee.
2. Little or no provision for collection and cancellation of losses was being made.
3. Notes received in payment for the initial franchise fees and tangible assets (inventories and equipment) often did not bear interest, or the contract interest rate was unreasonably low, say 4 to 6 percent.
4. Many of the franchisors had financial interests in the franchisees through stock ownership, options or obligations to purchase the franchisee's business, etc.[14]

For those interested in pursuing the matter further Holton recommended the reading of an article on the subject by Archibald McKay in the January 1970 *Journal of Accountancy*.

Doty enumerated other malpractices then current, which may be directly related to the above but are not necessarily so:

1. Contingent liabilities are co-mingled with general corporate funds in the franchisor's operations, that is, cash deposits on franchise fees which are refundable—as almost all in fact are—and on which substantial performance has not been completed. Some amounts involved are material, and an unanticipated run on the bank in the form of refund requests could have a serious effect on a franchisor's liquidity.
2. I also question the classification of a franchisor's advances for properties under construction as a current asset, when no long-term financing arrangement has yet been finalized. . . . Without the firm assurance provided by a financing commitment, however, the franchisor is gambling, and so is his auditor.
3. Another accounting abuse is the issuance of an audited balance sheet which reflects as a fait accompli on the closing date a material, such as a large lease

or debt financing, which occurred after the fiscal closing date, but within the following ninety days. The place for material subsequent events is in a footnote, and not on the statement itself.

4.   Finally, I dispute the practice of recognizing the full carved-out profit on long-term equipment lease contracts in the first year.[15]

There is no way of knowing how widespread these practices are today, but presumably they have been limited by being brought to light, and by the catastrophies which overtook firms engaging in them. Yet, the franchisor who seeks approval of his financial programs, the lender, and indeed prospective franchisees and their advisors in accounting, banking, and law, should be alert to the possible reemergence of any such practices which limit the stability of the franchisor. In the final analysis, perhaps, the period in which these practices flourished was merely one brief episode in the upsurge of the franchise system of marketing.

Money for Financing Franchisee Operations

The franchisee will require varying amounts of capital, depending on, among other things, the magnitude of the franchise which he seeks to acquire. The capital required to obtain a bulk ice cream outlet, a gasoline service station, or a doughnut shop is quite small compared with that needed to acquire a franchised motel, an automotive dealership, or a soft drink bottlership. Indeed, franchisees with several units may require as much capital as regional or otherwise limited franchisors, and the problems and opportunities faced by these multi-unit franchisees will be similar to those of franchisors. In fact, many franchisees have gone public, and their problems are as they are to franchisors, with the added restraints of the franchise contract between franchisor and franchisee.

Table 7-1 depicts the average (median) total investment and immediate cash requirements of franchisees just getting started, as reported to U.S. Department of Commerce people in their annual survey. There is a wide range within each kind of business, but only the measures of central tendency are shown to give the reader a ball park frame of reference as to the magnitude of investment requirements for the various franchises.

The median total investment for a hotel or motel franchiser was about $700,000 with an immediate cash requirement of $90,000. This investment requirement was the largest of any reported, although it should be noted that the U.S. Department of Commerce survey did not cover automobile dealerships, gasoline service stations, nor soft drink bottlerships, which presumably might require greater financial commitments. It should also be emphasized that these are median figures, and there was quite a wide range around the medians within each category of business. Investments in tax preparation franchises were generally not large. In fact, the median investment by franchisees was only $3,000, with a cash requirement of $2,000. Fast food restaurants, a large sector of the Type IV franchises, had a median investment of $75,000 with initial cash of $30,000. Again, it should be emphasized that these figures are medians, above which and below which 50 percent of the figures fall. One major fast food franchisor, for example, requires an investment of nearly $200,000, with initial cash of almost $100,000.

The capital requirements of franchisees are generally not negligible, and minority groups in particular have had difficulty in raising the funds needed, although various governmental agencies and other sources have taken special measures to provide funds for minority and indeed other groups. One dictum that may be overlooked by the neophyte in evaluating a franchise is that in a sound franchise the total investment should generally be recoverable within three to five years in addition to a going salary for the owner-manager. If the probability of doing so is not great, the franchise in question should be considered with caution.

Ordinarily the franchisor requires the franchisee to pay the franchise fee, or *front load*, out of the franchisee's personal savings. This requirement has a twofold effect: it gets the franchisee personally involved; and it tends to bring into the franchise system persons with at least some success. In other words, obtaining loans for this front money tends to negate, or nullify, the twofold merit of franchising. Moreover, franchisors tend to look askance at absentee owners or nonmanaging investors. Personal involvement of the investor franchisee in management of the operation is considered a definite advantage of franchising.

One of the keys to successful franchising is to develop a franchise package or program that does not require large-scale financing; and as has been noted, franchisors, either rightly or wrongly, have been one of the biggest sources of funds for franchisees (even though franchising has been viewed primarily as a means for securing funds by franchisors). The franchisor may accept notes in payment of franchise fees, he may cosign instruments with the franchisee, or his name alone on the franchise may itself lend such credibility to the operation that lenders will provide loans to the franchisee basically on the strength of his membership in the franchise system.

The aggressive retail-oriented commercial bank with experience in lending to small business is probably the franchisee's best prospect for funds. Loans from this source will be intermediate term, and a well-known franchisor name may be of considerable assistance to the would-be franchisee in securing a loan from the commercial bank. A good site will also be of value in helping to push through the loan; and if the loan is for financing equipment, a repurchase agreement from the franchisor will be of assistance. Some equipment manufacturers themselves, realizing the financing problem, will have working financial programs to assist in the sale of equipment.

Table 7-1

Total Investment and Start-up Cash Required, 1976

(Franchisee-Owned Businesses Only)

Kinds of Franchised Business[a]	Total Investment Median (In Thousands of Dollars)	Start-up Cash Required Median (In Thousands of Dollars)
Automotive products and services	40	20
Business aids and services		
Accounting, credit, collection agencies and general business services	15	6
Employment services	25	15
Printing and copying services	42	15
Tax preparation services	3	2
Miscellaneous business services	14	10
Construction, home improvement, maintenance and cleaning services	25	10
Convenience stores	60	13
Educational products and services	22	15
Fast food restaurants (all types)	75	30
Hotels and motels	700	90
Campgrounds	250	75
Laundry and dry-cleaning services	50	20
Recreation, entertainment, and travel	32	11
Rental services (auto, truck)	90	35
Rental services (equipment)	95	6
Retailing (nonfood)	50	20
Retailing (food other than convenience stores)	60	20
Miscellaneous	28	10

Source: U.S. Department of Commerce, Industry and Trade Administration, *Franchising in the Economy 1976-1978* (Washington, D.C.: U.S. Government Printing Office, 1978), p. 47.

[a]Does not include automobile and truck dealers, gasoline service stations, and soft drink bottlers, for which data were not collected.

The U.S. Government's Small Business Administration (SBA) is also a likely place to look for a franchise loan: for construction, for buying equipment, for working capital, and so on. The borrower, however, must first try sources such as banks, other private lenders, and governmental agencies before the SBA can enter the picture. In fact, if the borrower lives in a city of more than 200,000 population, he must be turned down by at least two banks before approaching SBA, and then he must agree not to discriminate in employment or services to the public. For the most part, the SBA acts only as a guarantor of the loans; the agency has very little money to lend directly. SBA may guarantee up to 90 percent or $350,000, whichever is less, and if the agency makes the loan directly, the maximum amount is $100,000.

For the individual or firm seriously seeking venture capital and willing to research sources, a book that offers help is *Guide to Venture Capital Sources*, which lists more than five hundred venture companies with suggestions on ways to conduct the search and the types and amounts of venture capital which the companies prefer. The book costs $49.50 and may be obtained from Capital Publishing Corporation, 10 La Salle Street, Chicago, Illinois 60603.

8 The Real Estate Program

The real estate program undertaken by the franchisor will depend upon the product or service involved, the age of the company, the optimum franchise size required to minimize distribution costs, and a host of other factors.

Theoretical Discussions of Franchise Locations

The type of franchise will also have an important bearing upon the real estate program. For example, the program for Type I franchises (*dealerships*), in which the franchisee stores, sells, and services the manufacturer's (franchisor's) products (as in the automobile field), may be quite different from that in which the franchisee buys the use of the tradename and techniques of the franchisor, as in the Type IV franchises. Both types of franchises, however, deal with the general public at the retail level and are similar to that extent. Locations favorable to retail operations must therefore be obtained.

In franchised distributorships (Type II franchises), however, the franchisee acts as a wholesaler to other businesses, such as franchised Coca-Cola bottlers do, and the bottlers certainly do not require retail sites. This real estate problem is quite different from that in the Type I, III, and IV franchises. (Actually, in the United States, at least, sites for most bottler operations were acquired years ago.)

For a new franchisor the matter of how the company wishes to expand will be paramount. Does the franchisor, for example, wish to expand by granting franchises for relatively large areas (or master franchises), or is the franchisor's objective to cover the (entire) nation on a unit-by-unit basis?

Another significant question is whether the franchisor has the desire and the financial capability to acquire and own, or assume the prime lease on, the site, or whether the franchisee is expected to acquire the site.

If the franchisor company is relatively young, maximum efficiency in expansion will probably be achieved by his proceeding to develop area by area across the nation, rather than by leap-frogging, for example, from Pittsburgh, Pennsylvania, to Los Angeles, California, to Butte, Montana. It would be difficult if not impossible for a new company to service properly from Pittsburgh, for example, a single franchisee in a village in Texas or one in Montana or some other isolated or distant place. On the other hand, if key areas having high market potential are rather thoroughly developed with a number of units, then servicing costs per unit can be minimized.

153

Some franchisors prefer to open a new area with a company-owned unit and use it as a base for local expansion. Later, this unit may be franchised or perhaps be continued as company-owned. The unit may serve as a training site for franchisees and even as a district or regional headquarters.

The prospective franchisee should be perceptive, or sensitive, to the franchisor's plans so that he is not left holding a rather pointless franchise miles away from any others and from the parent company's corporate or regional headquarters.

Site selection is generally a two-step process: first, the selection of the locality which the franchisor wishes to enter; and second, the selection of the location for the particular unit. Several factors must be taken into consideration in determining whether to franchise in a particular locality, and if so, how many franchises to place there and where to put them. The answer to the first question will depend not only upon the distance of the area from headquarters but also upon market potential, that is, the number of consumers for the product or service being sold and, incidentally, the number of potential franchisees available—a number which is assumed to be adequate in this discussion.

Somewhat obliquely related to site selection is an excellent empirical and theoretical analysis of optimal franchise size in the automobile field by Pashigian, who prepared a doctoral thesis at Massachusetts Institute of Technology on the franchise system in the distribution of automobiles.[1] Even though the study was limited to automobile dealerships, it illustrates an approach having many ramifications in other fields as well.

The major portion of the Pashigian study was devoted to the measurement of economies (of scale) which result from larger dealerships, made possible by the auto manufacturers' restricting, or limiting, the number of franchises they grant. The analysis leads to a determination of the optimal number of dealerships for profitable operation in local markets. (An analysis of this type will also indicate the ease with which new manufacturers can enter the industry.)

According to Pashigian and quoted here as food for thought,

> Given the retail demand for the manufacturer's product, the manufacturer would be interested in selecting that number of retailers which would minimize the distribution cost of any given volume of sales. Distribution costs would be minimized by selecting enough retailers so that each retailer operated at the minimum point of his long-run average cost schedule.[2]

Selection of Areas for Expansion

One of the first problems for the franchisor is to determine what measurable variables are related to sales of his product or service. Government statistics from the Census of Population and the Census of Business may be used as a guide; but even before using these, one should know what kind of people patronize the unit: whether interurban travelers or neighborhood residents, whether old or young, whether male or female, and whether high or low on the socioeconomic scale. The results of these analyses of pilot unit patrons can then be used to estimate market potential in prospective areas for expansion. Added to the analysis of market potential, of course, must be an analysis of competition, actual and potential, and of the cost of real estate and of servicing units in the area proposed for expansion.

General Considerations

Objective. The primary objective of market analysis and site selection is to predict dollars of sales and profits at a given location. It is quite possible that a site which is unsatisfactory for a take-out fried chicken operation would be quite satisfactory for a hamburg stand: that is, dollar sales and profits might be satisfactory for the hamburg unit but not for the fried chicken restaurant and conversely. Certainly a car wash and a hamburg stand do not require the same kind of site.

Types of Areas. Areas are generally classified in three categories: roadside, shopping center, and downtown (walk-in). In evaluating the respective kinds of sites, the evaluator proceeds differently. For example, for the downtown site, one would count (clock) pedestrian traffic all days and hours of the week. Nearness to theaters, churches, stadia, and other attractions is of primary concern. Close-by office buildings are a definite asset to the downtown location. Contrary to earlier expectations, some fast food chains have become quite successful in downtown locations in the United States, and overseas it would appear that central cities hold the only profitable sites.

The shopping center location requires a different orientation. The evaluator should investigate the developer and proceed with the keen awareness that big anchor tenants (such as department stores) are supported by the smaller tenants in the sense that smaller tenants may pay disproportionately much higher rent, and if patronage of the larger stores is not as high as projected, the small tenant cannot pay his bills. On the other hand, an adequate supply of customers for the shopping center does not necessarily mean adequate customers for the small units. One must also ask if the objectives of the franchise operation are compatible with those of the shopping center. For example, are the hours the shopping center is open compatible with those of the franchise unit?

It is the free-standing roadside unit on the open highway or imbedded in the community that so much effort is expended upon. One reason for this effort is the fact that selection of the site is followed by construction of the building for the franchise operation, and this fact raises further questions:

1. Will the franchisor operate with or without a real estate broker?
2. Who will handle the construction?
3. Will there be standard building plans, or will each site and building be treated individually?
4. Will the company employ a full-time architect, one or more draftsmen, and a construction supervisor, or will their functions be handled on a part-time basis?

Initial Site Survey. Once a city has been selected for one or more franchise sites, the evaluator should make a physical survey of the city, driving up and down the commercial and other areas during different hours and even flying over the area if possible. Major consideration should be given to accessibility of various locations, population, competition, economic stability, and trading area boundaries. In downtown areas, pedestrian traffic should also be studied.[3]

During the initial survey, the evaluator should visit the chamber of commerce, banks, the regional planning commission if there is one, newspapers and real estate trade journals, power companies, and real estate firms.[4]

The initial survey will guide the franchisor (and franchisee) to further effort, either in the confirming of various sites or in their rejection.

Factors Relating to Store's Volume of Business. Once the initial survey is completed and several alternative sites have been identified, the task of formulating a detailed estimate of expected gross sales (and net income) from stores on those sites begins.

One of the first matters to investigate carefully is the zoning of the sites.[5] Local ordinances regarding signs must also be checked to ascertain whether it will be possible to project the appropriate imagery.[6] Case admonishes against getting involved in legal and political problems over zoning.[7] If there is a potential zoning problem, go to some other site, he recommends. Even a court or zoning board victory may produce a loser: too many enemies may result, and the retail operation is there to make customers.

Gorman lists these specific factors to consider in evaluating the site:

1. Good arterial street, preferably without dividers down the middle—
    a marked highway with substantial traffic count is best
2. Far corner or midblock location with good visibility is superior
3. Traffic speed—15-20 mile speed limit is best
4. Traffic back-up at rush hours
5. Adequate frontage (110-200 feet)
6. Adequate curb cut width (35-40 feet)
7. Good housing and apartment combinations
8. Young families with many children
9. Proximity to
    a. Active stores
    b. Shopping centers

     c.   Recreational centers
     d.   Schools: high schools, colleges and universities
     e.   Twenty-four hour factories
10. Median family income
11. Future trends in population
12. Homeward bound side of street
13. Ethnic background of population
14. Educational level of population[8]

Loscocco asks whether a labor force is available.[9] Public transportation, too, is essential, he indicates. Also, it is desirable to check soil conditions at an early stage: removal of rock ledge, for example, can be very costly. As indicated in an earlier chapter, an employment service supplying live-in domestic help finds it necessary to locate its units near the source of supply of such help.

Sources of Information for Site Evaluation

These are sources of information useful in evaluating sites:

1. Highway traffic maps.
2. Police departments.
3. Rubin R. Donnelly Corp., Mt. Vernon, New York.
4. U.S. Chamber of Commerce (population surveys, distribution of income, regional planning reports, shopping center data, detailed maps, opinions of locations, present and future development areas).
5. Banks (can guide evaluator to reputable real estate firms).

Curt Kornblau in *Guide to Store Location Research* lists these sources of information for store location research:

1. Local government offices (including city, town, village, county): mayor; city manager; planning and zoning commission; clerk; engineer; assessor; school boards; courthouse; voter registration; housing authority; departments of building, health, welfare, fire, police, water, sewer, licensing.
2. State government offices: planning commission; departments of commerce, highways, motor vehicles, health, labor; revenue or tax commission; liquor control board.
3. Federal government offices (local or regional): Post Office; Commerce Department; Bureau of Labor Statistics; Federal Reserve Bank; Social Security Administration.
4. Public utility companies: telephone; gas; electric power.
5. Transportation companies: bus and streetcar lines; railroads; taxicabs.
6. Welfare agencies: especially well-organized house-to-house campaigners.

7. Universities: especially departments of marketing, geography, sociology, business research bureaus.
8. Newspapers and other advertising media.
9. Business groups: Chamber of Commerce; real estate boards.
10. Other business firms: banks; insurance companies; food store suppliers.
11. Compilers of maps, city directories, mailing lists.[10]

Consolidation of Demographic Information

Once the data are collected, the problem becomes one of consolidating the information to provide some meaningful evaluation of the site. The evaluator should stay alert remembering that the objective of data collection is to provide an estimate of the sales potential of a certain type of unit or outlet on the site.

There are three basic methods of consolidating the information which has been collected: the inspectional methods, the analog method, and the multiple and partial correlation, or regression equation, methods. In the final analysis none of these methods is perfect by any means, and the decision as to whether to locate on a site must rest on judgment. For one thing, one must consider the cost of the site after predictions of gross sales are made.

Inspectional Methods

Raffel recommended what is essentially an inspectional method which requires mapping the city tract by tract, as follows:

1. Put in median income for each area by color.
2. Put in major highways, expressways, and interstate highways in existence and under construction.
3. Plot population density on map.
4. Mark shopping centers and stores in plazas.
5. Clock and record on map traffic counts at peak and trough periods.
6. Check and plot crossing areas.[11]

On the basis of these factors plotted on the map, the desirability of various sites may be estimated on a rational and experiential basis.

If, as is increasingly becoming the case with motel sites, the problem is one of estimating gross sales of an operating property being taken over by a chain, the evaluator may obtain actual gross revenue figures for the current operation—and possibly for competitors. On the basis of these figures with adjustments for renovations and management and name changes, and consumer demand, estimates of gross sales can be rather precise on a judgmental, or inspectional, basis.

Analog Method

In a sense, analog methods are akin to inspectional or judgmental methods of site evaluation and selection. Applebaum presents a detailed case example of determining sales potential for a supermarket (Bull's Super Markets) by the analog method.[12]

The basic question, of course, was "How much business could Bull's realistically expect to do there [at or near the intersection of two streets]?" The bench mark for reference (the *analog*) was developed from three stores having similar market characteristics. Detailed data on these analogs were collected, tabulated, and averaged, for example, drawing power, population, per capita sales, and competition. These averages, adjusted on a judgmental basis for differences in areas, were then used as bases for estimating sales potential for Supermarket X, the projected new store.

So much for the analog method. If operational data are available from analogous stores, then this method can be quite helpful in evaluating a new site. The method can be most helpful when data from a variety of stores are available so that truly analogous stores can be selected. To the extent that the analog differs from the site from which projections are made, judgmental revisions in estimates must be made. When limited operational experience is available, as with new franchisor firms, one must "guesstimate." Perhaps this guesstimating in the last analysis is based upon little analogs that the decision-makers carry in their heads—stereotypes, so to speak, which may or may not be valid.

Use of Multiple Correlational Analysis

Cella described a statistical method that he developed for the Oklahoma Restaurant Association and applied with considerable success to the evaluation of restaurant sites.[13] This method, however, is dependent upon data from a considerable number of units already in operation and would be of little value to the franchisor in the developmental stages, except as a guide as to what to aim towards (a not undesirable use of such methods by any means).

In essence, what Cella attempts to do is predict a store's (restaurant's) gross sales from measurable factors which are related to operating units' sales. In other words, from census reports, utility reports, and establishments' records, he records factors influencing the volume of sales of units, such as population of the drawing area, income, number of competitors. For a given restaurant chain, he prepares charts depicting the relationships between each of these predictor variables and gross sales, the criterion against which the predictor variables must be validated. He then computes the coefficients of correlation between each variable and the criterion gross sales and combines the variables with what is termed *a multiple correlation*. The *coefficient of determination* is computed to ascertain whether all of the sales are accounted for; if not, additional variables are added until the coefficient is 100.

By utilizing proper statistical analysis, Cella prepares an equation that will enable the analyst to predict sales from the various measured factors. Some factors are not obtainable from census and other publications, such as type of neighborhood, decor of the establishment, capability of the managers. He has people rate these variables for each store on a nine-point scale.

For restaurants, at least, Cella claims very accurate and worthwhile results. The method, which is well known to statisticians, can be applied to other types of chains: gasoline service stations, motels, grocery stores. Cella emphasizes, however, that new equations must be developed for each different chain—for hamburgs, for chicken, for tacos. In fact, one of the uses of this type of analysis is in selecting a profitable menu from among several types of menus, hamburg, for example, where a chicken menu has been unprofitable. The projection of sales can also be used as a norm against which the actual performance of the unit can be gauged.

Obviously, correlational analyses of this type can only be made if a sizable number of units is already in operation. The method, however, is theoretically very sound, and beginning firms should plan data collection so that such analyses can later be made.

Methods of Acquiring Real Estate

Once the site has been evaluated, that is, sales projections have been made, negotiations must be undertaken to secure as favorable a price and terms as possible. Some companies insist upon owning or at least holding the primary lease on the property. Petroleum marketers operate thus, as does McDonald's. In fact, at one time, a third of McDonald's net income was derived from real estate.

Gorman, a former real estate executive with McDonald's, described eight types of real estate acquisition thus:

1. *Build-to-Suit.* In the build-to-suit arrangement, the landowner (usually of about 25,000 square feet) adds the building and improvements including a paved parking lot. Typically, he supplies the lessee a twenty-year prime term lease with two five-year options to renew; and if the lessee is alert, an option to purchase the propery.
2. *Ground Lease with Subordination.* Typically, the lessor grants a lease for fifteen to twenty years with the option to renew with subordination of the real estate (land) to the first mortgage, which usually covers the building cost.
3. *Straight Ground Lease without Subordination.* The landowner grants the financial institution or individual the right to build on the land without subordinating his ownership to the mortgage holder on the building. As a rule the landowner eventually owns the building.

4. *Lease with Option to Buy*. This is the simple lease, with the lessee having the option to purchase over a number of years.

5. *Cash Purchase*. This is a straightforward and probably the best method of doing business, with a bank furnishing 65 percent to 75 percent of the total cost of the package.

6. *Subordinated Land Purchase*. This, of course, is similar to any subordinated land purchase, but the sale is designed to avoid inordinate income taxes. The seller takes 29 percent or less of the purchase price to meet requirements of the Internal Revenue Code for an installment purchase.

7. *Downtown or Walk-in Store Lease*. In the downtown locations the lessor ordinarily provides the store renovations, usually with a ten-year lease and from two to four five-year options to renew. Occasionally part of the rental may be applied against the purchase price of the location. The rental charge is often a percent (4 percent to 5 percent) of gross sales less insurance and taxes.[14]

8. *Lease-back Package-Deal Programs*. Large firms often secure the financial backing of big lending institutions (insurance companies, for example) to buy a package of say ten completed free-standing unit franchise locations, thus eliminating the need for separate negotiations for each parcel of real estate. The finance firm buys the sites and leases (rents) them back to the franchisor. The franchisor can then plan and move ahead for quite some time, concentrating on other phases of the operation besides real estate. Beside Gorman, Phil Fine describes this approach in *Franchising Today 1966-1967*.[15] The franchisor under this arrangement has great leeway and flexibility in choosing and developing locations anywhere in the United States.

The reader who is interested in delving further into store location research should read Applebaum, particularly Appendixes 2 and 3.[16]

Franchisor-Franchisee Relations

Franchisor-franchisee relations is a broad term which might in a sense cover the entire spectrum of franchising. In a narrower and more specific sense, however, the term is used to describe the continuing relationship between franchisor and franchisees following acquisition of the franchise. The term covers in particular the measures that the franchisor adopts to maintain wholesome relations between himself and the franchisee or franchisees.

Measures to initiate and maintain good franchisor-franchisee relations are instituted for a variety of reasons, the most important ones being (1) to motivate franchisees to perform at a high level in terms of internal operations and of marketing, (2) to facilitate the adoption of new ideas, (3) to obtain new ideas from franchisees, and (4) to head off legal problems in the antitrust and trademark and trade name fields.

The maintaining of wholesome franchisor-franchisee relations goes hand in hand with good field supervision, and it is in the type of field supervision exercised, or the lack of it, that franchisor-franchisee relations are initiated and maintained. It is apparent for this reason that the franchisor's first line field supervisor is a most important cog in the franchise network. Moreover, it should be noted that the franchise salesman, by whatever name he is called, is the franchisor's first personal contact with the prospective franchisee. This first contact may set at the stage for a long-term relationship, and it is unwise to leave the beginning of this relationship to chance.

The term *motivation* or *motivating the franchisee* appears often under the heading franchisor-franchisee relations. Motivation is almost synonymous with stimulation of franchisees to sell more, or euphemistically, "to develop the market." A particular facet of this problem in the franchise field involves the franchisee who has made a great deal more money than he ever dreamed of making and is content to "coast," even though he has not developed his market or territory to the fullest extent possible. The problem here is a complex one for the franchisor: he often has neither the capital nor the inclination to buy back and operate big franchises; other purchasers are rare because of the capital required, and if they do have the large amount of capital required to buy the older, well-established franchise, they want to be absentee owners and not operators.

The Chicken Delight Case

One of the most striking examples of the shipwreck of a substantial franchise chain as a result of poor franchisor-franchisee relations, is the case of Chicken Delight, in which litigation was the end result. In 1969 Chicken Delight had more than six hundred franchisees, according to William T. Morgan, Jr., president, but the company was in the throes of a multimillion-dollar class-action lawsuit brought by franchisees.[1] The franchisor, Chicken Delight, had sold trade name franchises with illegal tying arrangements, the most conspicuous one being the obligatory purchase of paper goods by the franchisee from the franchisor.

Once the class-action lawsuit had been filed, the company did everything possible to prevent disintegration of the system. Among the things done were the following, according to Morgan:

1. Implementation of cooperative advertising programs, paying participants dividends out of company funds.
2. Establishment of training centers with professional staffs to retrain existing operators, as well as new franchisees.
3. Establishment of communications and advisory committees that meet for the express purpose of making certain that lines of communication were open.
4. Introduction of new products anticipating market needs.
5. Mailing of monthly house organ, *Chicken Delight News,* to all franchisees for purposes of reporting franchise activities across the country, food preparation and operating suggestions, and other matters of general interest.[2]

These things that Chicken Delight did are standard programs designed to initiate, maintain, and improve franchisor-franchisee relations, but unfortunately they came too late.

During the years of litigation in which the case went to the United States Supreme Court, the system disintegrated. Many franchisees dropped out of the chain, others ceased to pay the franchisor, and franchisor services were withheld. Eventually, not much more than the trade name remained; and it was finally sold by Consolidated Foods Corporation, which had acquired Chicken Delight.

Other franchisor chains have undoubtedly been threatened by similar catastrophes, although it has been possible to settle many suits out of court before litigation went so far. Hostile relations between franchisor and franchisees set the stage for lawsuits and other damaging assaults upon the integrity of the system, and sharp lawyers can always find some way to harass opponents in the legal arena.

These observations lead to another point which is quite simple: when the franchise company is young and small, it may do things that it may not do when it gets big, with resources that become fair game for others presumably wronged. In this day of acquisitions of smaller firms by giants, this bit of wisdom is particularly timely.

Setting the Stage Psychologically for Good Relations

Leonard Korot discussed the origins of franchisee unrest and some of the remedies.[3] One factor contributing to franchisee unrest has at various times been the franchisor's concentration on earnings per share of stock and on the price action of the common stock on the New York Stock Exchange or wherever it is sold.

Korot described the nineteenth-century management concepts to which the "mechanical man" was basic. All that was necessary for management to do was to set work standards, make sure the employee was nourished and had periodic opportunity to rest and go to the toilet, and provide each supervisor with a stopwatch.

This concept was greatly modified as a result of the experiments of Roethlesberger, a young Harvard professor whose work at the Hawthorne plant of Western Electric Company is now classic. The female workers at Hawthorne improved production despite degradation of the working conditions as a result of being part of the experimental group being given special attention. The women "felt important," and their productivity spurted despite lowered illumination and extreme heat or cold.

As a result of these experiments and the labor union movement, management changed its view from that of the "mechanical man" to that of the "Big Daddy" role. Health benefits, vacations, sick leave, cafeterias, decent restrooms, and many other fruits of the Big Daddy role were instituted. According to Korot, changes have taken place in Big Daddy's self-concept, but his role has remained the same. Walnut desks, reserved parking, Cadillacs, and so on have been added to health benefits, air conditioning, and the other fruits of his role.

Korot continued, "One cannot divorce franchisees from other people, one cannot separate franchising from other current movements—of the young, the black, of women's libbers." The need and desire of the franchisee is for "a piece of the action"—psychologically, the need for dignity, the need for worthwhileness, the need for significance as a multidimensional human being.

Korot summarized with this:

I am not advocating a free-form management utopia in which everybody does his own thing. Management absolutely requires discipline, requires strong leadership—but it is successful, over the long run, only if the corporate needs are highly correlated with the emotional needs for the people who constitute the company. And those needs as I have said are *not to run the company* but to feel included, to feel significant, to feel respected as a human being.

Bruce J. Walker's Study

As discussed briefly in chapter 2 in connection with the advantages and disadvantages of franchising to the franchisee, one of the more penetrating available studies of franchisor-franchisee relations was that made by Dr. Bruce J. Walker for his doctoral dissertation at the University of Colorado.[4]

Because of financial limitations so common to many doctoral studies, various aspects of methodology could be improved (for instance, the sampling), but Walker's study does tend to point to certain conclusions with respect to the existing state of franchisor-franchisee relations, and the need for continuing systematic research by individual franchisors to assess satisfactions and dissatisfactions of their own franchisees and reasons therefor.

Walker's emphasis upon the need for continuing research in the area of franchisor-franchisee relations is in line with what large companies have been doing for many years. For example, more than twenty years ago, General Electric Company, General Motors Corporation (a major franchisor, incidentally), Pittsburgh Plate Glass Company, and other large companies were instrumental in my initiating and publishing studies of employee attitudes and the effectiveness of different methods of communicating with employees under the sponsorship of the Association of National Advertisers[5] (although one should hasten to emphasize that franchisees are not employees, even though franchisee ties to parent companies are more akin to those of employees than to those of customers and other "publics"). Because franchisees are not employees, it is even more important that their attitudes be assessed and modes of two-way communication between them and franchisors be evaluated.

Psychological Findings in Walker Study

Walker's study was premised upon the work of the late eminent psychologist Maslow in the field of human motivation. In other words, the study sought to answer the basic question: What human motives are best satisfied by the franchisee's operation of the franchise, and what motives are not so well satisfied? The psychological needs depicted by Maslow and studied by Walker in his work on franchising are the need for security (security as a franchisee in the system); the social need (chance to develop close friendships, opportunity to help other people); the need for self-esteem (prestige of own franchise in system, feeling of prestige of franchisee position among friends); the need for autonomy (independence in thought and action, authority connected with position, opportunity to determine work methods and procedures); and the need for self-actualization (feeling of worthwhile accomplishment, opportunity for personal growth and development, feeling of fulfillment from being a franchisee).

Walker found that most franchisees' social motives and desires to be independent were indeed adequately gratified by their positions as franchisees. However, franchisees in the five franchise systems which he studied tended to be less than satisfied in terms of self-esteem, self-actualization, and security.

Curiously, the search for security is probably one major factor motivating persons to acquire franchises; yet there was a significant deficiency in the satisfaction of this motive among franchisees surveyed by Walker. Several factors probably lie at the root of this deficiency—one of them may simply be that franchisees feel basically more insecure to begin with than do persons among the general population, and even though the security motive is partially satisfied by the success of the franchise, a significant residual of insecurity may remain.

It is most important to note that "most franchisees considered themselves independent businessmen—rather than employees or semi-independent businessmen—at least to the point of having sufficient decision-making authority and operational freedom." In dealing with franchisees, the franchisor must keep this feeling in mind. To operate counter to the franchisee's belief that he is independent can only bring conflict and hostility.

Another of Walker's findings is particularly significant: franchisees who had larger operations tended to be more often satisfied with their franchises than were franchisees who had smaller operations. By "larger operations" is meant a larger number of individual retail units owned, a larger number of employees, larger sales volume, and higher income.

As has been emphasized, franchisor-franchisee relations begin with the first contact between the two parties.

Glossing over the drudgery connected with the position, exaggerating probable earnings, and otherwise improving what is being sold might sell more franchises than completely forthright, realistic presentation. But what must be considered and frequently has been overlooked is that the nature of this informational package affects the eventual attitudinal states of franchise buyers.[6] In Walker's study "prospects oversold" was the third most frequently mentioned reason for general dissatisfaction with the franchise.

Franchisor exaggeration during the sale of franchises has been noted by Vaughn with strong admonitions against the practice.[7] Ozanne and Hunt's study revealed that 37 percent of franchisees felt that franchisors overestimated (13 percent "greatly overestimated") profits during negotiation; whereas only 7 percent reportedly underestimated profits.[8] Thus, although the majority of franchisors neither overestimated nor underestimated profits, there was a significant excess of alleged "exaggerations" over "underestimates," and consequently, seeds sown for franchisee dissatisfaction later. (Interestingly, "Franchisees who report that franchisors overestimated profits earned substantially lower incomes from franchising than those who report no overestimate or an underestimate of profits.")[9]

Walker Results Summarized

Walker in two articles appearing in *Franchise Journal* and in a speech at the Southern Marketing Association Meetings added further findings pertinent to franchisor-franchisee relations and summarized his studies.[10]

In brief these are his salient points:

1. General satisfaction with the franchise was the rule rather than the exception (77.1 percent of the franchisees responding in Walker's survey experienced general satisfaction with their franchises).

2. The most common sources of *satisfaction* as verbalized by the particular franchisees who replied were being one's own boss, and excellent income.

3. The most common sources of dissatisfaction as indicated by respondents were poor financial return, lack of franchisor support, and prospects oversold.

4. There was considerable variation from franchise system to franchise system, and there was in the franchise package no single feature to which the majority of franchisees pointed with great satisfaction or dissatisfaction. For example, many franchisees in one system found satisfaction in factors seldom mentioned by franchisees in other systems, factors such as prestige or professional status; good hours; and continuous challenge.[11] This fact is understandable in view of the wide diversity in types of franchise systems and indeed between individual franchises within the broad types.

5. Being with a company having a national image or well-known name was most often mentioned by franchisees as the most beneficial single element in the franchise package, but that element was mentioned by fewer than one-quarter of the respondents. Other elements mentioned favorably by at least 10 percent of the respondents were centralized purchasing power, being part of an established national organization, good advertising, and sales programs.

6. The most undesirable elements indicated by franchisees responding were absence of continuing support and royalty rate or an excessive override in view of the small amount of continuing support. However, these individual elements were specified by less than one of every four franchisees.

7. In Walker's words, "... it must be concluded that elements of the franchise package and aspects of the position itself represent different things to different people."[12]

Thus, widespread generalizations about the reasons for people buying franchises and about the franchise-package features most important to franchisees are not supported by Walker's study. Each type of franchise system is different from the others, and, indeed, one might almost conclude that individual franchisees seem to have little in common with each other. Only through careful study of his own franchisees will the franchisor executive be in a position to act to maintain a high level of satisfaction and to reduce points of friction between the franchisee and himself. It should be noted again, however, that the large majority of franchisees in Walker's study expressed general satisfaction with their own positions in life, a finding which is essentially in agreement with results of the Wisconsin and Conference Board studies. (On the other hand, one cannot ignore the many class-action suits brought by franchisees against franchisors.)

Although not necessarily supported by statistical evidence from the Walker study, certain recommendations or suggestions do appear to flow from it. These six suggestions to franchisors appear worthy of note:

1. Eliminate distortions and exaggerations in recruitment.
2. Recruit franchisees from persons earning less than $10,000 per year and from sales groups. These groups appear to be somewhat more often satisfied with their franchises than others.
3. Augment what flows from headquarters to franchisees on the basis of continuing checks with franchisees to ascertain their wants and needs. To defray expenses of additional forms of support the franchisor might charge fees for them. There is an old adage that people do not appreciate what they do not pay for. Continuing "reminders" of what the franchise package has meant to franchisees—that is, site selection, assistance with opening—should be maintained.
4. Initiate or facilitate two-way communication with franchisees, through
   a. periodic monitoring of them,
   b. a franchisee council, and
   c. face-to-face and oral contacts.
5. Develop procedures to reduce need deficiencies and increase satisfactions. Feelings of self-esteem and security must be enhanced, but often these feelings are so unique to the individual that the person must be dealt with on an individual basis, and mass campaigns may not accomplish the task.
6. Encourage acquisition of a second unit and possibly more units by successful franchisees to increase satisfaction with the system and reduce boredom.

Obviously, these suggestions are just that, suggestions. It cannot be over-emphasized that every system has its own parameters, but these are some available alternatives. Their adoption, timing, and relative emphasis are within the sole domain of the individual companies, and based, I hope, on sound research designed to elicit the facts about the company's franchisees' attitudes.

Any business, of course, must keep alert to things that might disturb the employer-employee relationship, and as has been emphasized before, the situation in franchise systems in particularly sensitive because the franchisee, despite possessing many characteristics of an employee, is an independent businessman, tied to the franchisor by a contract, or franchise agreement, but still independent. Also, for some reason, perhaps, because of the peculiar relationship—half independent and half free—franchising seems to have attracted a great deal of attention in legislative bodies, in courts, and in the public press, if not because of some alleged overselling of the franchise or nonperformance on promises, then because the retail outlet is ugly or inappropriate in the neighborhood. Generally, however, franchisees appear to be well pleased with their situations, as shown by the Vaughn survey of small businessmen reported on earlier and by the other older studies. More than 80 percent of the franchisees queried in the Vaughn survey reported they would buy the franchise again.

Formalized Communication Programs

As one well-known public and employee relations executive put the matter years ago, "You have to do right. Doing right comes first, but that's not enough. People have to know you are doing right. You have to tell them." And the process of telling them is the communication program.

What are some devices for communication between franchisor and franchisee—or media for communication, one might better ask? The major medium and one that should continually be uppermost in the company program is the personal visit, or if the visit itself is impossible, the telephone call.

One apt example of the impact and rich imagery which may surround the personal visit by franchise executives was recently covered in no less a medium than *Time* magazine (25 April 1977, p. 77). The article reports on "store day" at McDonald's, when the Company's top executives work the day behind counters at retail sites across the nation. *Time* pictures McDonald's senior chairman and founder, Ray Kroc, facing a customer across the counter in a unit in San Diego, and depicts Edward Smith, McDonald's president, picking up a spatula to flip burgers.

The personal letter is still another variant of the personal message from the franchise executive to the franchisee. A basic feature of these three variants of the personal message is that the original communicator, or franchise executive, has the opportunity for feedback from the franchisee. The personal confrontation sets the stage for give-and-take between the parent company and the franchisee, and this give-and-take increases the chances that the message will be understood properly and acted upon, if action is the goal. Obviously, the opportunity for or ease of personal interaction varies considerably as between the personal visit, the telephone call, and the letter. Sometimes, of course, personal interactions, with the biases and prejudices they may introduce, are not desirable, as in opinion research, legal documents, and accounting.

The more formalized mass communication media are

1. The newsletter, sent to franchisees at regular (or perhaps irregular) intervals.
2. The House Organ (Internal) sent to all franchisees at regular intervals. (Many companies also publish an external house organ, which although primarily a marketing aid, can double as an internal house organ as well.)
3. Advertisements in general media or the trade press, supplemented by frequent public relations inspired news stories.
4. Marketing, or merchandising aids—point-of-display posters, counter signs— supplied by the franchisor to the franchisee at periodic intervals, perhaps regularly.

The typical newsletter or house organ has a column or two of personals, pictures of noteworthy events, and several news stories. Often neglected but certainly a desirable part of the publication supported by the company is a section with executives' views on policies, programs, and legislation affecting the industry and the company specifically. The house organ is often of tabloid newspaper format and issued weekly. Lots of personal items increase readership and perhaps stimulate morale. My early studies of the readership and impact of internal house organs indicated that employees (as franchisees presumably would, also) did indeed read top executives' columns in house organs, a fact which surprised many top executives themselves.

Advertisements in general media (magazines, newspapers, television) can take several forms: advertisements to sell product, such as Kentucky Fried Chicken, Dunkin' Donuts, Big Macs, and so on. The advertisements can be directed to potential franchisees to sell franchises. And then some companies embark upon what is termed *institutional advertising* campaigns—to sell the company as contrasted with products. The advertisements, of course, have many incidental values: often they serve to build morale of parent company executives and, in some instances, the company head himself, and that is no small objective considering that the top executive is a highly paid individual who should perform in a commensurate manner. Often overlooked is the fact that this highly paid top executive has the same human motives, in varying degrees to be sure, as the person lowest on the totem pole, and his problems require solutions just as anybody else's.

Merchandising aids are obvious. What is often overlooked, however, is that these are communication devices to franchisees. Effective merchandising aids, for example, those Baskin-Robbins uses in selling ice cream, not only sell more product but help sell the franchisee on the company.

Daryl Motte describes two difficult types of franchisees who require special handling: the complacent franchisee, particularly the one "whose present success stretches beyond the wildest dreams he had when he signed" the contract; and the "demotivator"—the professional agitator—"the franchisee whose motivational problems take the direction of motivating fellow franchisees *against* the parent company."[13]

The complacent franchisee, the underachiever, is not motivated by promise of more money. Motte, an executive of Manpower, Inc., suggested stressing other rewards: for example, greater recognition and the social opportunities that will result from broadening the scope of his operations. The demotivator, the professional agitator, might better, perhaps, be terminated, but often he cannot be, and termination may only lead to further trouble. Motte advocates isolating him by

1. Avoiding attacking him frontally or openly.
2. Avoiding at all costs letting him rattle you.
3. Stressing the positive in all communications with all franchisees. Answer the agitator's objections and complaints without hinting that that is what is being done.
4. Manipulating meetings and favorable franchisees so they can confront the agitator—and by praising the agitator publicly when he does cooperate with the team.
5. Giving him a forum (other favorable franchisees) where he will be shown that his criticisms are groundless and that you don't fear him.

Franchisee Councils, Committees

One very effective communication device that has developed in franchising over the years is the franchisee advisory council, or committee. These councils may be formed for a variety of purposes—to formulate and execute advertising policy within a region such as New England, Massachusetts, or nationally for that matter, to serve as a purchasing cooperative. Or the council may have as its sole purpose the hearing of complaints that franchisees may want communicated to franchisor management with some force behind them. In many instances, more serious general problems such as the energy shortage and high costs may be the subject of debate and perhaps solution by the council.

Fast Food, Restaurant Business Magazine in its March 1974 issue carried an excellent summary of the subject in the fast food field under the pointed title "Franchisors and Franchisees: Partners in Profits." Starting with McDonald's dictum from a plaque on the desk of its president at the time, Fred Turner, "Tell each other the truth," the article goes on to survey various fast food companies' adoption of and attitudes towards councils: Howard Johnson's, with the first in the business, Marriott's, Burger King's, A&W International's, Lum's, Dog and Suds', Bonanza's, Mister Donuts', and Shakey's.

The councils are structured in various ways. For example, the Eastern New England McDonald's Operators' Association, Inc. has a membership covering ninety-five units, of which thirty-three are company-owned and sixty-two operator-owned. Each operator has just one vote, regardless of the number of units he owns; likewise, the company-owned units as a group have just one vote. Altogether there are twenty-four votes. This is purely a business group which provides franchisees with opportunities to specify advertising at the regional level, conduct group purchasing, and engage in other business functions. There is also a national advisory group for advertising, which is controlled by franchisees.[14]

Another illustration of advisory groups is provided by Manpower's, which works thus:

> Franchisees through a subcommittee choose their own representatives. Membership rotates. Various subcommittees meet regularly during the year and once a year a week-long meeting of the main committee is held at company headquarters. The Committee's role is purely consultative but the members fully understand why this situation exists.[15]

Motivation plans are used to reduce absenteeism, encourage employee suggestions, stimulate recruitment of new personnel, and so on. Motivation plans typically exclude cash because it is considered deserved reimbursement. Instead, trips to Florida, the Caribbean, or some other exotic place are one type of incentive. Tickets to Broadway productions are another.

Benefit plans to hold the franchisees' key employees—and, indeed, franchisees themselves—covering hospitalization, long-term disability, death benefits, retirement, and stock options are becoming increasingly popular. The large petroleum companies—CITGO, Mobil Oil Company, Atlantic Richfield, and others—started the trend and others have followed suit. Surprisingly, these very desirable plans often do not cost the franchisor a cent.

The Franchisor's Public Image

The franchisor's public image, created by his posture, his architecture, his forthrightness, are an important factor in franchisor-franchisee relations. If, when he visits the franchisee, the franchisor (or his representative) drives up in a Cadillac limousine, stops for only a moment, and speeds on, the franchisee's reaction is apt to grow hostile. On the other hand, if he demonstrates he knows what he is talking about, shows no haste in leaving, and sincerely tries to aid the franchisee, the reaction is most likely to be favorable. If the franchisor takes every opportunity to obtain a kickback from suppliers, his reputation will not be the best with franchisees, and one well-known supplier, at least, recommends against the use of supplies for profit.[16]

The architectural plan developed for the unit is very important. "We don't want one of those things in our town" is a statement that is becoming more and more familiar to franchisors' (and franchisees') ears. As Selame has pointed out, franchisors should "try to understand what the town fathers are actually saying when they plan negative zoning codes," and Selame advises franchisors to consult the most recognized architectural, landscape, and graphic designers.[17] "Speak the truth through competent design consultants," Selame says.[18] By proceeding properly it is quite possible to insure good corporate identity and yet conform to existing (and future) building codes.

When discussing franchisor-franchisee relations we must include the enforcement of the franchise agreement, or contract, since it is in this area that franchisors and franchisees must come face to face. Enforcement of the contract, of course, must proceed from a sound base, that is, from a sound contract with enforceable clauses.

As Lifflander emphasized: "If you allow a franchisee to use your trademark in any way, you must, I repeat, *you must, be able to enforce your requirements as to the proper use of the mark.*"[19] Lifflander further adds, "The annals of trademark history are replete with colorful stories of how good marks were lost or diluted as a result of poor trademark administration."

Some franchise companies have permitted, even required, their franchisees to incorporate with a name containing the name or trademark of the franchisor. "This should never be permitted," Lifflander admonished. "The trademark is the key to quality control and frequently it is the foundation upon which otherwise legally indefensible practices in a franchise relationship become clearly valid."[20]

Use of the trademark and trade name must be rigidly policed. On-the-spot inspection teams and field supervisors are used by some franchisors. Many, if not most, insist "that their franchisee management or key employees attend training schools as a basic requirement of the enforcement procedure."[21]

Another common method of enforcement is to require the franchisee to submit production samples. Failure to comply with specifications can, with some agreements, result in termination on short notice.

It is imperative that the franchisor keep detailed records of control measures. Not only must the licensor retain control of the quality of products, he must also retain responsibility for quality. If the franchisor does not accept these responsibilities, the franchisee may terminate the agreement and continue to use the franchisor name, method, and procedures.

One should look at the other side of the coin, too, and ask if the restraint or element of control is necessary. If not, eliminate it. To continue with an unnecessary restraint is to fly in the face of antitrust laws and create hostility on the part of franchisees.

Mediation

Finally, it must be observed that relations between two parties cannot be expected to flow uninterrupted without at least some friction, and such friction may create considerable heat. After describing three major forms of misconduct in franchising uncovered by his year-long study with a blue ribbon panel of lawyers, Jerrold G. Van Cise recommended a National Mediation Panel within the industry to arbitrate disputes between franchisors and franchisees, and the Franchise Center at Boston College offered to set up such a panel.[22]

However, quoting from the author's testimony at the Federal Trade Commission Public Hearing:

> Van Cise further recommended a National Mediation Panel within the industry to arbitrate disputes between franchisors and franchisees.
>
> Four years have passed since the Committee report, and considerable publicity attended its publication; but no more than two or three requests for arbitration have come to us.[23]

It would seem that arbitration by a university group (or by the American Arbitration Association, as specified in many contracts) would be preferable to costly litigation with the seemingly necessary extreme positions, but as indicated in the author's FTC statement, the practice of arbitration seems far in the future.

10 International Franchising

The trend of American firms is to expand internationally, and most recently there has been a tremendous increase in foreign investment, particularly by Arabs, in the United States. Among foreign franchises in the United States, however, the most conspicuous are the automobile dealerships and distributorships, especially those based in West Germany and Japan. A study of the one thousand largest U.S. corporations revealed an increase from 50 percent with international operations in 1950 to 65 percent in 1960 to almost 100 percent with international operations by 1970; consequently the importance of world markets to U.S. firms is a topic receiving considerable attention.

Many years ago, Robert Weaver, an international management consultant, advised firms to enter world markets through licensing. Quoting from him:

> Foreign licensing is now one of the best ways to enter world markets with minimum risk, minimum investment of time and money—yet with substantial profits, particularly when profits are measured as return on investment.[1]

The soft drink bottlers were the first American franchisors to go abroad, and now they have penetrated the Iron Curtain countries, including the Soviet Union. The automotive manufacturers, of course, were not far behind in their sallies abroad.

Aside from Canada, Europe is most likely to be the first target of international expansion by an American firm, and well it should be. Europe has tremendous market potential and a higher economic growth rate than the United States. There are, however, many contrasts between Europe and the United States. For example, Europe is a complex of many different countries with many different languages, and the population density is much greater.

What would seem to be particularly favorable to franchising in Europe is the high incidence of small retailers with a larger share of sales volume, although there has been a sharp decline in the share of the market held by small retailers in recent years in Europe.

Advantages of Franchising Abroad

There are many reasons to franchise abroad, as contrasted with expanding by some other method. Here are some reasons for franchising abroad as enumerated by Lifflander:

1. Franchising makes it possible to expand abroad without committing large amounts of money, particularly in countries where capital may not be available locally or where funds may not be repatriated or profits remitted.
2. Franchising diversifies methods of creating income.
3. New business is generated through franchising.
4. Future markets are protected at minimal cost by franchising.
5. Industrial property rights such as trademarks and patents are protected.
6. Skilled management for company-owned operations is lacking for overseas operations, making it advantageous to turn over the operation there to locally recruited franchisees.
7. Language barriers can be better overcome by franchisees recruited locally in the foreign countries.
8. Early expansion through franchising protects against competitive business.
9. It helps insure against seasonal fluctuations in domestic business.
10. It provides the opportunity to exploit "spillover" advertising and public relations.
11. Franchising helps overcome particular problems in foreign countries.
12. It helps with labor problems in foreign countries.
13. It helps overcome threat of expropriation.
14. Franchising helps avoid production and distribution problems.
15. It overcomes nationalistic restrictions on foreign ownership.
16. It provides outlets for surplus or outmoded United States products.
17. It provides for maximum utilization of accumulated experience and know-how.
18. It accommodates certain existing customers.
19. It helps acquire reciprocal benefits from foreign participants.
20. It assists in the economic development of other countries.[2]

The U.S. Department of Commerce summarizes thus the advantages that U.S. franchisors have found in penetrating foreign markets: (a) entry into the international market with minimum risk, (b) minimum investment of time and capital, and (c) maximum opportunity for new business ventures.[3]

How to Proceed Internationally

According to Weaver:

> The most practical approach to an international program for franchisors seems to me clearly to be a licensing program, getting a substantial overseas partner—one who *knows* that particular market—giving you the benefit of working with competent nationals on a very low-investment basis, with plenty of control and lots of profit potential with low risk.[4]

The following steps should be taken in order to franchise abroad:

1. Assure that the concept is viable, or at least not obviously in error.
2. Assure that the American franchisor has the capitalization to fulfill foreign obligations in training, supply, advertising, and whatever other fields expertise is promised.
3. Thoroughly investigate the market for such a program.
4. Adapt the program for foreign operations.
5. Determine financing channels.
6. Plan competent overseas representation.
7. Phase in one or two countries.
8. Determine how, when, where, and under what conditions fees and various charges can be collected.
9. Adapt program for different merchandising requirements.
10. Scrutinize and prepare to cope with competition in ways quite different from those in America: trade associations, for example, have different status, and business ethics may be quite different from those in the United States.

The temptation to franchise an entire country may be difficult to resist, particularly if separate fees are involved, but various authorities, including David Seltz, have recommended against trying to sell a whole country at a time.[5]

It should be remembered that initial costs will be heavy abroad. For example, translation into French, German, Italian, Spanish, and even into idiomatic English for the United Kingdom will be quite expensive. Local styles in advertising will probably be considerably different from those in the United States, and knowledgeable advertising people will be required locally. Field coordination and supervision will entail sizeable travel costs, and international financial manipulations will bear scrutiny.

Of course, legal problems will arise. As Lifflander asks, "What courts will have jurisdiction? Which taxes are whose burden? Which laws should apply?"[6] And, how will the old problem of termination proceed? (Nearby Puerto Rico is particularly difficult in this respect.)

The risk in foreign ventures should not be ignored. Stehlin describes an experience of a British auto manufacturer thus:

> We went into Mexico several years ago and built a very expensive franchise system selling a product that we manufactured in England. There are many countries that are having a nationalistic trend, and several years ago Mexico passed a law saying all manufactured automobiles had to have 60 percent of the contents manufactured in Mexico. This left us with two alternatives: Build a five million dollar manufacturing plant or get out of the market. Needless to say, a small manufacturer chose the latter. We had to abandon the market.[7]

Some curious and interesting quirks arise in transporting U.S. programs abroad. The meaning of slogans or advertising themes may be twisted. Lifflander notes: "... our famous registered slogan, 'Hertz Puts You in the Driver's Seat' when translated into French means 'Let Hertz Make You a Chauffeur.' " As mentioned earlier, a native of Nigeria, where Manpower was advertising, wrote the company in all seriousness: " 'I would like to have your catalogue.... I would like to become a better man.' He was translating 'Manpower' as a way to become more powerful as a man. He wanted a catalogue of our 'talismans,' as he called it, our good luck charms. He wanted to buy one."[9] Lifflander recalls an incident from one of the new African republics.[10] A would-be franchisee sent in a few hundred dollars and then asked when he should expect to receive the twenty new Fords that he expected Hertz was going to send him!

Attitudes of European
Prospective Franchisees

Seltz lists some of the attitudes of the average European prospective franchisee that differ from those in the United States:

1. He wants the franchisor to get involved: "If your program is good, try it yourself."
2. He doesn't mind paying high royalties—higher than in the U.S. Budget Rent-A-Car obtains 10 percent overseas, for example.
3. He resists front-load fees.
4. He does not object to obligatory product purchases—Wimpy's front money, for example, is only $600, with a 2 percent royalty, but they are in the meat packing business overseas.
5. He likes the idea of paying the franchise fee over a period of time.
6. He would like to tie into an existing business.
7. He admires American know-how but it must be proved in his case.
8. He moves very slowly and is perhaps less money motivated than U.S. prospects are.[11]

Seltz notes that large suppliers overseas are interested in becoming master franchisees, with rights to an entire country or a good portion of it.

Some Special Problems

To an American negotiating abroad can be quite different from what it is in the United States. Foreigners obtain an image of American businessmen through motion pictures and are wary. They are apt to feel that they should also engage in gangster tactics as they see Americans do in the movies. More bargaining is also expected abroad, and "I shall see" or a referral to the board of directors are apt to be polite no's, or dodges. When asking the American for adaptations of the program to meet local conditions, the foreigner may merely be trying to get a lower price.[12] In Newfoundland the new business entrant meets the prime minister, and in some countries as in French-speaking Quebec, the prospective business negotiator starts by visiting the Roman Catholic priest in the local community.

According to *Service World*, McDonald's had to research completely the channels of food distribution in every country it entered and, for example, train meat distributors in Japan how to prepare hamburger patties that would fulfill specifications.[13] Because European beef is grass-fed rather than grain-fed as in the United States, hamburgers there taste slightly different from those in the United States. In several countries standardized hamburger buns are difficult to come by because bakers pride themselves on their individuality. Kentucky Fried Chicken had to try a thirteen-piece cut of chicken rather than the usual nine-piece because of variations in chicken sizes there.

Withdrawing funds from some countries is apt to be most difficult, and banking and financing have to be carefully worked out. In France and Germany altering existing shops is by law almost impossible.

Protecting trademarks abroad, especially in Australia, may pose serious problems. Hertz communicated with franchisees in English until it discovered that many of its franchisees did not really understand English. When the company began communicating with licensees in their own language, many problems were solved.

Land alone in Europe can cost $225,000, the same as a hotel costs in the United States. Although policing franchisees abroad is extremely important, the cost is apt to be prohibitive. There are several less costly approaches:

1. Certified accountant's statements
2. Temporary help services as spot checkers
3. Review forms with key questions and evidence of fulfillment of advertising and product information requirements
4. Photography
5. Cross checking of complaints

The U.S. Department of Commerce calls attention to six problems faced by American franchisors operating internationally:

1. Official limitations on royalty payments or licensing and trademark contracts. In some cases royalties on trademarks and brand names are taxable and payable by the franchiser whether he is domiciled in or out of that particular country.

2. Problems may exist in the protection of trademarks as no facility exists for their registration.

3. In some cases franchising arrangements remain solely the concern of contracting parties and there are no regulations to safeguard franchising agreements. Tie-in arrangements are discouraged and sometimes forbidden.

4. In some countries, a significant percentage of ownership share of the business activity is required by local nationals; in others, aliens cannot own real estate property and in others, they cannot own retail businesses.

5. There are also import restrictions on equipment. This may impose a significant problem with respect to equipment or systems considered essential to the distinctiveness of the end-product or the end-service.

6. Wide economic variation as a result of inflation and currency valuation, exchange controls, and price ceilings on products pose problems affecting various types of franchising business categories.[14]

Increase in International Units of American Franchisors

Many investigators have called attention to American franchisors' plans for foreign expansion,[15] and U.S. Department of Commerce surveys between 1971 and 1976 show that these plans have indeed materialized. In 1971, as shown in table 10-1, there were 156 U.S. Type III and IV franchisors with units outside the United States in addition to the Type I and II franchisors outside the United States, that is, automotive dealerships, gasoline service stations, and soft drink

Table 10-1
Total Number of Establishments outside United States: U.S.-Based Franchisors, 1971-1976

	Number of Franchisors	Total Number of Units	Percentage Increase in Units over Prior Year
1976	234	12,348	12.6
1975	222	10,964	13.5
1974	217	9,663	1.6
1973	208	9,509	54.5
1972	175	6,153	82.9
1971	156	3,365	

Source: U.S. Department of Commerce. *Franchising in the Economy 1976-1978, 1975-77, 1974-76, 1973-75, 1972-74, 1971-73* (Washington, D.C.: U.S. Government Printing Office, 1978, 1977, 1976, 1975, 1974, 1973).

Note: Does not include automobile and truck dealers, gasoline service stations and soft drink bottlers, for which data were not collected.

bottlers. By 1976 the number of Type III and IV American franchisors with foreign units had grown to 234 firms, representing an increase of 50 percent in the five-year period.

More spectacular, however, was the increase in units—from 3,365 foreign units in 1971 to 12,348 units in 1976, a 267 percent jump. Interestingly the big spurt in units, according to the U.S. Department of Commerce figures, was in 1972, with an increase of 82.9 percent, as shown in table 10-1. The franchising of foreign units declined sharply, however, in 1974, with hardly any growth in 1974 over 1973—a situation probably due to the petroleum shortage and economic recession.

*Countries in Which American
Firms Franchise*

Of American franchisors' 12,348 units outside the United States in 1976, almost half (5,187, or 42 percent) were in Canada, according to the USDC survey results shown in table 10-3. The United Kingdom, with 1,793 units (or 15 percent of the total) of American franchisors and Japan, with 1,626 units (or 13 percent of the total) were next in frequency of international units. At least some

**Table 10-2
Kinds of Franchised Businesses outside United States:
U.S. Franchisors**

Kind of Business	Number of Foreign Units	Percentage of Foreign Units
Fast food restaurants	2,620	21.2
Rental services (auto, truck)	2,342	19.0
Automotive products and services	1,610	13.0
Construction, home improvement, maintenance, and cleaning services	1,189	9.6
Business aids and services	1,176	9.5
Retailing (nonfood)	972	7.9
Educational products and services, rental services (equipment), convenience stores and miscellaneous	843	6.8
Retailing (food other than convenience stores)	495	4.0
Laundry, dry-cleaning services	438	3.5
Campgrounds, hotels, motels	370	3.0
Recreation, entertainment, travel	293	2.4
Total	12,348	99.9

Source: U.S. Department of Commerce, *Franchising in the Economy 1976-1978* (Washington, D.C.: U.S. Government Printing Office, 1978), p. 42.

Note: Does not include automobile and truck dealers, gasoline service stations and soft drink bottlers, for which data were not collected.

American units, however, were located in other European countries, Australia, the Caribbean, Mexico, Africa, South America, New Zealand and Central America. Again, it should be pointed out these figures do not include automobile and truck dealerships, gasoline service stations, and soft drink bottlers, for which data were not collected by U.S. Department of Commerce.

Kinds of Franchised Businesses
outside United States

Fast food restaurants, auto and truck rental services, and automotive products and services (excluding new car dealerships) were most frequently the kinds of businesses which American franchisors had established outside the United States by 1976, as shown in table 10-2. Other establishments by American franchisors found outside the United States in 1976 included: construction, home improvement, and maintenance and cleaning service units; business aids and services; nonfood retailing; educational products and services; equipment rental services; convenience stores; other types of food retailing; laundry and dry cleaning services; campgrounds and hotels and motels; and recreational entertainment and travel services. Hertz was so far flung by 1969 that Lifflander, a Hertz executive, could boast, "You can now rent a Hertz car from one of these people (franchisees) in New Caledonia, or Pago Pago in the South Pacific, or in Kampala, Uganda, deep in Central Africa."[16]

In a series of articles based upon surveys by the United States Department of Agriculture, Philip B. Dwoskin points out that the fast food industry represents an important market for exports by U.S. agriculture.[17] "On the foreign scene," he summarizes, "U.S. fast food firms included in the update study expect to generate about $1.6 billion in sales by 1980 of which about $655 (million) is export potential for both U.S. and foreign food producers and processors . . . about $1.1 billion additional potential by 1980 will consist of exports of non foods such as kitchen equipment, paper goods, and furniture."

Franchising in Various Countries

Canada

As shown in table 10-3, American franchisors' foreign outlets are most heavily concentrated in Canada. In 1976, for example, 42 percent of all U.S. franchisors' foreign establishments were in Canada, due obviously to the many social, economic, cultural, and geographic ties between the two countries. Table 10-4 indicates the rapid growth in the numbers of American units in Canada—from

Table 10-3
Number of Units in Various Countries: U.S. Franchisors, 1976

Country	Number of Units		Percentage of Units
Canada	5,187		42
United Kingdom	1,793		15
Japan	1,626		13
Other European	1,490		12
Australia	691		6
Caribbean	347		3
Mexico	272		2
Other Asian	205		2
Other	737		6
Africa		309	
South America		199	
New Zealand		139	
Central America		90	
Total outside U.S.	12,348		101

Source: U.S. Department of Commerce, *Franchising in the Economy 1976-1978* (Washington, D.C.: U.S. Government Printing Office, 1978), p. 42.

Note: Does not include automobile and truck dealers, gasoline service stations and soft drink bottlers, for which data were not collected.

1,557 establishments in 1971 to 5,187 in 1976. The number more than tripled in the five-year period, according to survey figures from the U.S. Department of Commerce. Curiously, there was an actual drop in the number of American units in Canada from 1973 to 1974, probably due to the Arab oil embargo, the consequent recession, and the taking over locally by Canadians of the American establishments. The uptrend had resumed, however, by 1975, and 1976 marked a new high in the number of American units in Canada.

There was a wide variety in kinds of franchised businesses of American firms

Table 10-4
U.S. Franchisors' Growth in Units in Canada, 1971-1976

Year	Number of Units
1976	5,187
1975	4,313
1974	3,974
1973	4,410
1972	2,758
1971	1,557

Source: U.S. Department of Commerce, *Franchising in the Economy 1971-1973*, p. xx; *Franchising in the Economy 1972-74*, p. 16; *Franchising in the Economy 1973-75*, p. 16; *Franchising in the Economy 1974-76*, p. 25; *Franchising in the Economy 1975-77*, p. 21; *Franchising in the Economy 1976-1978*, p. 6.

in Canada in 1976, with automotive products and services and fast food restaurants being the leaders, each having about a fifth of the total units, as shown in table 10-5.

Thus, American franchising has caught hold in Canada with few apparent obstructions to its continued success. Where governmental control may be exercised, it occurs at the local level.

Canadian based franchisors have been multiplying, too, and the numbers of their units have been increasing dramatically, as suggested by *Foodservice & Hospitality*'s annual surveys of foodservice and lodging franchising in Canada which were begun in 1974. Quoting from the fourth annual survey, conducted in 1978:

> The emergence of new Canadian franchise organizations along with the dazzling growth of existing units combined to increase total franchising industry sales by more than 123.4% in 1977 over 1976. Total number of franchise units has risen 21.5% and the average sales per unit has jumped 57.4%, the 1977 franchising in the foodservice and lodging survey shows.[18]

In 1974 the survey indicated that there were 1,952 units in the Canadian foodservice and lodging field with a total sales volume of $449,855,000. By 1977 the survey showed 2,914 units with a sales volume of $1,345,200,000. Average annual sales per unit jumped from $233,000 in 1974 to $461,633 in 1977. Much of this volume reflected the adoption of Canadian generated franchise concepts alongside American ones.

Table 10-5
Kinds of Franchised Businesses of U.S. Firms in Canada, 1976

Kind of Franchised Business	Number of Units	Percentage of Units
Automotive products and services	1,146	22
Fast food restaurants (all types)	1,047	20
Business aids and services	622	12
Retailing (nonfood)	561	11
Rental services (auto, truck)	499	10
Construction, home improvement, maintenance, and cleaning services	462	9
Laundry and dry-cleaning services	329	6
Campgrounds, hotels, motels	209	4
Educational products and services, rental services (equipment), convenience stores, miscellaneous	204	4
Retailing (food other than convenience stores)	65	1
Recreation, entertainment, travel	43	1
Total units	5,187	100

Source: U.S. Department of Commerce, *Franchising in the Economy 1976-1978* (Washington, D.C.: Government Printing Office, 1978), p. 42.

And the Canadian firms are themselves expanding internationally, as this quotation from the survey indicates:

> As the small Canadian market becomes crowded, Canadian franchise operators are already looking overseas, or south of the border. . . . Pizza Delight is pushing into the United States franchising scene, as well as Captain Scott's Fish & Chips, Randax Food Systems Co., Country Style Donuts, Dixie Lee Co., Mr. Submarine Ltd. and Pizza Patio in Japan.[19]

United Kingdom

Between 1971 and 1976 there was an uninterrupted yearly increase in the number of units which American franchisors had in the United Kingdom, according to figures shown in table 10-6, which were derived from the U.S. Department of Commerce surveys. This trend confirms the department's earlier predictions that British interest in franchising was favorable to its development despite some adverse publicity due to ill-conceived ventures there.

By 1976 American franchisors had 1,793 units in Britain, or 15 percent of U.S. franchisors' total foreign establishments. Fast food restaurants were the predominant kind of business, but auto-truck rental services; automotive products and services, construction, home improvement, maintenance, and cleaning services, and the broad category including educational products and services were also well represented among the Type II and IV franchisors surveyed by the U.S. Department of Commerce, as shown in table 10-7. However, all kinds of franchised businesses were evident in the United Kingdom.

American franchising has thus caught on in Great Britain, and there appear to be no serious obstacles to its continued growth there, with whatever regulations there are being imposed by the Department of Trade and Industry.

Under the title, "Franchising: Fresh Force in Retailing," Elinor Goodman

Table 10-6
Growth in U.S. Franchisors' Units in United Kingdom, 1971-1976

Year	Number of Units
1976	1,793
1975	1,709
1974	1,265
1973	1,042
1972	586
1971	195

Sources: U.S. Department of Commerce, *Franchising in the Economy 1971-1973*, p. xx, *Franchising in the Economy 1972-74*, p. 16; *Franchising in the Economy 1973-75*, p. 16; *Franchising in the Economy 1974-76*, p. 25; *Franchising in the Economy 1975-77*, p. 21; *Franchising in the Economy 1976-1978*, p. 6.

Table 10-7
Kinds of Franchised Businesses of U.S. Firms in United Kingdom, 1976

Kind of Franchised Business	Number of Units	Percentage of Units
Fast food restaurants (all types)	433	24
Educational products and services, rental services (equipment), convenience stores, miscellaneous	371	21
Rental services (auto, truck)	257	14
Automotive products and services	256	14
Construction, home improvement, maintenance, and cleaning services	208	12
Retailing (nonfood)	115	6
Business aids and services	114	6
Recreation, entertainment, travel	22	1
Campgrounds, hotels, motels	11	1
Retailing (food other than convenience stores)	5	a
Laundry and dry-cleaning services	1	a
Total units	1,793	100

Source: U.S. Department of Commerce, *Franchising in the Economy 1976-1978* (Washington, D.C.: Government Printing Office, 1978), p. 42.
a Less than 0.5 percent.

published an article in the 6 December 1977, issue of London's *Financial Times*, which traced the development of franchising in Great Britain and suggested that close attention be given to it by those who wished to help small business. She placed the number of franchised establishments in Great Britain at about two thousand units, with annual sales volume of about two hundred fifty thousand pounds. She mentions Kentucky Fried Chicken and Wimpy bars as leaders in the United Kingdom with Dayvilles (ice cream), Dyno-Rod, and Servicemaster also prominent. Pit Stop, Holiday Inns, and others have also done well in the United Kingdom. Also mentioned in an earlier publication by Mendelsohn were Budget Rent-a-Car International, Inc. and Five Minute Car Wash.[20] Goodman contends that brewers in eighteenth century England were the originators of franchising, but J. Lyons with its Wimpy hamburger units was the first successful modern franchise system in Great Britain—Orange Julius did not do well there, and Tandy switched to company-owned branch operations after an initial try at franchising. To protect itself from anticipated punitive governmental measures, arising, perhaps, from disappointments with pyramid sales plans, the English formed the British Franchise Association, a trade association similar to several others which have sprouted around the world.

Mendelsohn elaborates upon the following twelve considerations that are important to a foreign firm planning expansion in the United Kingdom:

1. Whether to operate in the United Kingdom as a branch or subsidiary—the question of relative tax systems governs here.
2. Differences in social habits, in attitudes, tastes (especially food), and so on (as revealed by local market surveys).
3. The United Kingdom must be considered a foreign country—even to America.
4. Will volume be sufficient to support the operation? For instance, specialized franchise schemes?
5. Criteria for site selection—roadside locations are not successful in the United Kingdom.
6. Cost of equipment in the United Kingdom.
7. Cost of employing staff, the availability of staff, labor laws, the cost of leasing premises.
8. Arrangements for suitable training. Will approach and methods in operating manuals need revision?
9. Differences in the legal systems.
10. Have the Town and Country Planning Acts and local by-laws for the conversion of premises been adequately taken into account?
11. The exchange Control Act of 1947 for countries outside the sterling area.
12. Differences in lease schemes in England.[21]

There are subtle outward differences between the United Kingdom and other countries, particularly the United States that require attention. For example, the United States drinks cold drinks but the United Kingdom drinks barrels of warm beer. Thermometers on ovens are notoriously inaccurate.

Japan

Japan was early seen as a fertile ground for American franchisors, and indeed it has been.[22] Total Japanese units of American franchisors in Types III and IV categories rose from 49 in 1971 to 1,626 in 1976, as shown in table 10-8. This increase represents a thirty-fold jump. The number increased ten-fold between 1971 and 1972 alone, a situation which had led the Japanese business study team which toured the United States in 1972 to exclaim: "Japan's franchise business has entered a stage of 'franchise boom' which once caught on in the United States."[23] By 1976 Japan was third among all countries in the number of foreign units which U.S. franchisors had, with 13 percent of all foreign units of U.S. Types III and IV franchisors, as shown in table 10-3.

Fast food restaurants (26 percent) and food retailing units other than convenience stores (25 percent) together comprised about half of all U.S. units in Japan (table 10-9). It should be noted that the U.S. Department of Commerce surveys, upon which the figures are based, do not combine doughnut, ice cream

Table 10-8
Growth in U.S. Franchisors' Units in Japan, 1971-1976

Year	Number of Units
1976	1,626
1975	1,364
1974	1,238
1973	862
1972	525
1971	49

Sources: U.S. Department of Commerce, *Franchising in the Economy 1971-1973* p. xx; *Franchising in the Economy 1972-74*, p. 16; *Franchising in the Economy 1973-75*, p. 16; *Franchising in the Economy 1974-76*, p. 25; *Franchising in the Economy 1975-77*, p. 21; *Franchising in the Economy 1976-1978*, p. 6.

and certain other specialty shops with fast food restaurants but show them separately in the food retailing group other than convenience stores.

Most kinds of franchised businesses were represented in Japan in 1976—construction, home improvement, maintenance and cleaning, educational products and services, recreation, entertainment and travel, automotive products and services, and auto-truck rental services.

Here are some breakdowns of sales by type of franchise as estimated by the Japanese business study team:

Franchised establishments	*Total sales in Japan (in percents)*
Eating	36.4
Laundry-linen supply	24.1
General retail stores	18.2
(Total franchise sales is 100 percent)	

The study team estimated that the retail and leisure fields would register an annual rate of increase of more than 50 percent; eating and drinking establishments and laundry-linen supply fields, annual gains of 42 and 30 percent, respectively.

Average payments by the franchisee to the franchiser were of smaller amounts in Japan than in the United States, as shown by these average figures: franchisee fee, $1,100; mortgage, $2,077; royalty, 1.87 percent of sales; and advertising and publicity, 0.98 percent of sales.

According to the Japanese study team, franchising grew so rapidly in Japan because of the radical changes in business environments there. Among the changes were: (1) transformation of the industrial structure from heavy goods and chemical orientation to a consumer goods orientation; (2) labor shortage

Table 10-9
Kinds of Franchised Businesses of U.S. Firms in Japan, 1976

Kind of Franchised Business	Number of Units	Percentage of Units
Fast food restaurants (all types)	415	26
Retailing (food other than convenience stores)	400	25
Construction, home improvement, maintenance, cleaning services	304	19
Educational products and services, rental services (equipment), convenience stores, and miscellaneous	190	12
Recreation, entertainment, travel	166	10
Automotive products and services	60	4
Rental services (auto, truck)	58	4
Business aids and services	17	1
Retailing (nonfood)	14	1
Campgrounds, hotels, motels	2	a
Laundry and dry-cleaning services	0	a
Total units	1,626	102

Source: U.S. Department of Commerce, *Franchising in the Economy 1976-1978* (Washington, D.C.: Government Printing Office, 1978), p. 42.
aLess than 0.05 percent. Figures add to more than 100 percent due to rounding.

and wage increases under a full-employment economy; (3) soaring of land prices; (4) the inroads of foreign fast food and motel businesses into Japan; and (5) the increase in savings of general workers and their growing will to do business on their own.

The Japanese study team anticipated that the following areas would receive emphasis in franchising over the next few years: merchandise development, managerial know-how, obtaining good franchisees, and human relations in franchisor-franchisee relations.

In a series of studies in the U.S. Department of Agriculture, Philip B. Dwoskin et al. have focused on the Japanese fast-food industry "to aid the Foreign Agricultural Service (FAS) in planning its market development program in Japan by determining present and potential markets for U.S. processed, semiprocessed, and bulk commodities in that industry."[24] In brief: "The first Western-style menu franchise chain operations got underway in 1970 and began to change the character of Japan's fast-food industry. By 1973, the Japanese fast-food industry was comprised of 43 fast-food chains, of which 24 served Western-style menu items."[25] Thirteen of the Western style firms operate under licensing, or franchise, arrangements, after buying the franchise rights and continuing to pay a royalty fee of 2.5 percent to 3.5 percent per annum.

Among the American fast-food firms which have entered the Japanese market are: Kentucky Fried Chicken, McDonald's, International Dairy Queen, and A&W International. By 1978 McDonald's had 131 units in Japan, and Kentucky Fried Chicken has plans for 300-400 Japanese units by 1980. In addition to these firms, Dunkin Donuts and Mister Donut have established units across the country, the latter with well over 100 units there. Dairy Queen has contracted to open 500 units in Japan. Franchisor trade missions to Japan and other countries are sponsored by the U.S. government.[26]

After exhaustively interviewing Western-style Japanese fast food executives, Dwoskin and Havas record these advantages of U.S. products in the Japanese market:

> . . . with very few exceptions, Japanese Western-style fast food executives regard them highly, respect U.S. fast-food technology, and believe strongly in the necessity of sticking to the specifications, food and nonfood, of the franchise agreement. Wholly owned Japanese operators of Western-style fast-food enterprises also believe in faithfully copying U.S. fast-food operations in terms of style, furnishings, and menu. Western-type fast-food outlets are growing much more rapidly than the rest of Japan's food service industry because firms are backed by some of the strongest financial interests in Japan. U.S. fast-food technology and expertise are being used almost totally, allowing Japanese operators to avoid many of the problems U.S. fast-food operators had to resolve by trial and error in the early developmental stage of the U.S. industry. The affluence of the Japanese economy and changing life styles, particularly of the younger generation, create a fertile environment for Western style fast-food growth . . .[27]

The U.S. Department of Commerce notes that an effective point of contact for American franchisors interested in entering the Japanese market is the Japanese Franchise Association, Room 601, Roppongi Royal Mansion 6-8-14, Roppongi, Minato-ke, Tokyo. The Association has prepared in Japanese a helpful paperback: (U.S.A. Franchising Enterprise/American-No Franchise Kigyo/), published by Tokyo Keizai, Kabushiki Kaisha, Otsuka Building 2-12-1 Misakicho Chiyoda-ku, Tokyo.

So far as legalities are concerned, trademarks, brand names and images, and so on are well protected in Japan, and there appear to be no oppressive laws or regulations hindering franchising.

Continental European Countries

There was an increase in the number of units of American franchisors in continental European countries between 1971 and 1976, as shown in table 10-10, but with a drop in numbers of units between 1973 and 1974—a situation stemming from the worldwide recession and Arab oil boycott and necessitating a pullback by American firms except in the most rewarding places.

Table 10-10
Growth in U.S. Franchisors' Units in Continental European
Countries, 1971-1976

Year	Number of Units
1976	1,490
1975	1,331
1974	1,177
1973	1,429
1972	866
1971	619

Sources: U.S. Department of Commerce, *Franchising in the Economy 1971-1973*, p. xx; *Franchising in the Economy 1972-74*, p. 16; Franchising in the *Economy 1973-75*, p. 16; *Franchising in the Economy 1974-76*, p. 25; *Franchising in the Economy 1975-77*, p. 21; *Franchising in the Economy 1976-1978*, p. 6.

In the continental European countries somewhat more than half of the American units in 1976 were in auto and truck rental services, with business aids and services a distant second, as shown in table 10-11. Fast foods in general have not fared so well on the European continent, although Wimpy's, from the United Kingdom, has done well, and others such as McDonald's are making headway. The French like their *petits bistros*, and the Italians love to sit and talk by the hour over their coffee. The Germans wondered about the war activities of Colonel Sanders and thought the firm was perhaps a travel agency; it eventually pulled out of Germany.

France. So far as the individual Continental European countries are concerned, franchising has probably met with the greatest success in France. Not only have many American franchisors done well in France, but numerous franchises have been generated within the country. The French Franchise Federation is very active, and the French contribute support to the European Franchise Federation. Four university theses (three doctoral) have been written in France on franchising, beginning with Jean Boursican's at the Université des Sciences Sociales de Toulouse followed by Michele Weill's at the Université Aix Marseille II, André Rolland at the Université de Rennes, and Dominique Baschet, at the Université de Droit, d'Économie et de Sciences Sociales de Paris. Weill also studied at the Boston College Franchise Center. Weill's office (Department of Management, University of Toulon) publishes the monthly *Bulletin of the French Franchise Federation*, which is cosponsored by the Fédération Européene de Franchising. Also, the French actively support the annual European symposia on franchising, the third of which was held in Brussels, Belgium, in October 1977, with the theme "Franchiser-Franchisee Relations," and featuring a speech on the subject by Jacques Cafler, Directeur General du Marketing

Table 10-11
Kinds of Franchised Businesses of U.S. Firms in Continental
European Countries, 1976

Kind of Business	Number of Units	Percentage of Units
Rental services (auto, truck)	781	52
Business aids and services	174	12
Retailing (nonfood)	134	9
Construction, home improvement, maintenance, cleaning services	119	8
Fast food restaurants (all types)	103	7
Campgrounds, hotels, motels	59	4
Laundry and dry-cleaning services	47	3
Educational products and services, rental services (equipment), convenience stores, and miscellaneous	45	3
Recreation, entertainment, travel	11	1
Retailing (food other than convenience stores)	10	1
Automotive products and services	7	—
Total units	1,490	100

Source: U.S. Department of Commerce. *Franchising in the Economy 1976-1978* (Washington, D.C.: Government Printing Office, 1978), p. 42.

Prouvost Masurel, and President of La Fédération Française du Franchisage.[28] The program was arranged by the Comité Belge de la Distribution. The book by Teston, *Le Franchising et les Concessionaires* (Paris: J. Delmas & Co., 1973), is the one book in France about franchising.

A rough quantitative picture of French franchises exclusive of the hotel-restaurant, automotive sales, and gasoline fields may be obtained from a survey made by the French publication, *Commerce Moderne* in 1977 and summarized in the June 1977 issue of the Bulletin of the French Franchise Federation, *Franchising*. The summary is shown as table 10-12: more than half of all French franchisees have shops selling items of special interest to the housewife—ready-to-wear, infant wear, wedding clothes, Morocco leather footwear, wool hosiery, sewing machines, and household linen. Of 7,562 franchisees, 4,609 were in this category.

However, French franchisors covered diverse fields: equipment for the house, specialized businesses and services, as well as personal wear items. *Commerce Moderne* listed ninety different French franchisors having 7,562 franchises in four business categories.

Among the French originating franchises are the following: Catena (Do-it-yourself hardware); Promo-France (men's, women's junior's, infant's wear);

Table 10-12
French Franchises, 1977

	Franchises	Franchisees
Equipment for the house		
Furniture	5	277
Pottery, hardware, garden	9	928
Decoration, carpets	5	95
Household, hi-fi, radio	4	11
Kitchen equipment	3	10
Subtotal	26	1,321
Personal items		
Ready-to-wear	11	393
Infant wear	4	190
Wedding clothes	1	138
Footwear, Morocco leather	5	403
Sewing machines, woolens, hosiery	7	3,422
Household linen	2	63
Subtotal	30	4,609
Specialized businesses		
Beauty shops	4	454
Sports, leisure time (recreational)	2	22
Gift shops	3	31
HBJO	6	169
Photo	2	50
Delicacies (foods)	5	132
Subtotal	22	858
Services		
Pressing	3	368
Transportation	1	91
Auto, trailer, truck rentals	3	128
Temporary help	1	3
Matrimonial agencies	1	30
Breakdown service	1	8
VPC boutiques	2	146
Subtotal	12	774
Grand total (excluding hotels and restaurants)	90	7,562

Source: Translated and adapted from the *Bulletin de la Fédération Française du Franchisage* (FFF) *Franchising* 45 (June 1977):613-614.

Note: On the occasion of a special issue (406, 8 June 1977) *Commerce Moderne* published a list of French franchises with their addresses and the number of franchisees. In summary one obtains the figures in the table for the different sectors. These figures constitute no more than approximations since the census was not exhaustive.

Korrigan (hosiery—150 plus stores); Quelle (a photo company); Prenatal (baby carriages, games, textiles—310 plus stores); Levitan (furniture—62 stores, started in 1956); Carrefour (supermarkets, started in 1960); OBI-Seramo (grocery stores); SOS-Derrange (radios, electronics, started in 1961); Clarins (massages—80 stores or more, started in 1957); and Pronuptia (wedding gowns and accessories), founded in 1958 by the late Henri Micmacher and now worldwide, including in the United States.

There are two case studies (an original and a revision) on Carrefour prepared under the supervision of faculty members of the Harvard Graduate School of Business Administration. Probably one of the best known French franchises internationally is Yoplait, a brand name yogurt, whose development has been guided by the Stanford educated Charles G. Seroude, a prominent authority on franchising. The very active French Franchise Federation's monthly *Bulletin*, prepared by Mrs. Michel Weill under the direction of Marc Goguet and an editorial committee of persons prominent in French franchising, maintains an up-to-date flow of information on franchising in France as well as other countries.

The December 1976 issue of the *Bulletin* carried an interesting article by Jean-Paul Clement, a Paris lawyer, which summarized financial and legal aspects of franchising in France. He estimated that the sale of goods through franchised outlets and voluntary chains which are moving towards franchising comprised about 20 percent of all retail trade in France.

Clement also commented on the export of French franchises, which has made headway in recent years. Pingouin Stem has put 12 units in Germany, 141 in Belgium, and 182 in Spain; Rodier has established 65 units in Germany, and 10 in diverse countries. Prenatal has 12 units in Germany, 19 in Belgium, 32 in Holland, 62 in Italy, 45 in Spain, and 25 in various countries. Rodier in September 1977 opened its third American franchise—on Madison Avenue, New York. These are just examples. Yoplait and Cofran were early exporters of franchises, but they are manufacturing types. French franchisors, Clement says, recognize the absolute necessity of developing not only in the European Common market but also in the United States.

Germany. Although franchising has not developed so fast in Germany as in France, franchise systems have been increasing in the Federal Republic of Germany, and there have been several publications on the subject in Germany. Günther Mathieu in a speech at Boston College in 1977 presented table 10-13, which depicts the German situation in 1972. Fifty-nine franchise systems were identified in Germany in 1972; of those, 33 were of German origin. The 59 franchisors had 10,756 franchisees, more than half of whom were in the automobile retail trade field. Although a broad sample of business sectors were represented by the 59 franchise chains, miscellaneous nonfood retail enterprises and beverage production had relatively large numbers of franchisees, as shown in table 10-13. Mathieu estimates there were more than 100 franchise systems operating in Germany in 1977 and possibly 150 by 1978.[29]

One reason for the rather slow development of franchising in Germany was the prior existence of various types of cooperatives, buying groups, and associations of small businesses, but many of these have gravitated towards the

Table 10-13
Franchise Systems in the Federal Republic of Germany, Spring 1972

Economic Sector	Line of Business	Number of Systems	Of German Origin	Number of Franchisees
Industry	Beverage production	8	3	950
Trade	Wholesale trade			
	Dairy products	2	2	40
	Retail trade			
	Automobiles	3	1	6,000
	Construction machines	1	0	1
	Mineral oil	1	0	30
	Building components			
	tools	7	4	250
	Food	3	3	250
	Furniture, carpets	3	2	150
	Other nonfood	7	7	1,900
Services	Restaurants, hotels	5	2	25
	Car rentals, taxis	4	3	350
	Dry cleaning	3	1	420
	Real estate	2	2	150
	Training	2	0	120
	Bookkeeping	2	2	100
	Pipeline cleaning	2	0	10
	Other (part-time work)	4	1	10
Total		59	33	10,756

Source: *Infratest Industria*; see Hubertus Bohm, "Franchise Zwischen Boom und Bangen" ("Franchise between Boom and Bust"), in *Absatzwirtschaft* 2d ed., 1972, as quoted by Günther Mathieu in a speech at Boston College, 8 March 1977, "Franchise Development in Germany."

franchise type of organization, with its more rigid central controls. As Gross notes, since Europe has long had these associations of small businessmen, the structure of franchising has erected upon quite a different foundation in Europe than in the United States, where the early stimulus to franchising was the desire of manufacturers to extend their distribution systems.[30]

Dr. Walther Skaupy contends that Germany has few people with enough money to buy a franchise and that the door is therefore open to persons with wealth or companies looking to diversify to secure master, or area, franchises and have them exploited by management specialists or even by operators from the franchisor company.[31] He thinks the outlook in this respect is favorable for either German or American nationals. He also sees an opportunity for sophisticated franchisors to take over the poorly managed dealerships and concessions and inject them with sound modern management methods. Just within the past year the German Franchise Association was formed, with Dr. Skaupy as its first president, and franchising in Germany is experiencing a sharp upsurge. For one thing, prices in full service restaurants are becoming so high that the "bargains" in fast food units are increasingly attractive. This situation, in fact, exists throughout Europe. Perhaps indicative of a trend is the recent purchase of American fast food firms, Lum's and IHOP (formerly International House of Pancakes) by the German firm, Wienerwald.

However, there are psychological blocks to franchising among Germans, according to Skaupy.[32] Potential franchisees are little inclined to submit to a strict system of controls. They are also little inclined to efface themselves behind the system's name, marks, and symbols. He contends that franchisees will not accept long-drawn and overly detailed contracts such as those prevalent in the United States. The preamble is particularly important—that is, the basis of the system must be spelled out. German law does not provide for registration of the service marks and recommendation of prices is difficult in Germany. Generally, however, antitrust is less complicated.

Here are some franchise companies *originating* in Germany, according to Skaupy:

1. *Nordsee* (Bremerhaven). Specializes in sale of seafood. Has more than three hundred company-owned outlets with snack bars attached. Developed a franchise chain and in 1971 had eighteen franchisees with plans for great expansion.
2. *Seifenplatz.* Has more than five hundred outlets selling cosmetic and soap products. Relatively few, however, are franchised.
3. *Bremer Modell.* Distributes milk products of all kinds. Operates under tradename *fz FrischdienstZentrale.* The franchisor, a Bremen company, has concluded delivery agreements with groups of clients all over the country. Franchisees are the wholesale dealers who ship products, and so forth, of whom there are relatively few.
4. *Musterring.* Has at least one hundred fifty franchisees of furniture and household equipment of about ninety manufacturers.
5. *Norddeutsches Modell.* Set up by Knechtel company in Bremen, it distributes construction components (for example, prefab doors and windows) through franchisees, who can subfranchise on occasion.
6. Others in construction, toys, office equipment, dry cleaning, real estate agencies, household equipment, furniture, temporary help.[33]

Gross and Skaupy's 1977 book, which I have reviewed in detail elsewhere,[34] describes and evaluates numerous franchises currently operating in Germany. These include the food and beverage systems such as Coca-Cola and McDonald's, Hallmark Cards and Gifts, Bremer Modell, Manpower, and others. The book also contains excellent chapters on the expansion of franchising in Europe, and especially on the legal aspects of franchising in the Federal Republic of Germany.

In addition to the scholarly book by Gross and Skaupy, the first edition of which appeared in 1968, Professor Bruno Tietz, Director of the Institute for

Trade and Commerce, University of Saarbrücken, West Germany, introduced in 1969 a series of seminars on franchising which were held at the Gottlieb Duttweiler-Institute, Rüschlikon, Switzerland. Professor Tietz's attention to franchising stemmed from his interest in the dynamics of retailing.

University dissertations on franchising continue to appear in Germany, the latest being Alfred Görge's in business administration under the direction of Professor Eberhard Dülfer at Marburg University. It was published in 1979 with the title *Die Internationalisierung von Franchise—Systemen.*[35]

Other Countries on Continent. The Benelux and Scandinavian countries as well as Spain have been exposed to franchising, and this mode of distribution seems to be catching on in those countries. For example, Pillsbury's Burger King in cooperation with Banco del Noroeste moved into Spain as early as 1974, and more recently Professor Jose Paz-Ares, a business law professor at the University of Madrid, has published several articles in the area of franchising.

The Comité Belge de la Distribution, as indicated earlier, sponsors the annual symposia on franchising of the European Franchise Federation, and Dr. F.W.J. Schalen, of the Netherlands, is one of Europe's leading franchising consultants. Of course, the Type I and II franchise systems (manufacturer-retailer dealerships such as in the automobile field and manufacturer-wholesaler-ships in soft drink production) have been well accepted in these countries for some time, as have the hotel and motel chains. On the other hand, even though there is a franchise association in Italy, few authorities would consider that country to be a glowing prospect for franchising.

Gross and Skaupy have a rather detailed country-by-country and franchise-by-franchise review of franchising in Europe, naming franchising authorities in the respective countries, such as Herbert Giesen (Stockholm), G. Christiäensen (Belgium), C. Seroude (France), Martin Mendelsohn (Great Britain), and so on.[36]

Australia

Next in numbers of units of American franchisors was Australia, with the total of 355 units in 1971, increasing to 691 units in 1976. The rise in number of units during this period was rather consistent year by year except for 1973, when the world wide recession seemed to put a damper on American franchises in Australia. Year-by-year figures are shown in table 10-14.

Australia appears to be a fast-food haven for American firms—about a third (32.4 percent) of all American franchised units in 1976 were in this category, as shown in table 10-15.

However, practically all business categories were represented in Australia by American franchisor firms; the exceptions being laundry and dry cleaning

0

Table 10-14
U.S. Franchisors' Units in Australia, 1971-1976

Year	Number of Units
1976	691
1975	643
1974	473
1973	430
1972	457
1971	355

Sources: U.S. Department of Commerce. *Franchising in the Economy 1971-1973*, p. xx; *Franchising in the Economy 1972-74*, p. 16; *Franchising in the Economy 1973-75*, p. 16; *Franchising in the Economy 1974-76*, p. 25; *Franchising in the Economy 1975-77*, p. 21; *Franchising in the Economy 1976-1978*, p. 6.

services and food retailing other than convenience stores, which showed no units there, as shown in table 10-15. Auto-truck rental services and business aids and services ranked next to fast food restaurants in number of American outlets in Australia as shown by the table. Other franchisor units were much fewer in number.

Three American fast food firms, Kentucky Fried Chicken, Pizza Hut, and McDonald's, dominate the market in Australia, and a survey found that

Table 10-15
Kinds of Franchised Businesses of U.S. Firms in Australia, 1976

Kind of Franchised Business	Number of Units	Percentage of Units
Fast food restaurants (all types)	224	32.4
Rental services (auto, truck)	190	27.5
Business aids and services	120	17.4
Retailing (nonfood)	119	17.2
Recreation, entertainment, travel	24	3.4
Construction, home improvement, maintenance, and cleaning services	7	1.0
Automotive products and services	3	0.4
Educational products and services, rental services (equipment), convenience stores, and miscellaneous	3	0.4
Campgrounds, hotels, motels	1	0.1
Laundry and dry-cleaning services	0	0
Retailing (food other than convenience stores)	0	0
Total units	691	99.8

Source: U.S. Department of Commerce, *Franchising in the Economy 1976-1978* (Washington, D.C.: Government Printing Office, 1978), p. 42.

Kentucky Fried Chicken was the most profitable firm in the country after Utah Mining Australia. Hartee's Restaurants, a subsidiary of Kellogg Food Products, had planned to open one hundred restaurants in Australia but closed down there after sizeable losses from the seventeen restaurants which they had opened. Kellogg had launched the project under a franchise arrangement with the American Hardee chain, changing the name to avoid confusion with other Australian companies. Meat pies were the favorite and practically the only food that Australians enjoyed until the American firms began to enter the market in the late sixties.

According to an article in the *National Times* of 27 February-4 March 1978, a McNair Anderson survey in December 1977 found that one quarter of the Australian population over thirteen had been to a Kentucky Fried Chicken outlet the previous month, and 12 percent of the population had been more than once. Although some disappointment was encountered in growth during the latest recession, McDonald's had plans for expansion. Beginning with the first unit in 1971, McDonald's had sixty-six outlets by 1978. About 20 percent of the average family's weekly grocery bill was spent on takeout or away-from-home eating in 1977 in Australia (as contrasted with 24 percent in the United States), and of this 20 percent, about 12.5 percent was spent in Kentucky Fried Chicken, McDonald's, or Pizza Hut units, according to the *National Times* article.

Another franchise trying to make headway in Australia against time worn customs is the convenient food store. Australian stores generally close Saturday and do not open again until Monday, but Seven-Eleven Food Stores, open for a minimum of sixteen hours a day (and some twenty-four hours a day), are opening in Melbourne, South Australia, and New South Wales. There were seven in suburban Melbourne by 1978, and plans were on the drawing boards to open one hundred more during the next three years—many in former service stations, where petrol will still be sold through the night.

Franchise conferences are now being held in Australia, and Howard Bellin, South Melbourne, has a thriving business as a franchise consultant, conducting conferences and publishing a newsletter. Dr. David Wadley, a professor in geography now at the University of Queensland, did his doctoral dissertation on franchising in the farm equipment field.

Specific American Franchisors
with Overseas Units

Overseas expansion by American franchisors has been so great that *Service World International* in its January-February 1975 issue was led to caption an article "Fast Food Still Top 'Export' from America," and the lead sentence described Pillsbury Company's Burger King's entry into Spain, as indicated earlier in this chapter. Two Spaniards, who were to direct the operation in Spain, were graduated from "Whopper College," Burger King's training school in Miami, Florida.

The story went on to describe the success of other fast firms abroad, beginning with Burger King's chief competitor, McDonald's. The latter was described as successful in Sweden, Germany, France, Holland, and England; its first restaurant in Sweden was reportedly headed for $2 million dollar gross its first year. Other sources indicate that McDonald's is successful in Australia, Japan and various other countries. By 1977, according to figures in the *Franchise Opportunities Handbook*, McDonald's had units in twenty-two countries in addition to the United States.[37]

Although *Service World* reports that Pizza Hut was in Germany and England, profits there were not so good, even though potentials were considered excellent there for Pizza Hut, as well as in Australia, the Netherlands, and New Zealand. As early as 1975 Kentucky Fried Chicken had more than seventy-five units in Japan with plans for several hundred more by the 1980s. Dairy Queen was also heavily involved in Japan, together with Mister Donut, Pizza Inn, Shakey's, Golden Skillet, and Dunkin' Donuts.

A perusal of *Franchise Opportunities Handbook* indicates that many other franchisors outside the fast food field are active abroad: the automotive, car rental, petroleum, hotels-motels, and soft drink firms, of course; but also: Manpower, Bernardi Brothers (car wash); the Cifer Corporation (auto glass repair, Canada and Switzerland, as well as the United States); Gail Industries (automotive cleaning products, worldwide); Robo-Wash (car wash, Europe and the Far East); Ziebart Rust Proofing (for cars, twenty-eight countries), just to name a few.[38]

European and Japanese automotive manufacturers have for many years franchised outside their own countries, and the American market, especially for Japanese cars, has been particularly fertile. Rootes Motors, of England, had three hundred fifty franchised dealers in the United States in 1965, and in 1964 had sold 250,000 cars in 163 countries using the franchise system of distribution. In the fast food field, the London based subsidiary of J.K. Lyons, Wimpy's, had early established units throughout Europe, and its acquisition of the American ice cream franchisor, Baskin-Robbins and the Tastee Freez chain bolstered its position in the international field.

France probably has the greatest international potential, with Charles Seroude's Yoplait and EPAC and Henri Micmacher's Pronuptia. Already in 1978, the location of the latter's stores required a map of the world.

Appendixes

Appendix A
A Franchise Contract

"A Franchise Contract" by Jerrold G. Van Cise. Reprinted from *Franchising Today* (1970), ed. by Charles L. Vaughn. (Lynbrook, N.Y.: Farnsworth Publishing Company, Inc., 1970), pp. 296-317.

Originally given as a speech at the Fifth International Management Conference on Franchising Sponsored by Boston College, this article met with approval by groups with diverse interests. The article was reprinted in the *Antitrust Bulletin*, entered into the *Congressional Record* by Senator Philip A. Hart and reprinted in booklet form by the International Franchise Association, with a foreword by the late Harry L. Rudnick, IFA Counsel.

A Franchise Contract

Ignorance of the law - at least in franchising - no longer is bliss. Franchisors who enter into unlawful agreements may be chained to injunctions;[1] their conduct may cost them treble damages;[2] and such violations may curb them with new regulations.[3] In franchising, therefore, standard equipment currently must include a lawful contract.

Knowledge of the law, however, need not increase sorrow - despite Ecclesiastes. This is because three principles are available to guide the pen of the draftsman in preparing a suitable franchise agreement. The first principle is that the contract should be *frank*. Complete disclosure of a proposed relationship between franchisor and franchisee is desirable in order to ensure that neither party may reasonably charge that thereby he was deceived by the other.[4] Second, its provisions should be fair. This franchise relationship should be so equitable that no party may convincingly claim that thereunder he was dominated by the other.[5] Finally, its contents should be *enforceable*. If either the franchisor or the franchisee should be tempted to breach the covenants thus openly and equitably entered into, he should not be in the position of a pot entitled to call the other an equally black kettle.[6] In short, if the franchise agreement is drafted so that the parties know what they are doing when they agree, like what they are doing when they perform, and fear what they may suffer if they sin, the resulting contractual relationship should be relatively non-litigious.

The legal tailor must of course cut his contractual cloth to conform to the contours of his client. For example, he may prepare a short document to clothe the distribution of standard appliances to established dealers - but any such "mini" contract would be far too short to cover an arrangement for serving distinctive foods in new service outlets. Moreover, he should attempt to design covenants which will look well on his client. Thus, provisions appropriate for hot dogs may not be suitable for live dogs. Nevertheless, his agreement should sufficiently adhere to the suggested three principles that neither party will hesitate to appear in public wearing the finished garment.

Possible contractual provisions embodying these principles are discussed below. Counsel for the individual franchisor or franchisee can best determine which, if any, of these provisions might be considered for inclusion or exclusion in his client's future agreements. The objective here has been solely to propose and not to dispose of illustrative issues relevant to the preparation of such new franchise contracts.

General Provisions

(1) *Description of parties:* A franchisor is accustomed to require an applicant
for a franchise to disclose many facts in order to enable the former intelli-
gently to exercise his right to select those with whom he wishes to deal.[7]
A franchisee, in his turn, should have an equal right to obtain access to
equivalent information with respect to the franchisor. Accordingly, a frank,
fair and enforceable franchise contract might provide for mutual access by
both parties to facts reasonably related to the business qualifications of
the proposed signatories.

The franchise contract, for example, might not only describe briefly
the parties but affirm that each had disclosed to the other, in writing, information as to his financial resources, previous experience, if any, in the franchised business and other relevant facts, and that each relies solely upon these
written representations and no others in executing the agreement. Preferably,
the franchisor should deal directly with the contemplated franchisee, and not
through a sub-franchisor having a less personal interest in protecting the franchised name, when these disclosures are given and received. If these steps
are taken, neither party thereafter may reasonably claim that he was misled
with respect to the qualifications of the other to discharge the contractual
obligations undertaken by him.

(2) *Nature of franchise:* The franchise which is to be granted to this franchisee is in essence a license authorizing him to engage in business in a manner associated with and identified by a trade name. This name is owned by
the franchisor and will remain so owned upon any termination of this license.
It follows that a contract conforming to our three principles should explain
the ownership of the franchised name and describe exactly what it covers.
Any subsequent restraint in this license might then be phrased in a manner
to indicate how its restriction is reasonably ancillary to the lawful main purpose[8] of protecting the good will represented by this trade name.

The franchise agreement therefore might affirm the ownership by the
franchisor of the trade name, state that the franchisee acknowledges this
ownership, describe the form and substance of the business identified by
this name, and refer to some of the unique features upon which the parties
rely to justify their contractual restraints.

(3) *Territory of franchise:* The franchise agreement at some point customarily identifies the area within which the franchisee is licensed to do business.
In addition, it often specifies a particular address in this area from which the
franchisee may solicit customers. Therefore it is essential that each party
know exactly what and where this area and/or location are. To date, the
courts have approved the grant of such limited, as distinguished from un-
limited, territorial licenses.[9]

The franchise agreement might not only identify the licensed area and/or location, but - possibly by cross-reference to the relevant papers - describe the criteria used in determining the market potential of the franchise and represent that this criteria is known to and is satisfactory to both parties. If the franchisor wishes to lean over backwards, the document could also make provision for some equitable adjustment or even a possible removal of the franchisee to a new location within the franchised territory in the event that the criteria used should subsequently prove to be erroneous or become outmoded.

(4) *Protection from competition:* The franchisee will probably desire to know the extent to which he will obtain exclusive rights in this franchised territory, and in this event the franchisor should tell him. An applicant should not be permitted to assume that he will be protected from competition if this will not be the case.

The franchisor may lawfully provide in the franchise contract, if he so elects, that in the franchised territory he will solely license the franchisee. He may also promise that neither he nor anyone associated with him will open up a company outlet there. The franchisor may not, however, undertake that any other franchisee located in any other market will not tranship into the licensed territory.[10]

(5) *Representations by franchisor:* Following the execution of such a contract, some franchisees have asserted that erroneous representations by the franchisor had been made with respect to the assistance which the franchisee was to receive and the profits which he was to earn. Moreover, such assertions on occasion have been found to be justified.[11] If proven, any such franchisees would have actionable claims for deception and failure of consideration against their franchisor.

The franchise agreement therefore might reduce to writing any representations which had been made to the franchisee in order to induce his execution of this document, and contain an acknowledgment from the franchisee that no others had been made either orally or in writing. In addition, supplementary instructions might be issued to the franchisor's personnel requiring them to limit their promises to what they have been authorized in writing to make.

(6) *Representations by franchisee:* Likewise, at times, franchisees have claimed that they had been high-pressured into signing their franchise contracts before they had had adequate time in which to study their terms, check on the representations made or obtain professional advice on the foregoing. They have also asserted on varying grounds that they did not knowingly and willingly enter into their contractual obligations. If substantiated, any such conduct could invite proceedings from the Federal Trade Commission.[12]

The franchise agreement accordingly might contain a blank to be filled in by the franchisee specifying the period during which he has had in his possession a copy of this document. In addition, it might provide for a representation by the franchisee that he has had adequate time in which to review all aspects of the proposed contractual arrangements, and a statement that he is freely signing after having submitted the document to his counsel and having received his advice. As further insurance - against a possible claim that even this acknowledgment was obtained by unethical means - an option might be given which permits the franchisee within a reasonable time thereafter to change his mind and to receive back an equitable portion of any monies deposited by him. In short, the franchise contract might be so drafted as to evidence on its face that any future charges of fraud made by the franchisee are instead acts of fraud committed by this franchisee.

Start-Up Provisions

(7) *Deposit of fee:* We now leave the general and turn to the more specific contractual provisions, starting with any fee which may be required before the franchise grant is to take effect. Franchisors vary in whether or not they insist upon the payment of any such initial fee by a franchisee upon the execution of the franchise contract. Some waive any such requirement; others seek an amount to cover some or all of their costs in launching the franchisee in business; and still others charge what they consider to be the market value of the franchise grant. Needless to say, federal and state laws with respect to fraud, taxes and securities[13] must be consulted when these decisions are made.

A frank contract might list all start-up charges; a fair contract might disclose the justification for each; and an enforceable contract might avoid vague commitments giving rise to disputes over the adequacy of the consideration received for any such payment. A generous agreement might provide that any such fee is to be considered as a mere deposit to be returned in part or in whole in the event that, for some reason, the franchisee never commences to engage in business under the franchisor's name.

(8) *Land and building:* Many franchisors undertake, in part consideration for this franchise fee, not only to make available a distinctive design of building which is uniform to all of its franchisees, but also to secure a desirable business location, to lease it from its owner, and to sublease it to the franchisee. They may also offer to finance the construction of the building which is to be used by the franchisee. If these services are contemplated, the extent of any such undertakings should be spelled out; the charges for any land and building thus obtained should be itemized; and any acceptance of these arrangements should of course be optional.

The leasing of land and buildings may not safely be tied to the acceptance by the franchisee of his franchise license from the franchisor.[14]

A franchisor therefore might expressly state in his contract that a franchisee has the option either to obtain his own land and building (conforming to the standards, blueprints and specifications of the franchisor), or to lease such land and building from the franchisor. He might also take care to limit any charges for any leased property to the prevailing rates in the community plus a reasonable return for his real estate services. In this manner, both the language of the contract and the confirming facts of the marketplace will establish that the lease of property and the license of the trade name are independently entered into and thus are independently enforceable.

(9) *Equipment and facilities:* Many franchisors likewise discover that they must locate equipment and facilities appropriate for use by their franchisees in their business operations and must undertake to finance their supply to their franchisees. This ancillary line of business activity also is proper, provided again, that the franchisee understands what is offered, has the opportunity to check upon the reasonableness of each charge, and may reject any or all items insofar as they are available in comparable form and substance elsewhere. Except where they represent unique and indispensible items only available from the franchisor, any requirement that equipment and facilities be purchased solely from the franchisor is hazardous.[15]

The franchisor here also might spell out in his contract that the franchisee has the option either of making his own arrangements for the purchase of equipment and facilities meeting the specifications of the franchisor or of obtaining them from the franchisor. The prices charged by the franchisor for these items - once again - might be based on competitive price levels plus a reasonable return for special services provided by the franchisor. As in the case of the previous provision relating to real property, a transaction of sale and a license of rights should in form and in fact be offered and accepted on their individual merits in the absence of special facts making them to a degree interdependent.

(10) *Training of applicant:* Whether or not franchisors furnish land, building and facilities, they must of course undertake to make sure that their franchisees are qualified to deal with the public in a manner conforming to the standards represented by their franchised names. At times, a franchisee may be sufficiently informed of his duties by written communications from his franchisor. Normally, however, he should receive some more or less intensive training in the unique demands of his franchised business from his franchisor.[16] It is essential, accordingly, that the franchise agreement disclose in adequate detail the nature, duration and additional cost, if any, to the applicant, of the training that will be required of an applicant for

a franchise before he will be entitled to engage in business under the franchised name.

Amplifying a prior suggestion, a franchise contract might provide that a franchisee who changes his mind about becoming a franchisee during his training period may cancel his contract and receive back some or all of any deposit which he has previously made, upon condition that no use of any information thus far received by him will either be used by him or be disclosed to another. A provision of this nature will foreclose any subsequent charge by some franchisee that he has been misled into surrendering his life savings for and devoting his remaining lifetime to a franchise business unknown to and untried by him.

(11) *Transmission of standards:* Once the franchisor has arranged for the supply of land, building, facilities and training, he must communicate to his franchisee the standards which should be maintained by the latter when doing business under the franchised trade name. These standards normally are incorporated in manuals and other written communications, which convey to the franchisee the specifications, procedures and other trade secrets of the franchisor. The establishment and enforcement of these standards are not only permissible, but are essential, in trademark licensing, in order to safeguard the public which patronizes the franchised business in reliance upon its identification with the franchised trade name.[17]

These standards of the franchisor preferably should be objective in nature, capable either of written definition or of scientific determination where this is feasible. Their nature should conform to the description of these franchise controls contained in the franchise contract, so that the franchisee was aware of their restrictive features before he undertook to be bound by them. Provision might be made for reasonable changes in these standards by the franchisor in the light of subsequent experience and new developments. Any authorization of capricious changes from time to time at the whim of the licensor, however, should be avoided. For any attempt to use the device of alleged standards to maintain arbitrary controls over independent businessmen would cause suspicious franchisees and skeptical courts to consider them to be mere camouflaged procedures intended to impose collateral trade restraints upon the licensees.

(12) *Opening for business:* Eventually the franchisee is prepared to open for business. On this occasion, as an additional service offered in part consideration for the payment of any franchise fee, the franchisor as midwife customarily provides promotions, advisory personnel and other assistance in order to ensure the successful birth of this new entrant. These services are reasonably ancillary to the grant of the franchise and should raise no legal problem.

The franchise contract, however, might detail the specific forms of help which are to be provided. Too often franchisees believe that promised forms of assistance have not been given during these critical opening days, and thereupon rely upon this alleged default to justify their subsequent inadequate performance and even for their refusals to meet royalty obligations. A franchisor should, of course, take most seriously his obligations to assist a franchisee at the time he enters into the world of franchising. At no other time will his new franchised offspring need more solicitous and sustaining support.

Operating Provisions

(13) *Assistance in purchasing:* Once the franchisor has assisted a franchisee to open for business, the former in most cases makes available to the latter a continuing purchasing service. This service may be limited to the mere listing of suppliers which can meet the franchise specifications or may also extend to the offer of goods and services for sale to the franchisee. The supply of this additional merchandising service is subject to the same principles as are applicable to the furnishing of land and facilities, namely that it may be provided so long as the franchisee is not coerced into using franchisor-designated sources when competitive merchandise of comparable form and quality is available.[18]

The franchisor, it follows, might state in his franchise contract the nature of the purchasing service which he will provide to his franchisee, *i. e.*, specifications, lists of qualified suppliers and/or qualified merchandise. He may further bind his franchisee to purchase from him such of the distinctive franchise goods as cannot be secured from others, and to refrain from obtaining any substitute commodities from others which do not meet his objective specification standards.[19] These specifications, of course, should seek only to ensure the uniform and distinctive nature of the franchised goods and services, and thus should not consist of numerous, irrelevant differences whose objective is solely to discourage the use of competing sources of supply. If the franchisor wishes to win friends in government and influence courts in litigation, he might also assure the franchisee that otherwise he is free to select his sources of supply. Once again, it would be helpful if both the franchisor's contract provisions and his competitive pricing could demonstrate that his franchisees are not captive markets foreclosed to competition.

(14) *Guidance in bookkeeping:* The franchisor will probably also desire to aid the franchisee to keep his operating costs down to a minimum. He may therefore make available to the franchisee certain business forms, systems of cost control, procedures of record keeping, and even computer services. In addition, he may specify how receipts and expenditures are to be recorded, when bank deposits are to be made, and to what extent monies may be drawn down by the franchisee.

Whatever service of this nature is to be given, however, might be so identified in the franchise contract that the franchisee will be sufficiently put on notice with respect to the benefits he is to receive and the controls he is to accept before he is bound by its contractual terms.

(15) *Management and promotions:* The franchisor may likewise wish to furnish to the franchisee merchandising support of the nature which a chain gives to its store managers. For this reason he might plan to provide field services, refresher courses, communications of marketing developments, disclosures of new advances, and periodic inspections. These subjects might therefore be covered in his franchise contract.

Whether or not the franchise contract promises to supply one or more of these forms of merchandising assistance, however, it might at least bind the franchisor to offer to the franchisee a coordinated program of local sales promotions, public relations projects and national advertising. Thus it might contain a covenant that the franchisor will devote for this purpose a specified percentage of the royalty payments which are received by him. Preferably, the agreement might provide that the franchisor will receive a sufficiently large royalty to be able to underwrite all of this advertising activity; because an arrangement that the franchisor is to supply promotions which are to be paid for by the franchisee could conceivably provoke a claim - however absurd - that the franchisor is using his grant of a franchise to tie up the purchase from him by his franchisee of an important competitive service.[20]

(16) Recommendations on sales: The franchisor, finally, will be most anxious to assist the franchisee in deciding what goods or services should be offered, in what markets, and at what prices. Accordingly, the franchisor might direct his franchisee to offer for sale only the unique products and services identified by the licensed trade name[21] provided, as previously stressed, that the latter may obtain reasonably equivalent supplies where available from any sources meeting the franchisor's specifications.[22] He might also bind the franchisee to engage in business at least in defined markets[23] - if the franchisee remains free to sell elsewhere without being penalized.[24] Finally, he might even suggest resale prices[25] so long as he does not require any observance by the franchisee of these suggested prices[26] (unless they are fair traded). A franchisor whose captive outlets compete with franchised outlets should take particular care not to check on whether these recommendations with respect to prices are being observed.[27]

The franchise contract, it follows, might provide that the franchisee is licensed to do business solely at the franchised premises and solely in the franchised goods and services. It might further provide that the franchisee undertakes to use his best efforts to promote the sale of these franchised goods and services "primarily" to designated customers and/or in defined markets. If it should add that advice on prices may be given to the franchisee, it might go on to state that such advice of course is entirely optional. Any compulsory regimentation of resale prices not only could result in an unenforceable contract and treble damage liability - but fines and jail for the franchisor. Such a price for the privilege of price-fixing would seem to be unduly high.

(17) *Performance by franchisee:* Thus far, the discussion has related principally to the obligations of the franchisor. It is now in order to turn to the duties of the franchisee. In return for his receipt of the franchise grant and these franchisor's services, the franchisee may be required to exploit effectively this grant and these services. Thus, while he must be free to purchase from qualified sources other than his franchisor, he can be obligated separately to identify products coming from his franchisor and aggressively to display and sell the latter.28 Again, as observed above, although he is free to advertise and sell anywhere, he can be required to devote his best sales efforts primarily in the markets for which he is responsible.29

The franchise contract might therefore make clear exactly what will be required from the franchisee in the way of merchandising efforts. Among such subjects, which might properly be covered, are the hours during which the franchised premises are to be open, the size of the sales force which is to be employed, the signs that are to be erected, and the displays of merchandise that are to be made. Supplemental provisions to ensure the protection of the "sales image" of the franchised name might include the unique features to be preserved, the quality controls to be maintained, the laws to be observed, the standards of cleanliness and service to be met and the good will of customers to be achieved. Some franchisors go further and impose sales quotas negotiated with and accepted as reasonable by the franchisee before the signing of the franchise agreement. The sum of these requirements, as well as their individual provisions, however, should not exceed what is reasonably ancillary to the success of the franchise relationship.

(18) *Reports and royalties:* As further consideration for the franchise grant and the franchisor's services, the franchisee may of course also be required to report and to pay royalties computed on the basis of his earnings. The franchise contract would be misleading, however, if it did not clearly identify both the rate of royalty to be paid and any other supplemental charges which are to be made. Criticism might be avoided, moreover, if it could be demonstrated that the continuing royalties which are charged bear a reasonable relationship to the value of the continuing benefits which are conferred.30

The franchise contract therefore might take pains to specify, in the manner discussed above, the various benefits for which the royalty is charged to the franchisee. The reasonableness of this royalty, when compared with the rights granted and the services provided, might be reviewed with and acknowledged in writing to be acceptable' by the franchisee. Thereupon appropriate recording, reporting and payment procedures might be established. Subsequently, the franchisor would be well advised so generously to provide his promised services to the franchisee that the latter will hesitate to jeopardize their receipt through any failure on the latter's part to make the royalty payments when they are due.

(19) *Insurance and taxes:* The franchisee should, of course, assume the responsibility for keeping in force general liability and product liability insurance of a defined coverage, for paying all taxes, and for keeping the franchised premises in good order, condition and repair.

Needless to say, these obligations also should clearly be spelled out in the franchise agreement and thereby be knowingly accepted by the franchisee when he signs.

(20) *Confidentiality of disclosures:* The franchisee should also agree to keep confidential all information, procedures, specifications, manuals and other communications in the nature of trade secrets which are received by him in writing from the franchisor. Writings containing mechanical details such as the hours of doing business had best be segregated, however, and not included in this category.

The franchise contract might therefore declare that any such information represents confidential disclosures which remain the property of the franchisor and, insofar as practical, shall be returned to the latter upon the termination of the agreement. In addition, the franchisee might covenant not to disclose such information to third parties - and to assume the burden of proving that he is not using it should he engage in a comparable form of business - during the period of the franchise agreement and for a reasonable time thereafter.

Termination Provisions

(21) *Renewal of terms:* There remains for consideration what might happen if the franchise relationship should come to an end. The provisions on this subject might distinguish between two types of franchisors. Thus, on the one hand, where a franchisor creates and continues to retain solely for himself a business of producing and selling a finished product, and merely authorizes distributors to resell this product in the form in which it is received, it seems reasonable for him to grant to these distributors for short periods of time franchises to resell his commodity, and to give no automatic right on the part of these franchisees to demand successive renewals of their franchise grants. This is because the law does not permit the franchisor to tie

up these franchisees[31] and it seems only equitable for him to be permitted to withhold any comparable right by the franchisee to tie up the franchisor. The most that such a franchisor might be required to do would be to promise that, in the event their franchises are not renewed, these franchisees will have an option to turn back to him their inventory of the franchised merchandise, at their cost including freight and taxes. If buildings and facilities were specially designed to handle the franchised product, the franchisor might also underwrite the cost of the franchisee in converting them to other uses.

But, on the other hand, a franchisor who licenses his trade name and know-how to a franchisee, in order to enable the latter not merely to add a new label to one of his lines of products but to create an entirely new local business, might be well advised to franchise such a new entrant for a substantial period of time. In addition - if the franchisor does not wish to be subject to charges of unjust enrichment - he might accord to any such franchisee, who is not in default of his franchise obligations, a right to receive successive renewals of his license. In the latter case the local franchised business may have been built up as much through the efforts of the local franchisee as due to the contributions of the franchisor, and each should be entitled to continue to benefit from the fruits of his work. Possibly, however, an undertaking to discuss changes in the relative rights and obligations of the parties at the time of renewal might also be included, provided that each party is free to agree or disagree to any such proposed change.

(22) *Transfer of rights:* Whether or not a franchise contract is renewed, the franchisor traditionally reserves the privilege to assign his rights and obligations thereunder to a third party of his choosing, but he does not always permit any such transfer by the franchisee. The latter restriction is currently under attack in some quarters on various grounds, such as that it lacks mutuality and possibly constitutes a restraint upon alienation.[32]

The franchise contract, accordingly, might provide that a franchisee may transfer his rights and duties to any individual (or a corporation controlled by an individual) who meets defined standards and will assume the transferor's obligations; but that some specified prior notice must be given by the franchisee to the franchisor of any such transfer, whether in whole or in part. Any such privilege of transfer might also apply in the event of death. In view of the fact that the performance of a franchisee is so dependent upon the personal ability and integrity of the individual involved, moreover, the franchisor might reserve the right either to veto the franchisee's transfer to anyone not meeting the agreed standards or to purchase back the franchise at the price being offered by the proposed transferee. The franchisor might further promise that his consent to any such transfer would not unreasonably be withheld.

(23) *Terminations for cause:* A franchise relationship may, of course, come to an end even if a renewal or a transfer of the franchise grant is permitted. Thus, a substantial breach by a party of his contractual obligations - not corrected after he is placed on notice of his default - will justify cancellation of the franchise agreement by the other party. Accordingly, what constitutes such a breach might be spelled out in the franchise contracts. For example, failure on the part of the franchisor to provide the promised services, and on the part of the franchisee to pay the agreed royalties, would be such a proper cause.

In view of the Washington spotlight upon alleged arbitrary terminations of franchise grants, a franchisor might prepare for his possible appearance on Capitol Hill by explaining what he means when he states that the lack of adequate promotion of the franchised business in his area of primary responsibility by the franchisee may constitute good cause for termination. If any such a provision should be incorporated, the draftsman might identify objective and unobjectionable yardsticks to be used in measuring the performance of the franchisee, e. g., a significant decline in his relative position in his market when his sales volume is compared with the sales volume of competitors and other franchisees over a period of years, failure to carry adequate inventories, financial instability, poor service, and bad relations with consumers. The franchisor may not, however, unreasonably reserve the right to claim that a franchisee's failure to measure up to the average sales volume of all franchisees constitutes good cause for cancellation, because in that event he will be claiming a right at any time arbitrarily to cancel out up to half of his franchisees whose individual sales volume also would be less than the average for all franchisees. Incidentally, even if the franchisor has good cause to cancel out a franchisee, he might lose his right to do so should he seek to exercise it pursuant to some unlawful plan, *e. g.*, to control resale prices.[33]

(24) *Terminations without cause:* Even without a substantial breach by a party of his obligations, it may be desirable to permit either party at any time to cancel the franchise agreement upon the payment of an appropriate price. Businessmen who are unhappy with each other had best not be forced to fight each other on the same franchise bed. The terms of any such divorce of the franchised parties, needless to say, including what would constitute a fair price, must depend upon the facts of the particular franchise relationship.

A possible provision on this subject in a franchise agreement might be that the franchisor may, by appropriate advance note, cancel the franchise rights of a franchisee, without cause, provided that he pays to the latter the cost of the franchisee's inventory including freight and taxes plus the fair value of the franchisee's business measured by the present worth of the probable future income of the latter. In his turn, the franchisee might be permitted to surrender his franchise prior to the expiration of his franchise agreement, but only in the event that he either obtains a substitute franchissee acceptable to the franchisor or goes out of business and covenants not to reenter a comparable business in the franchised area during a reasonable period of time.

(25) *Obligations on termination:* The preceding discussion has identified certain obligations which might be acceptable to the parties, upon the expiration of the franchise, with or without cause. Other duties might also be imposed in such an event.

For example, to the extent possible, each party might undertake to return to the other any property belonging to the latter which has not been purchased by the former as part of the termination settlement. In particular, confidential manuals, promotional material and signs using the franchised name should be turned back. Again, along the lines of a previous suggestion, the franchisee might either covenant not to enter into a competing business in the franchised area for a short period of time, or agree to assume the burden of demonstrating that he is not using any franchised knowhow should he engage in any such business during this period of time. Above all, the franchisee should discontinue his use of the franchised name.

(26) *Resolution of disputes:* In the event of any disputes arising between the parties, in connection with any of the above matters, each might undertake, upon the request of the other, to attempt to agree upon the appointment of a mutually acceptable mediator who could try to bring the parties together. In this role any such mediator might be empowered to make non-binding recommendations for resolving the controversy.

Any such disputes which are incapable of resolution by such mediation however might, at the option of either party, be submitted to binding arbitration. Thus it might be provided that any claim by either party should be settled solely and exclusively by arbitration in accordance with the then prevailing rules of the American Arbitration Association.

(27) *Relationship of parties:* The franchise contract should of course state that each party is an independent contractor and thus is neither an agent nor a legal representative of the other. No one should hold himself out to the public as being any such agent or representative.

Preferably - although this is not usually the custom   the franchisee might be required to feature his name in signs, readily seen by the public, which identify him as a franchisee licensed to use the franchisor's name. Such precautions - if supplemented by holding the contractual controls to a minimum - might help to defeat attempts by public or private persons to make the franchisor liable for any actionable shortcomings on the part of the franchisee.

(28) *Miscellaneous other provisions:* Other points which might be covered in the franchise contract are the places at which notices should be given, the law which should govern, the separability of the provisions and the right of the franchisor unilaterally to waive any of the restraints imposed by him upon the franchisee. There might also be a statement that all terms which are binding between the parties have been incorporated in writing in the franchise agreement.

CONCLUSION

One word of caution in closing. The franchise contract should, as stated at the outset, be frank, fair and enforceable. The draftsman of this document should not be so open-minded in protecting the franchisee, however, that his brains fall out in failing to safeguard the franchisor. Thus he should not fear to empower the franchisor to "coerce" and "dominate" the franchisee if any such restraint is reasonably necessary to prevent the latter from using the licensed name to destroy the franchisor or to defraud the public. But any excessive controls, which are not thus reasonably ancillary to the lawful main purpose of franchising, should be avoided. Our three guiding principles might be supplemented with a fourth: "Too much of anything is bad, except whiskey."

Authorities

1. J. G. Van Cise, "Franchising and the Supreme Court" in *Franchising Today, 1967-1968* (Vaughn & Slater eds., 1968), p. 133

2. *Albrecht v. Herald Co.*, 390 U. S. 145 (1968); *Perma Life Mufflers, Inc. v. International Parts Corp.*, 392 U. S. 134 (1968)

3. See, *e. g.*, Senate Bill S. 2321, 90th Cong., 1st Sess. (Aug. 21, 1967)

4. See, *e. g.*, "Report on Findings of the Special Committee on Unfair and Deceptive Practices in Franchising," to be published in May in *Franchising Today, 1968-1969* (Vaughn & Slater eds.) (hereinafter "Report of Special Committee")

5. *FTC v. Texaco, Inc.*, 393 U. S. 223 (1968)

6. *Perma Life Mufflers, Inc. v. International Parts Corp., supra,* note 2

7. *United States v. Colgate & Co.*, 250 U. S. 300 (1919)

8. *United States v. Addyston Pipe & Steel Co.*, 85 Fed. 271 (6th Cir. 1898), aff'd, 175 U. S. 211 (1899)

9. *U. S. v. Arnold, Schwinn & Co.*, CCH 1968 Trade Cases Para. 72, 480 (D. Ill. 1968)

10. *United States v. Arnold, Schwinn & Co.*, 388 U. S. 365 (1967); *United States v. Sealy, Inc.*, 388 U. S. 350 (1967)

11. Report of Special Committee, *supra,* note 4

12. Sec. 5 of the Federal Trade Commission Act, 15 U. S. C. 45

13. See, *e. g.*, 49 *Op. Att'y. Gen.* (Cal.) 124 (1967) (holding that two types of franchises are "securities" under California law and that a third type is not); see, also, M. Coleman, "A Franchise Agreement; Not a 'Security' Under The Securities Act of 1933," 22 ABA *Business Lawyer* 493 (Jan. 1967)

14. *Northern Pacific Ry Co. v. United States*, 356 U. S. 1 (1958)

15. *Atlantic Refining Co. v. FTC*, 381 U. S. 357 (1965)

16. *Arthur Murray, Inc. v. Horst*, 110 F. Supp. 678 (D. Mass. 1953)

17. *Dawn Donut Co. v. Hart's Food Stores, Inc.*, 267 F .2d 358 (2d Cir. 1959)

18. *FTC v. Brown Shoe Co.*, 384 U. S. 316 (1966); *Albrecht v. Herald Co., supra,* note 2; *FTC v. Texaco, Inc., supra,* note 5

19. *Susser v. Carvel Corp.*, 332 F 2d 505 (2d Cir. 1964), *cert. dismissed as improvidently granted*, 381 U. S. 125 (1965); *Carvel Corp.*, FTC Dkt 8574, CCH Trade Reg. Rep., 1965-1967 Transfer Binder 17,298 (1965)

20. *Cf. United States* v. *Loew's, Inc.,* 371 U. S. 38 (1962)

21. *Susser* v. *Carvel Corp.* and *Carvel Corp.*, both *supra*, note 19

22. *FTC* v. *Brown Shoe Co., supra,* note 18

23. *White Motor Co.* v. *United States,* 372 U. S. 253 (1963)

24. *United States* v. *Arnold, Schwinn & Co.* and
     United States v. *Sealy, Inc.*, both *supra*, note 10

25. *United States* v. *Colgate & Co., supra,* note 7

26. *United States* v. *General Motors Corp.,* 384 U. S. 127 (1966);
     Simpson v. *Union Oil Co.,* 377 U. S. 13 (1964)

27. *United States* v. *Container Corp. of America,* CCH 1969
     Trade Cases   72,675 (U. S. Sup. Ct., Jan. 14, 1969)

28. *FTC* v. *Sinclair,* 261 U. S. 463 (1923)

29. *White Motor Co.* v. *United States, supra,* note 23

30. *Cf. Brulotte* v. *Thys Co.,* 379 U. S. 29 (1964)

31. *FTC* v. *Brown Shoe Co., supra,* note 18

32. *United States* v. *Arnold, Schwinn & Co., supra,* note 10

33. *Albrecht* v. *Herald Co., supra,* note 2; *Simpson* v. *Union Oil Co.,*
     supra, note 26

Appendix B
The Franchise Agreement

"The Franchise Agreement" by Gerald G. Udell. Reprinted from *The Cornell Hotel and Restaurant Administration Quarterly* 13, no. 3 (August 1972), 13-21. Reproduced by permission of Author and Editor of *Quarterly*.

ANATOMY OF THE FRANCHISE AGREEMENT
172 Franchise Agreements Analyzed by 167 Contract Provisions

The anatomy of the franchise agreement has been developed through analyzing 172 different franchise agreements, of which 60% were fast food restaurants containing 95% of the provisions listed. These provisions are grouped according to similar elements and the frequency for each is given.

PAYMENTS TO THE FRANCHISOR

Franchise Fee — 78.8%
The franchise fee generally ranges from $500 to $25,000 and is in payment for the privilege of doing business under the franchisor's banner.

Non-refundable Fees — 36.0%
Often the franchise fee is fully earned and non-refundable once the franchise agreement has been signed.

Royalty — 76%
Generally based on a percentage (2–5%) of gross sales.

National Advertising — 40.7%
Franchisees are often required to contribute a percentage of gross sales for national advertising.

Local Advertising — 53.3%
Franchisee either agrees to spend a percentage of sales for local advertising or to pay the franchisor for doing so.

Security Deposits — 18.0%
Non-recurring payments such as grand opening or special promotions.

Special Payments — 26.1%
To insure faithful performance by franchisee. In case of violation, deposits are forfeited as liquidated damages.

Renewal Fee — 8.7%
Payment ($500–$1,000 +) to renew the franchise.

Service Fees — 12.4%
Payments to the franchisor for special services, such as accounting services. May be a fixed amount or percentage of gross sales.

Rental or Lease Payments — 26.1%
For equipment and property rental or lease.

Rent Adjustment — 2.3%
Allows franchisor to adjust rent or lease payments in the future.

Purchase — 78.6%
Payments for equipment purchased on installment plan.

Indirect Payments — 2.9%
Permits kickbacks and rebates to the franchisor from the franchisee's suppliers.

Penalties — 20%
Fines levied against franchisee for violations of contract or operating manual.

Termination Penalties — 8%
Penalties ($15,000 in one case) paid by franchisee in the event franchise agreement is terminated for any reason.

GENERAL CONTRACT PROVISIONS

Length of Contract Term — 78%
Term varies – usually between 10 and 20 years.

Option to Renew — 54.2%
Guarantees the franchisee's right to renew, usually for a specific period of time.

Exclusive Territory — 59.3%
Establishes a protected territory in which the franchisor may not authorize another franchise. A 1/2 mile radius is common.

Start-Up Date — 8.7%
Franchise must be in operation within a stated period of time or the agreement may be terminated by the franchisor.

Franchisor Confidential Disclosure — 51.8%
Prohibits the franchisor from disclosing information about the franchisee and his operation.

Hold Harmless — 57%
The franchisor is not responsible for the acts of the franchisee.

Act of God — 12.4%
Either one or both of the parties to the agreement shall not be held responsible for delays or failures caused by acts of God, riots, strikes.

No Waiver of Default — 61%
Failure to enforce a provision does not preclude the franchisor from taking action in the event of future violations.

Illegal Covenant — 56.4%
If a provision is declared illegal, the rest of the contract is not affected or tainted.

Legal Business — 11.2%
Requires the franchisee to engage in lawful business only.

Franchisee Confidential Disclosure — 1.2%
Prohibits the franchisee from disclosing information about the franchise operation.

Independent Contractor — 61.8%
States that the franchisee is not an agent or employee of the franchisor.

Operating Manual — 43.1%
Make the operating manual part of the franchise agreement.

Goodwill Payments — 5.8%
In the event that franchisor buys back the franchise there are no payments for goodwill.

Correction of Deficiency — 23.3%
Gives the franchisor the right to correct deficiencies and violations without franchisee's permission and to charge the cost to the franchisee.

Compliance with Local Laws — 53.6%
Requires franchisee to obey all local laws, regulations.

Franchisee Association Forbidden — 1.7%
Franchisee agrees not to join any association of franchisees.

Right to Future Revisions — 7.8%
Gives the franchisor the right to make changes in the operation in the future.

Franchisee Disability — 6.9%
If franchisee becomes sick or is unable to personally operate his business, the franchisor may, at his option and franchisee's expense, take over the operation until he is able to do so.

Arbitration — 23.3%
Disputes between the franchisee and the franchisor shall be settled by arbitration.

Site Selection — 7.8%
Provides that the site must have been approved before franchise agreement is effective.

MISCELLANEOUS CONTRACT PROVISIONS

Incorporation Permitted — 90%
Allows franchisee to incorporate his business.

Trademark Restrictions — 51.8%
Recognizes the franchisor's ownership and rights of trademarks, trade names and copyrights.

Distinctive Architecture — 20.9%
Recognizes building design and interior decor as unique and property of franchisor.

Good Ethics — 4.7%
Resures that franchisee uses good ethics in operating his franchise.

State of Interpretation — 12.2%
Specifies the state (and laws) in which the contract is interpreted.

Venue Clause — 7.0%
Specifies the state (and city) in which all legal matters will be heard and settled. Generally this is the home of franchisor.

Sub-Franchising — 6.4%
Permits franchisee to sub-franchise to others.

Civil Rights — 0.6%
Requires compliance with Civil Rights Act.

Full Time — 13.3%
Requires franchisee to devote full time and best efforts to the operation of his franchise.

Competitive Business — 27.5%
Prohibits franchisee from entering any competitive business during the time he is a franchisee.

Restrictions on Sale of Goods — 1.7%
Prevents franchisee from selling mixes, supplies and materials.

Product Service — 0.6%
Requires that the franchisee honor the guarantee given on work done by another franchisee.

Sales Quota — 0.6%
Establishes a sales quota for the franchisee.

Guaranteed Sales — 0.6%
Guarantees that sales will reach a stated level.

PROVISIONS OF UNIFORMITY

Physical Layout Approval — 27.1%
Franchisee must obtain franchisor's approval of the layout of his building and equipment.

Local Variations Permitted — 11.0%
Permits variations to conform to local law.

Days Open — 57.7%
Specifies the days the franchise must be open for business.

Hours Open — 57.0%

Specifies the hours during which the franchise must be open.

Product Line — 59.6%
Franchisor controls the products, services or menu offered by the franchisee.

Price Control — 28%
Franchisor controls the prices franchisee may charge.

Alteration Approval — 58.2%
No building or layout alterations without franchisor's approval.

PROVISIONS OF OCCUPANCY (PROPERTY)

Franchisee Owns — 26.7%
His own building.

Franchisor Owns — 32.0%
— and rents to the franchisee.

Franchisee Leases — 25%
— building directly from third party.

Franchisor Leases — 29.7%
— building and sub-leases to franchisee.

Lease Approval — 13.9%
Franchisor must approve franchisee's lease.

Notice of Non-Compliance — 2.3%
Leasor must notify franchisor of any violation of lease.

Lease-back — 2.9%
If franchisee owns his own building, he leases it to franchisor and subleases it back.

Lease Loss — 16.8%
If franchisee loses his lease, franchisor may terminate the franchise.

OBLIGATIONS OF THE FRANCHISOR

Analyze Reports — 26.4%
Franchisor agrees to analyze franchisee's reports and to advise him of any deviations from the norm.

Advertise — 27.7%
Franchisor agrees to advertise on the behalf of the franchisee.

Advise & Consult — 16.8%
Franchisor agrees to advise and consult with franchisee on a periodic basis.

Inspect — 12.8%
Franchisor agrees to inspect franchisee's operation on a periodic basis.

Advise of Changes — 32%
Franchisor agrees to advise franchisee of all changes and improvements.

Grand Opening — 24.4%
Franchisor agrees to provide grand opening assistance and training.

BOOKKEEPING

Bank Approval — 04.1%
Franchisee must obtain franchisor's approval of his bank.

Bookkeeping System Approval — 20.4%
Franchisor to approve franchisee's system.

System Required — 58.4%
Franchisee must use franchisor's system.

Annual Certified Audit — 26.7%
Franchisee must obtain an annual certified audit at his expense.

Margin of Error — 29.1%
If franchisee's books are in error by a fixed amount or a percentage during an inspection by franchisor, the franchisee must pay the cost of that audit.

Right to Audit Books — 43.7%
Franchisor may audit the franchisee's books.

Income Tax Copy — 15.7%
Franchisee must furnish franchisor with a copy of his tax return.

Periodic Reports — 75.8%
FrFanchisee must furnish franchisor with periodic reports (operating statements Profit & Loss).

Cash Withdrawal — 4.7%
Limits the amount of cash franchisee can take out of his business.

Profit Withdrawal — 11%
Limits the profits that can be taken out.

EMPLOYEE CONDUCT AND TRAINING

Uniforms — 37.9%
Employees must wear franchisor designed or approved uniforms.

Conduct — 32.6%
Franchisor sets standards for employees' conduct.

Number — 8.1%
Franchisor may determine the number of employees that must be on duty.

Right to Hire and Fire — 5.8%
Franchisor may hire and fire employees for the franchisee.

All Employee Training — 8.7%
All employees must complete franchisor training program.

Formal Training — 60.7%
Franchisee must complete franchisor's formal training course.

Subsequent Managers — 17.4%
All new managers must complete training.

Refresher Course — 11.6%
All franchisees must take periodic refresher courses.

Key Employees — 18%
Key employees must also take training.

OJT and Assistance — 18.6%
Franchisee and his employees will be given on-the-job training and grand opening assistance.

OPERATION

Right to Inspect — 71.4%
Franchisor has the right to inspect franchisee's property and operation.

Maintenance Required — 66.3%
Requires franchisee to keep the premises repaired and maintained.

Standard of Cleanliness — 72%
Requires franchisee to keep premises clean and up to franchisor's standards.

Standards of Product or Service Quality — 65.1%
Franchisee must meet franchisor standards.

Standards of Operation — 63.5%

Franchisee must operate his franchise at a level (standard) acceptable to the franchisor.

Inventory Control — 34.5%
Franchisee must maintain inventory levels set by franchisor.

Evaluation — 1.2%
Agreement specifies the system of evaluation to be used.

Parking Lot — 9.3%
Requires franchisee to maintain and clean his parking lot.

Slow Items — 1.7%
Specifies procedure for removal of slow items.

INSURANCE PROVISIONS

Franchisor Administration — 19.8%
Franchisor administers franchisee's insurance program.

Franchisor-Additional Co-Insured — 51.1%
Franchisee must co-insure the franchisor.

Cancellation Notice — 16.8%
Requires franchisee's insurance company to inform franchisor of any cancellations.

Approval of Company — 20.3%
Requires franchisee to obtain franchisor's approval of all insurance companies.

Proof of Insurance — 36.6%
Requires franchisee to provide franchisor with proof of his insurance.

Types of Insurance Required of Franchise:
Business Interruption Insurance 3.5%
Workmans Compensation 27.1%
Personal Liability 11.4%
Employer Liability 17.4%
Property Liability 66.8%
Product Liability 67.4%

PURCHASING

Paper Goods — May Buy — 37.8%
Franchisee *may* buy from franchisor.

Paper Goods — Must Buy (% included above)
Franchisee *must* buy from franchisor.

Operating Supplies — May Buy — 51.8%
Franchisee *may* buy from franchisor.

Operating Supplies—Must Buy (% included above)
Franchisee *must* buy from franchisor.

Equipment — May Buy — 66.3%
Franchisee *may* buy from franchisor.

Equipment — Must Buy (% included above)
Franchisee *must* buy from franchisor.

Signs — 54.2%
Franchisee may/must buy or lease signs from franchisor.

Vendor Approval — Paper — 42.3%
Franchisee must obtain franchisor's approval of paper good vendors.

Most franchisee headaches relate to operations and contract termination.

Vendor Approval — Operating Supplies — 50%
Franchisee must obtain franchisor's approval of suppliers (vendors) of operating supplies.

Vendor Approval — Signs — 19.8%
Franchisee must obtain franchisor's approval of sign vendors.

Standards — Paper Goods — 32%
Purchased paper goods must meet franchisor's standards.

Standards — Operating Supplies — 46.5%
Purchased operating supplies must meet franchisor's standards.

Standards — Equipment — 39.6%
Equipment must meet franchisor's standards.

Standards — Signs — 26.8%
Signs must meet franchsor's standards.

Price Restrictions — 4.6%
Prices charged franchisee by franchisor must be competitive.

Franchisor-Vendor Rebate — 1.9%
Rebates and kickbacks from franchisee's suppliers to franchisor are prohibited.

Vending Approval — 12.2%
Franchisee must obtain franchisor's approval of vending machines.

ADVERTISING

Franchisor Does Advertising — 25%
Franchisor does all advertising, both local and national.

Franchisor Fund Accounting — 6.9%
Franchisor must inform franchisee how all funds were spent.

Right to Enter and Destroy — 11%
Franchisor has the right to enter franchisee's place of business and destroy unauthorized advertising without franchisee's permission.

Signs Required — 50%
Franchisee is required to install and maintain signs.

Franchisor Approval — 66.2%
Franchisee must obtain franchisor's approval of advertising.

Advertising Committee — 5.6%
Franchisee must join a (regional) committee or association of franchisees. All advertising is either done by or approved by the committee.

PROVISIONS OF SALE OR TRANSFER

Franchisor Right of First Refusal — 32.4%
If franchisee wishes to sell, he must first offer to sell to franchisor.

Franchisee Right of First Refusal — 5.6%
If franchisor wishes to establish another franchise within a predetermined territory, he must first offer that franchise to the franchisee located within the territory.

Right of Inheritance — 33.1%
Heirs of franchisee have unqualified rights to the franchise after death of franchisee.

Limited Right of Inheritance (% included above)
Franchisee may not advertise that his franchise is for before taking over franchise.

No Right of Inheritance (% not available)
Heirs of franchisee may not inherit the franchise operations.

Franchisor Approval of Sale — 74.1%
Franchisee may not sell his franchise without franchisor's approval.

No For-Sale Advertising (% not available)
Franchisee may not advertise that his franchise is for sale.

Binding Upon Successors — 7%
The franchise agreement is binding upon the successors of the franchisee.

Stock Transfer Approval — 10.4%
If the franchise is incorporated, the franchisee must obtain franchisor approval to sell or otherwise transfer stock.

No Goodwill Payments — 26.2%
In case of sale (to franchisor) agrees that there will be no compensation for goodwill built up by the franchisee.

CONDITIONS OF TERMINATION

Failure to Pay — 19.8%
Franchisee failure to pay any bill or invoice promptly is a violation of agreement and basis for termination.

Franchisee Termination — 22.1%
States the conditions and terms under which franchisee may terminate the agreement.

Franchisor Termination — 98.4%
States the conditions and terms under which franchisor may terminate the agreement.

Immediate Cancellation — 42.3%
States conditions and terms under which franchisor may terminate the franchise agreement without advance notice or a "grace period."

Bankruptcy — 34.9%
Franchisor may terminate immediately if franchisee declares bankruptcy or goes into receivership.

Any Violation — 12.0% (estimated)
Any violation of the franchise agreement (and in some cases the operating manual) is grounds for termination of the franchise agreement.

Grace Period — 69.3%
Provides a grace period during which franchisee may correct deficiencies or violations before franchisor may terminate.

10-Day Grace — (% included above)
Grace period is ten days.

30-Day Grace — (% included above)
Grace period is thirty days.

Quality Standards — 6.4%
Franchise agreement may be terminated if franchisee does not meet quality standards.

Training Failure — 2.9%
Agreement may be terminated by franchisor if franchisee fails to complete required training.

PROVISIONS — AFTER TERMINATION

Covenant Not to Compete — Years — 56.4%
Franchisee agrees not to engage in a similar business for a stated period of time.

Covenant Not to Compete — Miles — 48.8%
Franchisee agrees not to engage in a similar business within a stated distance of (his former franchise or any franchise).

Covenant Not to Hire — 23.8%
Franchisee agrees not to hire employees of franchisor or other franchisee for a stated period of time after termination.

Covenant Not to Use System — 47.1%
Franchisee agrees not to use franchisor's system of operation for a stated period after termination.

Cease Operations — 48.8%
Franchisee agrees to immediately cease operations in the event of termination.

Change Building — 16.8%
Franchisee agrees to paint or otherwise alter building upon termination.

Remove Sign — 25.6%
Franchisee agrees to immediately remove signs upon termination.

Cost of Enforcement — 19.7%
Franchisee agrees to pay the cost of enforcing the above provisions.

PROVISIONS OF SALE AFTER TERMINATION

Equipment — 32.6%
Franchisee agrees to sell equipment back to franchisor at an agreed upon price.

Signs — 29.1%
Franchisee agrees to sell signs to franchisor at an agreed upon price.

Trademarked Supplies — 26.7%
Franchisee agrees to sell equipment to franchisor at an agreed upon price.

Regular Supplies — 18.1%
Franchisee agrees to sell all regular supplies to franchisor at an agreed upon price.

Appendix C
Sample Franchise Contract: Revised Chicken Delight Agreement

This agreement was a matter of public record in the San Francisco litigation involving Chicken Delight and its franchisees.

FRANCHISE AGREEMENT

This is a FRANCHISE AGREEMENT dated the . . . . day of . . . .
between CHICKEN DELIGHT, INC., an Illinois corporation, (hereinafter called
Chicken Delight) and . . . . of the
City of . . . . , State of . . . . , (hereinafter called Franchisee).

RECITALS

A. Chicken Delight, through expenditure of considerable money, time and
effort, has created and developed a successful, efficient and unique system of
preparing, packaging, merchandising and selling a limited menu of hot and cold
freshly prepared foods, particularly chicken, which are of a distinctive, uniform
and high quality, are prepared in accordance with Chicken Delight's specifications and methods, are packaged in distinctive packaging bearing Chicken
Delight's trademarks, are sold at and from specially and distinctively designed,
decorated and equipped stores operating under and prominently displaying the
Chicken Delight name, and are sold to customers in freshly prepared condition
for immediate consumption.

B. Chicken Delight is the exclusive owner of the trade name "Chicken
Delight," the trademarks "Chicken Delight," "Shrimp Delight," "Rib Delight,"
and "Pizza Delight" and other associated marks, designs and symbols, hereinafter collectively sometimes called the Chicken Delight name and marks, which
distinctively identify to the public the Chicken Delight stores, foods, system and
methods described above and which have therefore acquired great value,
goodwilln and public acceptance.

C. Franchisee desires a license to use the Chicken Delight name and marks
and Chicken Delight's system and methods of food preparation, operation and
merchandising, as described above, in the operation of a Chicken Delight store at
the location described below.

AGREEMENTS

In consideration of the above premises and of the mutual terms, promises and
conditions hereinafter set forth, the parties agree as follows:

1. Grant of Franchise

(a) Subject to all of the terms and conditions of this agreement, Chicken
Delight grants to Franchisee, and Franchisee accepts, a continuing non-exclusive
license and right to use (i) the "Chicken Delight" name and marks, and the
associated marks, symbols and designs owned by Chicken Delight, and (ii) Chick-
en Delight's distinctive system and methods of food preparation, operation and

merchandising, in the operation by Franchisee of a "Chicken Delight" store located at . . . . in the City of . . . . , State of . . . . , (hereinafter sometimes called "the franchised store") and in the preparation, sale and delivery of food products in connection with said Chicken Delight store. (b) Franchisee acknowledges and agrees that Chicken Delight is the exclusive owner of the words "Chicken Delight," the Chicken Delight name and marks, and all marks and names which are compounds or variations thereof, and that Franchisee's use of said marks and names shall be by virtue of and subject to the terms and conditions of this agreement only, and Franchisee shall acquire no proprietary interest in said marks and names. (c) Franchisee also acknowledges that Chicken Delight owns the goodwill symbolized by the Chicken Delight name and marks and agrees that same are to be used by Franchisee for the benefit of Chicken Delight and that Franchisee will expend his best efforts to upgrade same, and that Franchisee shall not use the words "Chicken Delight" or any variations thereof in Franchisee's corporate name.

2. Territory

"Franchisee's territory" will be the area described as follows: . . . .
. . . .
. . . .
. . . .
Franchisee will be primarily responsible for selling and promoting Chicken Delight food products throughout said territory and (if Franchisee offers delivery service) for making prompt and timely deliveries of hot fresh food and other authorized products to all Chicken Delight customers in said territory. Chicken Delight agrees that so long as this franchise agreement is in effect, it will not operate, and will not grant nay other license or franchise to operate, a "Chicken Delight" store within Franchisee's territory.

3. Services by Chicken Delight

In addition to the license to Franchisee of the Chicken Delight name and marks and the system and methods of Chicken Delight, Chicken Delight, to the extent practicable, will use its best efforts to provide Franchisee with the following services:

(a) Assistance in selection of a suitable location; furnishing of standard building plans and specifications; and assisting Franchisee in store installation.

(b) Developing and making available for purchase and use by Franchisee equipment, packaging, Chicken Delight batter preparation and barbeque rib seasoning, and certain other supplies and food items.

(c) Assistance in arranging for or informing Franchisee of other sources of supply for certain food items, packaging and signs which meet Chicken Delight's standards and specifications. Chicken Delight agrees that it will not receive any remuneration from any supplier of any such items for or on account of such supplier's sales or prospective sales to Franchisees or their utilization of the Chicken Delight trademarks.

(d) Providing confidential information, manuals, assistance, recommendations and training to Franchisee and/or his designated representative or employee(s) regarding Chicken Delight's food preparation methods, packaging, and merchandising, promotional, and operating techniques and methods.

(e) Providing Chicken Delight advisory personnel in connection with Franchisee's opening and, at the discretion of Chicken Delight, from time to time thereafter.

(f) National advertising of the Chicken Delight name and products.

4. Products and Services to be offered by Franchisee

The parties desire that the Chicken Delight name and marks continue to be publicly identified and associated with Chicken Delight stores which offer a limited menu of hot and cold freshly prepared foods and drinks, particularly chicken, which are of a distinctive, uniform and high quality in distinctive packaging bearing Chicken Delight's trademarks. To that end the parties agree as follows:

(a) *Use of Chicken Delight Name.* Franchisee will operate the franchised store only under the name "Chicken Delight," which name will be prominently displayed on and in the store.

(b) *Limitation on Food Products.* In operating the franchised store Franchisee will sell and promote the sale of only those food products and combinations thereof which are specified in the Chicken Delight "Operations Manual" and are prepared in accordance with the specifications and methods set forth in the Operations Manual. To the extent specified in the Operations Manual, and as described therein, Franchisee will be required to offer for sale chicken products, but the sale of other products specified in the operations manual will be optional with Franchisee. Chicken Delight may from time to time change or add to the operations manual whenever it deems such changes or additions reasonably necessary to protect the Chicken Delight name or marks or improve quality or service standards at Chicken Delight stores. Franchisee acknowledges receiving a copy of the Operations Manual, and the Operations Manual is hereby incorporated in and made a part of this agreement.

(c) *Packaging.* Franchisee will use his best efforts to assure that all food products sold at or from the franchised store will be sold only in the distinctive Chicken Delight packaging specified in the operations manual, which packaging will bear Chicken Delight's trademarks and meet Chicken Delight's quality and design specifications. However, Franchisee need not use such packaging where prevented from doing so by unavailability of packaging supplies.

(d) *Authorization of other products and packaging.* Chicken Delight may from time to time authorize the sale of products other than those specified in the operations manual and/or in packaging not bearing a Chicken Delight trademark, at Franchisee's and other Chicken Delight stores in Franchisee's local marketing area, but such authorization will be given and continued only if sale of such other products is compatible with the image and significance of the Chicken Delight name and marks as described above.

(e) *Deliveries, etc.* All foods cooked in the franchised store will be sold to customers hot and freshly prepared. Franchisee will allow customers to pick up purchased food products at the franchised store, and may allow products to be consumed on the premises if suitable seating arrangements are provided. Franchisee may offer delivery service, and, if so, will make prompt and timely deliveries of food products (in hot and freshly prepared condition if cooked in the franchised store) to all customers within Franchisee's territory who request such delivery, using delivery vehicles equipped with heat preservation ovens.

5. Purchases of Food and Supplies[a]

(a) *Batter preparation and Rib seasoning.* The parties recognize that the special Chicken Delight batter preparation and barbeque rib seasoning sold by Chicken Delight are processed and produced in accordance with specialized and secret formulae, ingredients and methods, and are essential to the distinctive and uniform taste and quality of certain of the food products sold at Chicken Delight stores. Therefore, Franchisee agrees to purchase from Chicken Delight the special Chicken Delight batter preparation and the special Chicken Delight barbeque rib seasoning, to be sold by Chicken Delight at its cost plus a sum not to exceed 20% thereof to cover the costs of handling, and Franchisee will not use any other batter preparations or rib seasonings in his Chicken Delight business.

(b) *Other food products.* Franchisee may purchase any and all other authorized food products from suppliers of his choice, provided that such foods are uniform and high quality and comply with the standards and specifications set forth in the operations manual.

(c) *Packaging.* Chicken Delight will make available for purchase by Franchisee, at Chicken Delight's cost plus reasonable handling charges, any or all of the Chicken Delight packaging to be used by Franchisee in the sale of food products. However, Franchisee may also purchase any or all of such specified packaging from any other supplier.

(d) *Availability from Chicken Delight.* To the extent practicable Chicken Delight will make available for optional purchase by Franchisee other supplies and some food products which Franchisee may wish to use in operating the franchised store, including various products bearing Chicken Delight's trademarks.

---

[a]Paragraph 5(a) retains a former Chicken Delight practice which probably constitutes a "tie-in." The cost control therein, however, was thought to render it safe, although the conservative attorney may wish to modify it to remove any questions.

6. Construction, Signs, etc.

The construction, appearance, design, fixtures and furnishings of the franchised store, both outside and inside, and any material alterations thereof, and the content, layout and design of all signs, placards, advertising and promotional materials and other written materials which Franchisee proposes to use on, in or in connection with the franchised store shall be as specified by Chicken Delight. Chicken Delight will make available for purchase by Franchisee, the signs to be utilized by Franchisee, but Franchisee may purchase such signs from other suppliers.

7. Franchisee's Operations

Franchisee agrees that the franchised store and all portions thereof, and all equipment, vehicles, supplies, food and other items used in Franchisee's Chicken Delight business will at all times be maintained in good repair and at a high degree of cleanliness and sanitation, and that Franchisee will at all times comply with the food preparation methods prescribed in the operations manual. Franchisee further agrees that the franchised store will at all times be well staffed with personnel who observe the highest standards of cleanliness, service and courtesy to customers, and will be open at all reasonable business hours including hours generally followed by competitive stores in Franchisee's market area. Franchisee agrees to comply with all applicable governmental food and sanitary laws and regulations and all other applicable laws and regulations.

8. Taxes and Indemnity

Franchisee agrees to pay any and all taxes, including but not limited to property, sales and income taxes, assessed or levied upon any real or personal property at the franchised store or arising from operation of said store, and will hold Chicken Delight harmless from any liability for such taxes. Franchisee further agrees to indemnify and defend Chicken Delight against and hold it harmless from any and all fines, suits, claims, demands, actions or liabilities of any kind arising from or connected with the use, condition or operation of the franchised store or the sale, use, consumption or condition of any products sold at or from said store.

9. Retail Sales Prices

Although Chicken Delight may from time to time recommend suggested retail prices to be utilized by Franchisee to maximize his sales and profits, and although Chicken Delight advertising may from time to time mention suggested retail prices, it is understood and agreed that all prices to be charged by Franchisee for all products sold by Franchisee will be determined in Franchisee's sole discretion.

10. Franchise Fees

(a) *Continuing License Fee.* In consideration for and as an essential condition of Chicken Delight's continuing licensing to Franchisee of the Chicken Delight name and marks and Chicken Delight's systems and methods of food preparation, operation and merchandising (and not as consideration for any of the services described in paragraph 3 above or any other services), Franchisee agrees that during the entire term of this agreement Franchisee will pay to Chicken Delight a continuing license fee equal to five percent (5%) of Franchisee's total gross receipts from sales at or from the franchised store, excluding sales tax (or other tax in the nature thereof), payable weekly and in the manner specified in paragraph 12 below.

(b) *Minimum Annual Fee.* If in any "franchise year" the total continuing license fees paid to Chicken Delight under paragraph (b) of this paragraph are less than $3,000.00, Franchisee agrees that within 45 days after the close of each such franchise year Franchisee will pay to Chicken Delight the difference between said sum of $3,000.00 and the continuing license fees actually paid in said franchise year. For purpose of this paragraph the "franchise year" shall be the 12-month period commencing on the date operation of the franchised store begins or on the date of this agreement, whichever occurs later, and upon each anniversary of said date.

11. Advertising

In view of the importance of publicizing the Chicken Delight name and marks by all reasonable means, Franchisee agrees to pay to Chicken Delight a local advertising contribution equal to four percent (4%) of the total gross receipts by Franchisee from sales at or from the franchised store, excluding sales tax (or other tax in the nature thereof), payable weekly in the manner specified in paragraph 12 below. Chicken Delight agrees that the amount of all such contributions by Franchisee and of similar contributions by other franchisees in Franchisee's local marketing area will be spent in the advertising and promotion of Chicken Delight's name and marks, Chicken Delight stores and Chicken Delight products in said local marketing area through various media which may include but are not limited to television, radio, newspapers, magazines, mailers and other promotional material. Notwithstanding the foregoing, Chicken Delight may, at any time, and on such reasonable conditions as it may prescribe, relinquish to a committee or other group chosen by a majority of franchisees in said marketing area, or to the individual Franchisee in the case of an isolated store, any or all of the responsibilities of collecting such contributions, deciding on the types, forms and contents of advertising and promotions for which such contributions will be used, making the arrangements for such advertising and promotions, and otherwise administering such contributions and the local advertising program.

12. Method of Payment—Reports

(a) *Weekly Report and Payment.* Franchisee agrees to mail or deliver to Chicken Delight, at the address stated in paragraph 22 (c) below, so as to be received by Thursday of each and every calendar week,

(i) An accurate report, in such form as Chicken Delight may prescribe, showing the dollar amount of all gross receipts received by Franchisee during the immediately preceding calendar week, (i.e., Monday through Sunday) reasonably itemized by product categories; and

(ii) Franchisee's check, money order or other form of payment in an amount equal to 9% of the total gross receipts received by Franchisee during the immediately preceding calendar week from all sales at or from the franchised store. This payment shall constitute Franchisee's continuing license fee and local advertising contribution based on said gross receipts of the immediately preceding week.

(b) *Other Reports*. To provide additional verification of Franchisee's gross receipts,

(i) Franchisee agrees to deliver to Chicken Delight, as soon as prepared, a copy of every sales tax report submitted by Franchisee to any state or other local governmental body and copies of all portions of Franchisee's annual federal and state income tax returns which pertain to Franchisee's "Chicken Delight" business; and (ii) upon reasonable advance notice Chicken Delight may examine all books and records of Franchisee pertaining to operation of the franchised store, the cost of any such examination to be at the expense of Franchisee in the event that a discrepancy of five percent (5%) or more is found to exist between actual and reported gross receipts.

13. Other Inspection

For the purpose of maintaining high standards of quality, cleanliness and service and insuring compliance with this agreement, Chicken Delight shall have the right to examine, at any time during business hours and without notice, the foods prepared and sold, the facilities maintained, the methods of operation employed, and the personnel employed by Franchisee in the operation of the franchised store.

14. Protection of Confidential Information

Franchisee agrees that during the term of this agreement and at all times thereafter neither Franchisee nor any of his agents, employees or representatives shall at any time disclose to any other person, or use for any purpose other than operation of the franchised store, any confidential information received from Chicken Delight as to Chicken Delight's methods and techniques of food preparation, operation and merchandising, recipes, specifications, or other kinds of confidential information, nor any of the contents of the operations manual or confidential written materials received by Franchisee from Chicken Delight, and that all such confidential information, manuals and written materials shall at all times remain the sole property of Chicken Delight.

15. Term

(a) *Commencement*. The term of this agreement shall commence on the first day of September, 1969. Franchisee agrees to deliver to Chicken Delight as soon as possible after execution, copies of any and all leases of the real property on which the franchised store is located, and of all renewals, extensions, modifications or additions to or of any such lease.

(b) *Duration*. Unless sooner terminated as authorized in this agreement, the term of this agreement and of all licenses and rights granted herein shall continue for a period of 10 years from the date of this agreement and shall be automatically renewed for two successive five year terms unless, at least 6 months before the beginning of any such 5 year term Franchisee gives to Chicken Delight written notice of non-renewal. Following the conclusion of the last such 5 year term this agreement and all rights and licenses granted herein shall continue from year to year unless terminated by either party by giving 60 days written notice to the other. *Provided*, however, that Chicken Delight agrees that upon any notice of termination given by Chicken Delight pursuant to this paragraph, and on the condition that Franchisee is not then in default under this agreement, Chicken Delight will negotiate with Franchisee in good faith for a new franchise agreement satisfactory to both parties.

16. Assignment of Franchise

The licenses and rights granted herein are non-transferable, and Franchisee may not assign, sell, transfer or sublet this franchise or any of Franchisee's rights or licenses under this agreement without Chicken Delight's prior written consent. Such consent will not be unreasonably withheld if the proposed transferee meets the requirements then in effect by Chicken Delight for a new franchisee, executes a new Chicken Delight franchise agreement under the standard terms than in effect, pays to Chicken Delight a $1,000 transfer fee as consideration for Chicken Delight's qualifying the transferee, preparing papers for the new franchise, and providing training and/or initial assistance to the new transferee and/or his designated representative(s) or employee(s), and Franchisee executes a one year non-competition agreement in favor of the transferee in form and content reasonably satisfactory to Chicken Delight and the transferee. In any event, Chicken Delight shall have the first right and option to purchase all assets of Franchisee's Chicken Delight store (including leasehold interests if any) and all licenses and rights of Franchisee hereunder, at any time that Franchisee receives and proposes to accept a firm bona fide offer to purchase the same, upon the same terms as such firm offer. Said option must be exercised by written notice given to Franchisee within 30 days after Franchisee notifies Chicken Delight in writing that Franchisee has received such a firm offer and proposes to accept it.

17. Termination by Chicken Delight for Breach

In addition to any rights and remedies provided by law, Chicken Delight may terminate this agreement and all rights and licenses granted herein, by 10 days written notice to Franchisee, if any of the following occur:

(a) Any default by Franchisee in the payment when due of any amount owing by Franchisee to Chicken Delight, or in the delivery to Chicken Delight when due of any report or statement required under paragraph 13 (a) of this agreement, if (i) such payment is not made or such report not delivered within 15 days after Chicken Delight gives Franchisee written notice of nonreceipt of and demand for such payment or report, or (ii) a failure by Franchisee to make such a payment or deliver such a report strictly within the time required by paragraph 13 (a) occurs in two consecutive weekly periods, or in three out of five consecutive weekly periods, or in five out of thirteen consecutive weekly periods.

(b) Any other breach of or default under any term of provision of this agreement by Franchisee if (i) Franchisee without legal excuse fails to cure such breach or default within 15 days after Chicken Delight gives Franchisee written notice thereof and a request to cure the same; or (ii) Franchisee intentionally repeats the same or a similar breach or default after Chicken Delight gives to Franchisee written notice of the prior breach or default and a request that it not be repeated.

(c) Any closure of the franchised store without good cause for more than 7 consecutive days at any time.

18. Termination by Franchisee for Breach

In addition to any other rights and remedies provided by law, Franchisee may terminate this agreement and all rights and licenses granted herein, by 10 days written notice to Chicken Delight, upon any breach of or default under this agreement by Chicken Delight which is not corrected within 15 days after Franchisee gives Chicken Delight written notice of said breach or default and a request to cure the same, or which is intentionally repeated by Chicken Delight after Franchisee gives Chicken Delight written notice of the prior breach or default and a request that it not be repeated.

19. Termination upon Bankruptcy, etc.

In addition to any rights or remedies provided by law this agreement and all rights and licenses granted to Franchisee herein, shall automatically and immediately terminate in the event of the commencement of any proceedings or taking of any action by or against Franchisee or any individual signing or guaranteeing this agreement, under any statute relating to insolvency, bankruptcy or the relief of debtors, or the appointment of a receiver to take possession of any of the property of, or an assignment for the benefit of creditors by, Franchisee or any individual signing or guaranteeing this agreement, or upon Franchisee's death, (if an individual) or dissolution or cessation of existence (if a corporation or partnership).

20. Options to Purchase on Termination

Upon any termination of this agreement for any reason whatever, whether by Chicken Delight, by Franchisee, by mutual consent or under paragraph 19, Chicken Delight shall have and may exercise either of the following options:

(a) An option to purchase from Franchisee all assets (including leasehold interest if any) of Franchisee's Chicken Delight store at a price equal to (i) Franchisee's actual cost thereof less depreciation taken by Franchisee for federal income tax purposes, if the termination is by Chicken Delight for breach or default under paragraph 18 hereof, or (ii) at a price equal to the fair market value of said assets upon any other kind of termination, (which value shall be determined by arbitration under the rules of the American Arbitration Association if the parties cannot agree on the same) or

(b) An option to purchase from Franchisee all cookers and fryers which Franchisee has at any time purchased from Chicken Delight, at a price equal to Franchisee's cost less the depreciation taken by Franchisee for federal income tax purposes.

Either of said options may be exercised by written notice given to Franchisee (i) at any time within 30 days after the giving of any notice of termination pursuant to paragraph 17 or 18, or (ii) at any time within 60 days after any automatic termination under paragraph 19 or the giving of any notice of termination or non-renewal pursuant to paragraph 17.

21. Obligations on Termination of this Agreement

Upon any termination of this agreement for any reason whatever, whether by Chicken Delight, by Franchisee, by mutual consent or under paragraph 19, immediately upon the effective date of such termination Franchisee shall:

(a) Remove from the franchised store and discontinue using for any purpose or in any way whatsoever, any and all signs, placards, packaging, advertising and promotional materials bearing any "Chicken Delight" name or mark or any other marks, symbols or designs owned by Chicken Delight, or any compound or variation thereof or any name or design substantially similar thereto; and

(b) Relinquish to Chicken Delight any telephone numbers then assigned to Franchisee's Chicken Delight store; and

(c) Return to Chicken Delight any and all manuals and other written materials of any kind or character received at any time from Chicken Delight; and

(d) Discontinue and forever refrain from any other use of any of the trade names, marks, systems and methods of Chicken Delight; and

(e) Pay to Chicken Delight all continuing license fees and advertising contributions owing or which become owing to Chicken Delight pursuant to paragraphs 10, 11, and 12 (a) of this agreement, and all other amounts owing or which become owing by Franchisee to Chicken Delight.

22. Miscellaneous

(a) *Injunction*. In the event of any breach or threatened breach of any term of this agreement by either party, the other party shall immediately be entitled to an injunction (including temporary restraining order and preliminary injunction) restraining the other party from such breach without showing or proving any actual damage sustained.

(b) *Nonwaiver*. No delay, omission or forbearance by Chicken Delight in the exercise of any right, power or remedy, nor any continuance by Chicken Delight to perform or accept performance after an event giving rise to such right, power or remedy, shall be a waiver of that or any other right, power or remedy; and the single or partial exercise of a right, power or remedy shall not prelude its further exercise. No waiver by Chicken Delight of any default or of any right, power or remedy hereunder shall operate as a waiver of any default, right, power or remedy on a future occasion.

(c) *Notices*. Any notice or demand which may or must be given under this agreement shall be deemed given when deposited in the United States mails, registered or certified, postage prepaid, and addressed to Chicken Delight at 1515 S. Mt. Prospect Road, Des Plaines, Illinois 60018 and to Franchisee at franchised store address.

(d) *No Agency, etc*. It is understood and agreed that no agency, employment or partnership is created between the parties, and the business to be operated by Franchisee is separate and apart from the business of Chicken Delight. In furtherance hereof, Franchisee shall clearly indicate in all letterheads, signs, etc. that it is a licensee of Chicken Delight.

(e) *Successors and Assigns*. Subject to the limitations upon assignment and transfer set forth in paragraph 16 hereinabove, all of the covenants, conditions and agreements herein contained shall be binding upon and inure to the benefit of the successors and assigns of the parties; and it is agreed that the rights of Chicken Delight hereunder may be assigned by Chicken Delight to any successor in interest of Chicken Delight.

(f) *Entire Agreement*. This agreement contains the entire agreement between the parties and supersedes and annuls all other agreements, contracts or arrangements whether written or oral, on the subject matter, and in entering into this agreement neither party has relied on any representation or agreements which are not contained herein.

In witness whereof the parties hereto affix their signatures.

                                        CHICKEN DELIGHT INC.
                                        an Illinois corporation

. . . . By . . . .
                Secretary   Vice President

. . . .
                Franchisee   Franchisee

The undersigned acknowledges that he has had in his possession a copy of this agreement for a period of no less than . . . . days; that he has read and fully understands all of the provisions of this agreement and has adequately reviewed all aspects of it; and that he has had full opportunity to review the same with counsel of his choice.

. . . .

         Franchisee   Franchisee

**Appendix D
Franchise Rule
Summary. Federal
Trade Commission
The Franchise Rule:
Questions and
Answers**

This is the Franchise Rule Summary as released by the Federal Trade Commission, December 21, 1978. Also included in Appendix D are eleven questions and answers about the Franchise Rule, released with the Summary by the FTC.

Franchise Rule Summary

The Franchise Rule, which is formally titled "Disclosure Requirements and Prohibitions Concerning Franchising and Business Opportunity Ventures," [16 Code of Federal Regulations § 436.] has been promulgated in response to widespread evidence of deceptive and unfair practices in connection with the sale of the types of businesses covered by the Rule. These practices often are able to exist because prospective franchisees lack a ready means of obtaining essential and reliable information about the business in which they are asked to invest their money and, frequently, their labor. This lack of information reduces the ability of prospective franchisees either to make an informed investment decision or otherwise verify the representations of the business's salespersons.

The Rule attempts to deal with these problems by requiring franchisors and franchise brokers to furnish prospective franchisees with information about the franchisor, the franchise business and the terms of the franchise agreement. Franchisors and franchise brokers must furnish additional information if they have made any claim about actual or potential earnings, either to the prospective franchisee or in the media. All disclosures must be made (i) before any sale is consummated and (ii) by means of disclosure documents whose form and content are set forth in the Rule.

The Rule requires disclosure of material facts. It does not regulate the substantive terms of the franchisor-franchisee relationship. It does not require registration of the offering or the filing of any documents with the Federal Trade Commission in connection with the sale of franchises.

The effective date of the Rule is July 21, 1979.

Businesses Covered by the Rule [§ 436.2(a)]

Either of two types of continuing commercial relationships are defined as a "franchise" and covered by the Rule.

The first type involves three characteristics: (1) the franchisee sells goods or services which meet the franchisor's quality standards (in cases where the franchisee operates under the franchisor's trademark, service mark, trade name, advertising or other commercial symbol designating the franchisor ("mark")) or which are identified by the franchisor's mark; (2) the franchisor exercises significant control over, or gives the franchisee significant assistance in, the franchisee's method of operation; and (3) the franchisee is required to make a payment of $500 or more to the franchisor or a person affiliated with the franchisor within six months after the business opens.

The second type also involves three characteristics: (1) the franchisee sells goods or services which are supplied by the franchisor or a person affiliated with the franchisor; (2) the franchisor secures accounts for the franchisee, or secures locations or sites for vending machines or rack displays, or provides the services of a person able to do either; and (3) the franchisee is required to make a payment of $500 or more to the franchisor or a person affiliated with the franchisor within six months after the business opens.

Relationships covered by the Rule include those which are within the definition of "franchise" and those which are represented as being within the definition when the relationship is entered into, regardless of whether, in fact, they are within the definition.

The Rule exempts (1) fractional franchises; (2) leased department arrangements; and (3) purely verbal agreements. The Rule excludes (1) relationships between employer/employees, and among general business partners; (2) membership in retailer-owned cooperatives; (3) certification and testing services; and (4) single trademark licenses.

The Disclosure Document [§ 436.1(a)]

All franchisors must furnish the document described in this section. The disclosure document requires information on the following 20 subjects:

1. Identifying information about the franchisor.
2. Business experience of the franchisor's directors and key executives.
3. The franchisor's business experience.
4. Litigation history of the franchisor and its directors and key executives.
5. Bankruptcy history of the franchisor and its directors and key executives.
6. Description of the franchise.
7. Money required to be paid by the franchisee to obtain or commence the franchise operation.
8. Continuing expenses to the franchisee in operating the franchise business that are payable in whole or in part to the franchisor.
9. A list of persons who are either the franchisor or any of its affiliates, with whom the franchisee is required or advised to do business.
10. Realty, personality, services, etc. which the franchisee is required to purchase, lease or rent, and a list of any persons from whom such transactions must be made.
11. Description of consideration paid (such as royalties, commissions, etc.) by third parties to the franchisor or any of its affiliates as a result of a franchisee's purchase from such third parties.
12. Description of any franchisor assistance in financing the purchase of a franchise.
13. Restrictions placed on a franchisee's conduct of its business.
14. Required personal participation by the franchisee.

15. Termination, cancellation and renewal of the franchise.
16. Statistical information about the number of franchises and their rate of terminations.
17. Franchisor's right to select or approve a site for franchise.
18. Training programs for the franchisee.
19. Celebrity involvement with the franchise.
20. Financial information about the franchisor.

The disclosures must be made in a single document, with a cover sheet setting forth the name of the franchisor, the date of issuance of the document, and a statement—whose text is set forth in the Rule—advising the prospective franchisee of the contents and purpose of the document. The document may not include information other than that required by the Rule or by State law not preempted by the Rule. However, the franchisor may furnish other information to the prospective franchisee which is not inconsistent with the material set forth in the disclosure document.

The disclosure document must be given to a prospective franchisee at the earlier of either (1) the prospective franchisee's first personal meeting with franchisor, or (2) ten days prior to the execution of a contract or payment of consideration relating to the franchise relationship. At that time, the franchisor or franchise broker must give the prospective franchisee copies of the franchisor's standard franchise agreement.

The information in the disclosure document must be current as of the completion of the franchisor's most recent fiscal year. In addition, a revision of the document must be prepared quarterly whenever there has been a material charge relating to the franchise business of the franchisor.

Earnings Claims [§ 436.1(b)-(e)]

The Rule prohibits earnings representations about the actual or potential sales, income, or profits of existing or prospective franchisees unless three prerequisites are met: 1) there is a reasonable basis for the representation; 2) the representation has been prepared in accordance with generally accepted accounting principles; and 3) the franchisor has evidence to substantiate every representation and such evidence is available to the prospective franchisee or to the Federal Trade Commission upon reasonable demand.

Whenever the franchisor or franchise broker makes a representation about earnings, either in the media or directly to a prospective franchisee, an earnings disclosure document must be furnished to every prospective franchisee. This document must include: (1) a statement describing the material bases and assumptions for each earnings representation made, including the number and percentage of outlets achieving the same results as those claimed, (2) cautionary language—whose text is set forth in the Rule—concerning the projectability of the representation to the prospective franchisee's future experience, (3) a notice that evidence to substantiate the representation is available for inspection upon reasonable demand, and (4) a cover page setting forth the name of the franchisor, the date of the document, and a statement—the text of which is set forth in the Rule—advising the prospective franchisee of the importance of the document.

Any earnings representation, other than one used in advertising, must be relevant to the geographic market in which the prospective franchisee's franchise will be located. The earnings disclosure document may not contain any information other than that required by the Rule or by State law not preempted by the Rule, and must be given to every prospective franchisee to whom the representation has been made at least ten days before the execution of a contract or the payment of any consideration relating to the franchise, or at the first personal meeting following the making of the representation, whichever occurs first.

Acts or Practices Which Violate the Rule

It is an unfair or deceptive act or practice within the meaning of § 5 of the Federal Trade Commission Act for any franchisor or franchise broker:

1. to fail to furnish prospective franchisees, within time frames established by the Rule, with a disclosure document containing information on 20 different subjects relating to the franchisor, the franchise business and the terms of the franchise agreement [§ 436.1(a)] ;
2. to make any representations about the actual or potential sales, income, or profits of existing or prospective franchises except in the manner set forth in the Rule [§ 436.1(b)-(e)] ;
3. to make any claim or representation (such as in advertising or oral statements by salespersons) which is inconsistent with the information required to be disclosed by the Rule [§ 436.1(f)] ;
4. to fail to furnish prospective franchisees, within the time frames established by the Rule, with copies of the franchisor's standard forms of franchise agreements and copies of the final agreements to be signed by the parties [§ 436.1(g)] ; and
5. to fail to return to prospective franchisees any funds or deposits (such as down-payments) identified as refundable in the disclosure document [§ 436.1(h)] .

Violators are subject to civil penalty actions brought by the Commission of up to $10,000 per violation.

The Commission believes that the courts should and will hold that any person injured by a violation of the Rule has a private right of action against the violator, under the Federal Trade Commission Act, as amended, and the Rule. The existence of such a right is necessary to protect the members of the class for whose benefit the statute was enacted and the Rule is being promulgated, is consistent with the legislative intent of the Congress in enacting the Federal Trade Commission Act, as amended, and is necessary to the enforcement scheme established by the Congress in that Act and to the Commission's own enforcement efforts.

State Franchise Laws

The Commission's goals are to create a minimum Federal standard of disclosure applicable to all franchisor offerings, and to permit States to provide additional protection as they see fit. Thus, while the Federal Trade Commission Trade Regulation Rules have the force and effect of Federal law and, like other Federal substantive regulations, preempt State and local laws to the extent that these laws conflict, the Commission has determined that the Rule will not preempt State or local laws and regulations which either are consistent with the Rule or, even if inconsistent, which would provide protection to prospective franchisees equal to or greater than that imposed by the Rule.

Examples of State laws or regulations which would not be preempted by the Rule include State provisions requiring the registration of franchisors and franchise salesmen, State requirements for escrow or bonding arrangements and State required disclosure obligations exceeding the disclosure obligations set forth in the Rule. Moreover, the Rule does not affect State laws or regulations which substantively regulate the franchisor/franchisee relationship, such as termination practices, contract provisions and financing arrangements.

The Uniform Franchise Offering Circular

The Uniform Franchise Offering Circular ("UFOC") is now accepted in satisfaction of the disclosure requirements in 14 States which have franchise registration and disclosure laws. The UFOC format is not identical to the disclosure format prescribed in the Rule. For example, there are minor differences in language on similar disclosure requirements; there are subjects about which the UFOC requires more disclosure than the Rule, and subjects where the Rule requires more disclosure than the UFOC. Even though the two documents are not identical in language, they are quite similar; in any event, both documents are designed to achieve the same result regardless of any minor variations in the means used to reach that result. Accordingly, the Commission will permit franchisors to use the UFOC format in lieu of the disclosure document provided by the Rule. This alternative use is limited to the UFOC version adopted by the Midwest Securities Commissioners Association, Inc., on September 2, 1975 plus any modifications thereof which do not diminish the protection accorded to the prospective franchisee which may be made by a State in which such registration has been made effective.

Certain provisions of the Rule still will control even if the UFOC format is used in lieu of the Rule's disclosure document, such as: (i) the persons required to make disclosure; (ii) transactions requiring disclosure; (iii) the timing of the disclosure; and (iv) the types of documents to be given to prospective franchisees.

The Commission's decision to permit use of a State disclosure document in lieu of its own document does not constitute Commission deferral to State law enforcement. The Commission is expressly providing for concurrent jurisdiction between the Commission and the States in appropriate instances. The Commission's action does not and is not intended to deprive the Commission of its responsibility to determine whether particular franchisors have complied with the Rule.

Commission Assistance

The Commission has prepared proposed interpretative guidelines to the Rule in an effort to assist franchisors and franchise brokers in complying with the Rule. These interpretative guidelines are open for public comment through February 20, 1979. Final interpretitive guidelines will be issued after a review of comments received, and prior to the effective date of the Rule.

The Commission will furnish a formal advisory opinion about the relationship of the Rule to specific fact situations in accordance with its Procedures and Rule of Practice.

The Commission's franchise staff will furnish informal staff opinions, in appropriate circumstances, upon written request.

The Franchise Rule: Questions and Answers

Q. What is a Trade Regulation Rule?

A. A Trade Regulation Rule sets basic standards for lawful business conduct. A Trade Regulation Rule may be issued by the Commission to prevent unfairness or deception in business dealings either by prohibiting certain acts and practices or by imposing affirmative obligations such as disclosure of pertinent information.

Q. What will this Rule do?

A. The Rule will require sellers of franchises and other business opportunity ventures to provide prospective investors with the information they need to make an informed investment decision. It will further protect investors by requiring that all earnings claims be documented, that the information investors receive is complete and accurate, and that they have adequate time to consider and evaluate the disclosures before making any final commitment.

Q. Who will be covered by the Rule?

A. The Rule is designed to cover sellers of franchises and business opportunity ventures. Generally speaking, it will apply to the sale of franchises of an entire retail business (e.g., a fast-food restaurant), and of distribution rights for trademarked products (e.g., an automobile dealership), as well as such business opportunity ventures as vending machine route programs. Businesses will, of course, need to compare their marketing arrangements with the Rule's definition of the types of franchises which are covered to determine whether they must comply with the Rule. The Commission staff is available for assistance in this regard.

Q. What penalties will a franchisor or franchise broker face for violating the Rule?

A. The penalties are substantial. The Commission will ordinarily be able to seek civil penalties of up to $10,000 a day for each violation of the Rule and may seek to enjoin continued violations. The Commission also may be able to seek additional relief in some cases.

Q. What prompted the Commission to issue the Rule?

A. The Commission began this rulemaking proceeding after receiving a significant number of consumer complaints about franchise and business opportunity venture sales practices. The rulemaking record alone contains over 5,400 pages of consumer complaint letters. Although the complaints covered many subjects, the root cause of the complaints was the same—the unavailability of reliable information essential for investors to make informed investment decisions and to verify the claims made by franchise salespersons.

Q. What kind of public participation went into the formulation of the Rule?

A. Public interest and participation in the rulemaking process has been substantial and widespread. The rulemaking record contains more than 5,400 pages of letters from consumers, some 5,000 pages of comment from affected businesses, and another 5,000 pages of comment from state and federal government agencies and members of the academic community. It also includes almost 2,000 pages of transcript from public hearings on the Rule.

Q. What is the time frame for implementation and enforcement of the Rule?

A. The Rule published today will take effect on July 21, 1979. The proposed implementation guidelines which accompany the Rule will be open for public comment until February 20, 1979, and will be published in final form before the effective date of the Rule.

Q. Does the Rule provide for consumer refunds? Does it give investors the right to sue for violations?

A. The Rule expressly requires that any refunds promised by the seller of a franchise or business opportunity venture be made. The Commission can sue to obtain appropriate relief for investors injured by a violation of a Rule. Although there is some question about whether federal courts will permit individual investors to sue for relief from a Rule violation, the Commission has publicly stated its view that private actions would add a valuable dimension to its own enforcement efforts. Even if the Commission's view is not adopted by courts at the federal level, investors may be able to obtain relief from state courts under State "Baby FTC Acts" and common law.

Q. What type of enforcement actions can be expected from the Commission?

A. We plan an active program of educating sellers of franchises and other business opportunity ventures about their compliance obligations, monitoring their compliance efforts, and proceeding against those who fail to comply.

Q. Will the Rule supersede State law?

A. The Rule will supersede only those few State franchise disclosure law provisions which provides less protection to investors. By setting minimum nationwide disclosure standards, the Rule should encourage individual States to continue to take an active regulatory role in providing even greater protection to investors.

Q. What steps should a would-be investor take before investing in a franchise or other business opportunity venture?

A. We recommend five basic precautions:

1. Study the required disclosure statement and proposed contracts carefully.
2. Consult with an attorney and other professional advisors before making a binding commitment.
3. Be sure that all promises made by the seller or its salespersons are clearly written into the contracts you sign.
4. Talk with others who have already invested in the business. Find out about their experiences.
5. If you are relying on any earnings claims or guarantees, study the statement describing the basis for the claims. Find out the percentage of past investors who have done equally well.

Notes

Chapter 1
The Nature, Scope, and History
of Franchising

1. "Cable Franchises Won by American Television for Four Communities," *The Wall Street Journal* (Eastern ed.), 29 March 1972, p. 4.

2. Kenneth W. Brown, "Franchising and Licensing: A Comparison," in "Franchising Today 1972," ed. Charles L. Vaughn (unpublished).

3. Charles Mason Hewitt, Jr., *Automobile Franchise Agreements,* Indiana University School of Business, Bureau of Business Research Study No. 39 (Homewood, Ill.: Richard D. Irwin, 1956), p. 7.

4. U.S. Department of Commerce, Industry and Trade Administration, Office of Consumer Goods and Service Industries, *Franchising in the Economy 1976-1978* (Washington, D.C.: U.S. Government Printing Office, 1978).

5. Charles L. Vaughn, *The Vaughn Report on Franchising of Fast Food Restaurants: Six Categories of Franchises* (New York: Farnsworth Publishing Company, 1970), p. 8.

6. Urban B. Ozanne and Shelby D. Hunt, *The Economic Effects of Franchising: Report Prepared for the Small Business Administration, Graduate School of Business, University of Wisconsin* (Washington, D.C.: U.S. Government Printing Office, 1971), p. 2-2.

7. Charles L. Vaughn, "Growth and Future of the Fast Food Industry," address to Annual Marketing Conference, Atlantic Pizza Delight Franchisees. Hilton Hotel, Montreal, Quebec, Canada, 9 April 1976.

8. U.S. Department of Commerce, *Franchising*, p. 30.

9. William P. Hall, "Franchising: New Scope for an Old Technique," *Harvard Business Review* (January-February 1964), pp. 60-72.

10. Charles L. Vaughn, "Growth and Future of Franchising," in *Franchising Today 1969*, ed. Charles L. Vaughn (Lynbrook, N.Y.: Farnsworth Publishing Company, 1969), pp. 265-287.

11. U.S. Department of Commerce, *Franchising*.

12. Jane Wallace and Betsy Raskin, *Institutions/V.F. Magazine, The 13th Annual Institutions 400 Issue*, (Chicago: Cahners Publishing Co., 1977).

13. Charles L. Vaughn, "Growth and Future of the Fast Food Industry." *The Cornell Hotel and Restaurant Administration Quarterly* 17, no. 3 (November 1976), pp. 31-39.

14. U.S. Department of Commerce, Domestic and International Business Administration, Consumer Goods and Services Division. *Franchise Opportunities Handbook* (Washington, D.C.: U.S. Government Printing Office, 1977).

15. Donald N. Thompson, *Franchise Operations and Antitrust* (Lexington, Mass.: D.C. Heath and Co., 1971), pp. 19-40.

16. Ernest Henderson, Sr., "Franchising Yesterday," in *Franchising Today 1966-1967*, ed. Charles L. Vaughn and David B. Slater (Albany, N.Y.: Matthew Bender, 1967), p. 239.

17. Andrew B. Jack, "The Channels of Distribution for an Innovation: The Sewing Machine Industry in America, 1860-1865," in *Explorations in Entrepreneurial History* (February 1957) (Cambridge, Mass.: Harvard University Research Center in Entrepreneurial History, 1957), pp. 113-141.

18. Thompson, *Franchise Operations and Antitrust*, p. 20.

19. Hewitt, *Automobile Franchise Agreements*, p. 240.

20. Ibid., p. 242.

21. Thompson, *Franchise Operations and Antitrust*, p. 21.

22. Alfred P. Sloan, Jr., *My Years with General Motors* (Garden City, N.Y.: Doubleday, 1964), p. 301.

23. Bedros Peter Pashigian, *The Distribution of Automobiles: An Economic Analysis of the Franchise System* (Englewood Cliffs, N.J.: Prentice-Hall, 1961).

24. Ko Ching Shih and C. Ying Shih, *American Soft Drink Industry and the Carbonated Beverage Market: A Statistical Analysis and Graphic Presentation*, Studies of American Industries, Series No. 2 (Morton Grove, Ill.: Shih and Shih, 1965), p. 12.

25. Ben Ginsberg, *Let's Talk Soft Drinks* (Springfield, Mo.: Mycroft Press, 1960), p. 35.

26. Shih and Shih, *American Soft Drink Industry*, pp. 139-141.

27. Ginsberg, *Let's Talk Soft Drinks*, p. 38.

28. Harry Kursh, *The Franchise Boom: How You Can Profit In It*, rev. ed. (Englewood Cliffs, N.J.: Prentice-Hall, 1968).

29. Ginsberg, *Let's Talk Soft Drinks*, p. 38.

30. Ibid., p. 41.

31. Kursh, *Franchise Boom*, p. 6.

32. John G. McLean and Robert W. Haigh, *The Growth of Integrated Oil Companies* (Boston, Mass.: Division of Research, Graduate School of Business Administration, Harvard University, 1954).

33. Ibid., p. 291.

34. Ibid., p. 294.

35. Hall, "Franchising: New Scope," pp. 60-72.

36. Ibid., p. 61.

37. Ibid., p. 62.

38. Ibid., p. 65.

39. Burton M. Sack, "The Trend in Company-Owned vs. Franchised Units at Howard Johnson Company: Underlying Causes," in *Franchising Today 1969*, ed. Vaughn, pp. 195-197.

40. Wallace E. Johnson, "The Story of Holiday Inns," in *Franchising Today* (1970), ed. Vaughn (Lynbrook, N.Y.: Farnsworth Publishing Company, 1970), pp. 157-158.

41. "The Burger That Conquered the Country," *Time*, 17 September 1973, pp. 84-92. Reprinted by permission from *Time, The Weekly News Magazine*, copyright Time, Inc., 1973.

42. Colonel Harland Sanders, "Remarks upon Receiving the Hall of Fame Award in Franchising," in *Franchising Today 1971*, ed. Charles L. Vaughn (unpublished), pp. 8-10.

43. Charles L. Vaughn, "Growth and Future of Franchising," in *Franchising Today 1969*, ed. Vaughn, p. 273.

44. Ibid., p. 265.

45. Charles L. Vaughn, "Growth and Future of the Fast Food Industry," *The Cornell Hotel and Restaurant Administration Quarterly*, p. 34.

46. U.S. Department of Commerce, *Franchising*, p. 36.

47. Hewitt, *Automobile Franchise Agreements*, p. 18.

48. Kevin P. Tighe, "Autowest, Inc. vs. Peugeot, Inc.: 'Good Faith' in Action," *Cars and Trucks* (February 1971), pp. 32-33.

49. Thompson, *Franchise Operations and Antitrust*, pp. 19-40.

50. David E. Krischer, "Franchise Regulation: An Appraisal of Recent State Legislation," *Boston College Industrial and Commercial Law Review* 13, no. 3 (February 1972), pp. 529-567.

51. Vaughn, *Franchising Today 1969*, p. 282.

52. Ginsberg, *Let's Talk Soft Drinks*, pp. 16-17.

Chapter 2
Marketing the Product or Service

1. For a more detailed account of some of these, see Harry Kursh, *The Franchise Boom: How You Can Profit In It* (Englewood Cliffs, N.J.: Prentice-Hall, 1968).

2. U.S. Department of Commerce, *Franchising in the Economy 1976-1978* (Washington, D.C.: Superintendent of Documents, 1978), p. 1.

3. For example, see E. Jerome McCarthy, *Basic Marketing: A Managerial Approach* (Homewood, Ill.: Richard D. Irwin, 1975).

4. *The New York Times*, 16 July 1975, p. 33m.

5. *The Wall Street Journal*, Tuesday, 22 August 1978, p. 16.

6. *Business Week*, 21 February 1977, p. 30.

7. *The Wall Street Journal*, Wednesday, 8 March 1978, p. 10.

8. *The Wall Street Journal*, Thursday, 28 April 1976, p. 1.

9. *Time*, 25 April 1977, p. 77.

10. *The Wall Street Journal*, Wednesday, 23 August 1978, p. 1, 29.

11. *Restaurant Business*, August 1974, p. 55, as quoted from Television Bureau of Advertising based on Broadcast Advertisers Reports.

12. Annual *Institutions 400* Issues (12th and 13th Editions), 1976, 1977.

13. For example, see *The Wall Street Journal*, Wednesday, 5 April 1978, p. 1: "Whopper War, Burger King Begins Big Hamburger Fight Against McDonald's . . . " Or *The New York Times*, Monday, 23 January 1978, p. D4, "A Wooing of the Young by Burger King."

14. Material provided by Paul H. Marcotte, vice-president, Director of Marketing, Convenient Food Mart, 8 May 1978.

15. U.S. Department of Commerce, *Franchise Opportunities Handbook*, June 1978, p. 110.

16. Ovid Russo, "Advertising Guidelines for Small Retail Firms," *Small Marketers Aids no. 160* (Washington, D.C.: U.S. Small Business Administration, January 1977).

17. McCarthy, *Basic Marketing: A Managerial Approach.*

Chapter 3
**The Advantages and Disadvantages of
Franchising to the Franchisor
and Franchisee**

1. Alfred P. Sloan, Jr., *My Years with General Motors* (Garden City, N.Y.: Doubleday & Company, 1964), p. 301.

2. Charles Mason Hewitt, Jr., *Automobile Franchise Agreements*, Indiana University School of Business, Bureau of Business Research Study no. 39 (Homewood, Ill.: Richard D. Irwin, 1956), p. 18.

3. Richard J. Boylan (executive vice-president, McDonald's Corporation), "Company-Owned vs. Franchised Operations," p. 14; William A. Conway (pres., Mister Softee, Inc.), "Company-Owned vs. Franchised Operations," p. 18; Dansby A. Council (pres., Council Manufacturing Company), "Company-Owned vs. Franchised Operated," p. 20; in *Franchising Today* (1965), ed. Charles L. Vaughn and David B. Slater (Chestnut Hill, Mass.: Boston College Press, 1965). Robert E. Bennett (vice-president, Hardee's Food Systems, Inc.), "To Franchise or Not—How to Decide: Pro-Why, How, Advantages," p. 19; Ernest Henderson, III (pres., Sheraton Corp. of America), "To Franchise or Not—How to Decide: Pro and Con," p. 33; in *Franchising Today 1966-1967*, ed. Charles L. Vaughn and David B. Slater (Albany, N.Y.: Matthew Bender and Company, Inc., 1967). Burton M. Sack (vice-president, Howard Johnson Company), "The Trend in Company-Owned vs. Franchised Units at Howard Johnson Company . . . Underlying Causes," p. 196; in *Franchising Today 1969*, ed. Charles L. Vaughn (Lynbrook, N.Y.: Farnsworth Publishing Company, Inc., 1969).

4. Hewitt, *Automobile Franchise Agreements*, p. 18.

5. Boylan, "Company-Owned vs. Franchised," p. 16; Conway, "Company-Owned vs. Franchised Operations," p. 18; Council, "Company-Owned vs. Franchised Operated," p. 21; in *Franchising Today* (1965), ed. Charles L. Vaughn. Sam A. Peterson (secretary and assistant general manager, Johnson Waxway Centers, Inc.), "To Franchise or Not—How to Decide: Pro-Why, How, Advantages," p. 18; Henderson, "To Franchise or Not," p. 37; in *Franchising Today 1966-1967*, ed. Charles L. Vaughn and David B. Slater.

6. Bennett, "To Franchise or Not," p. 22.

7. Boylan, "Company-Owned vs. Franchised," p. 16.

8. Ibid., p. 16.

9. Conway, "Company-Owned vs. Franchised Operations," p. 18.

10. Boylan, "Company-Owned vs. Franchised," p. 16.

11. Ibid., p. 16. Bennett, "To Franchise or Not," p. 22.

12. Boylan, "Company-Owned vs. Franchised," p. 17.

13. Conway, "Company-Owned vs. Franchised Operations," p. 18.

14. Council, "Company-Owned vs. Franchised Operated," p. 21.

15. Boylan, "Company-Owned vs. Franchised," p. 16.

16. Ibid., p. 16.

17. Bennett, "To Franchise or Not," p. 22. Henderson, "To Franchise or Not," p. 37.

18. Boylan, "Company-Owned vs. Franchised," p. 15. Bennett, "To Franchise or Not," p. 20. Lawrence E. Singer (president, Royal Castle System, Inc.), "To Franchise or Not—How to Decide: Con—Why Company-Owned Units," p. 24; William Ware (executive director, PKI Foods, Inc.), "Con—Why Company-Owned Units," p. 29; in *Franchising Today 1966-1967*, ed. Charles L. Vaughn and David B. Slater. Henderson, "To Franchise or Not," p. 37; Sack, "The Trend," p. 198.

19. Boylan, "Company-Owned vs. Franchised," p. 15; Singer, "Con—," p. 25; Ware, "Con—," p. 29.

20. Boylan, "Company-Owned vs. Franchised," p. 15.

21. Singer, "Con—," p. 25; and Ware, "Con—," p. 31.

22. Boylan, "Company-Owned vs. Franchised," p. 15.

23. Ibid.

24. Ibid.

25. Ibid.

26. Ibid.

27. Conway, "Company-Owned vs. Franchised Operations," p. 18.

28. Singer, "Con—," p. 24.

29. Ibid.

30. Ware, "Con—," p. 30.

31. Ware, "Con—," p. 29.

32. Singer, "Con—," p. 25.

33. Boylan, "Company-Owned vs. Franchised," p. 15.

34. Ibid., p. 17.

35. Robert M. Dias and Stanley I. Gurnick, *Franchising: The Investor's Complete Handbook* (New York: Hastings House, 1969). David D. Seltz, *How to Get Started in Your Own Franchised Business* (New York: Farnsworth Publishing Company, Inc., 1967).

36. Jerome L. Fels and Lewis G. Rudnick, *Investigate Before Investing. Guidance for Prospective Franchisees* (Washington, D.C.: International Franchise Association).

37. Bruce James Walker, *An Investigation of Relative Overall Position Satisfaction and Need Gratification Among Franchised Businessmen* (unpublished doctoral dissertation, Faculty of the Graduate School of Business Administration, University of Colorado, 1971).

38. Charles L. Vaughn, *The Vaughn Report on Franchising of Fast Food Restaurants: Six Categories of Franchises* (New York: Farnsworth Publishing Company, 1970), pp. 9-10.

39. Urban B. Ozanne and Shelby D. Hunt, *The Economic Effects of Franchising*, report prepared for the Small Business Administration, Graduate School of Business, University of Wisconsin (Washington, D.C.: U.S. Government Printing Office, 1971).

40. E. Patrick McGuire, Franchised Distribution, Conference Board Report no. 523 (New York: The Conference Board, 1971).

41. Walker, *Need Gratification.*

42. Vaughn, *The Vaughn Report*, pp. 9-10.

43. Ibid., p. 40.

44. Ozanne and Hunt, *Economic Effects of Franchising*, pp. 41, 42, 43, 48.

45. McGuire, *Franchised Distribution*, p. 16.

46. Ibid., p. 89.

47. Ibid., p. 87.

48. Ibid., p. 87.

49. Ibid., p. 91.

50. Ibid., p. 99.

51. Ibid., p. 99.

52. Walker, *Need Gratification*, pp. iv-v.

53. Ibid., p. 195.

54. Ibid., p. 195.

Chapter 4
Starting and Developing a Franchise
Operation as a Franchisor

1. John F. Angeline and William C. Hale, *Fast Food Franchising: 1970-1975* (Cambridge, Mass.: Arthur D. Little, Inc., 1970), p. 13.

2. Charles L. Vaughn, "Growth and Future of the Fast Food Industry," *The Cornell Hotel and Restaurant Administration Quarterly* 17, no. 3 (1976):38.

3. David D. Seltz, "Starting, Developing, Marketing, and Terminating the Franchise," in *Franchising Today 1972*, ed. Charles L. Vaughn (unpublished), pp. 69-74.

4. George F. Dillman, "An Overview: 'Starting and Developing the Franchisor Firm'," in *Franchising Today 1972*, ed. Charles L. Vaughn (unpublished), p. 4.

5. John H. Grant, "Starting, Developing, Marketing, and Terminating the Franchise," in *Franchising Today 1971*, ed. Charles L. Vaughn (unpublished), p. 82.

6. Ernest Henderson III, "Starting and Developing the Franchise Firm," in *Franchising Today 1972*.

7. Grant, "The Franchise," p. 80.

8. Ibid., pp. 80-81.

9. William Putt, ed., *How to Start Your Own Business* (Cambridge, Mass.: MIT Press, 1974).

10. C. Baumback and J. Mancuso, *Entrepreneurship and Venture Management* (Englewood Cliffs, N.J.: Prentice-Hall, 1975).

11. Joe Mancuso, ed. *The Entrepreneur's Handbook*, 2 vols. (Dedham, Mass.: Artech House, 1974).

12. James W. Schreier, *The Female Entrepreneur: A Pilot Study* (Milwaukee, Wisc.: Mount Mary College, 1974).

13. Franklin Wyman Jr., "An Established Company Takes the Franchise Route," in *Franchising Today 1969*, ed. Charles L. Vaughn (Lynbrook, N.Y.: Farnsworth Publishing Company, 1969), p. 222.

14. Ibid., p. 223.

15. Lois Lindauer, "Starting and Developing the Franchise Firm," in *Franchising Today 1972*, ed. Charles L. Vaughn (unpublished), pp. 2-3.

16. Wyman, "An Established Company," p. 222.

17. Henderson, "Starting and Developing," p. 3; Dillman, "An Overview," p. 4; Bronson H. Fargo, "Developing the Franchise Package," in *Franchising Today 1969*, p. 218.

18. Donald M. Smart, "Distribution of the Franchise through Individual Units, Territorial Franchises, and Master Franchises with Sub-Franchising Rights," in *Franchising Today 1966-1967*, ed. Charles L. Vaughn and David B. Slater (Albany, N.Y.: Matthew Bender and Company, 1967), p. 52.

19. Seltz, "The Franchise," pp. 74-79.

20. Dillman, "An Overview," pp. 8-11.

21. Aaron Rothenberg, "Network Plan for the Start-Up of a Franchise Operation," *Fast Food* 67, no. 11 (1968):105-108.

22. David D. Seltz, "The Elements of the Franchise Package—Its Demand, Acceptance, and Services," in *Franchising Today 1966-1967*, p. 43.

23. Ibid., p. 43.

24. Seltz, "The Elements of the Franchise Package," pp. 44-46.

25. E. Patrick McGuire, *Franchised Distribution,* Conference Board Report No. 523 (New York: The Conference Board, 1971), pp. 15-32.

26. Charles L. Vaughn, *The Vaughn Report on Franchising of Fast Food Restaurants: Six Categories of Franchises* (Lynbrook, N.Y.: Farnsworth Publishing Company, 1970), p. 10.

27. Dewey A. Dyer, *So You Want to Start a Restaurant* (Chicago: Institutions/Volume Feeding Management Magazine, 1971).

28. Jerrold G. Van Cise, "The Boston College Center's Special Committee on Unfair and Deceptive Practices in Franchising. The Chairman's Final Report," in *Franchising Today 1969,* pp. 185-192; also see Appendix B, pp. 291-351.

29. Lewis G. Rudnick, "Franchising: Proposed Legislative Solutions for a Troubled Relationship," *1972 National Franchise Directory* (Denver, Colo.: Continental Reports, 1972), p. 15.

30. "Special CFR Report on the Status of State Franchising Laws," Supplement to 23 July 1973 issue, *Continental Franchise Review* 6, no. 8, 23 July 1973.

31. Gladys Glickman, *Business Organizations, Franchising,* 15 (New York: Matthew Bender, 1976), pp. 3-17—3-50.1, 8-17—8.34.15.

32. Ray O. Burch, "Franchising: Remarks of Ray O. Burch before the 5th Annual Legal and Government Affairs Symposium of the International Franchise Association" (Washington, D.C.: International Franchise Association, 1972).

33. Jerrold G. Van Cise, "A Franchise Contract," in *Franchising Today 1969,* pp. 295-317.

34. Gerald G. Udell, "Anatomy of the Franchise Contract," *The Cornell Hotel and Restaurant Administration Quarterly* 13, no. 3 (1972):13-21.

35. Apparently illegal provisions in view of the outcome of the Chicken Delight litigation.

36. Glickman, *Business Organizations, Franchising.* (Updated annually.)

Chapter 5
Recruiting and Selecting Franchisees

1. Robert C. Townsend, "Marketing: Selling the Public," in *Franchising Today* (1965), ed. Charles L. Vaughn and David B. Slater (Chestnut Hill, Mass.: Boston College Press, 1965), p. 91.

2. Charles L. Vaughn, *Franchise Industry Training, 1967-1968* (Chestnut Hill, Mass.: Boston College, 1968).

3. U.S. Department of Commerce, *Franchising in the Economy 1976-1978* (Washington, D.C.: U.S. Government Printing Office, 1978).

4. *Convenient Food Mart Enterprise* (Chicago: Convenient Food Mart, 1974), 5 (no. 11), pp. 1, 9. (This is CFM's internal house organ, a periodical.)

5. Melvin J. Evans, "The Profile of a Franchisee," in *Franchising Today 1966-1967*, ed. Charles L. Vaughn and David B. Slater (Albany, N.Y.: Matthew Bender and Company, 1967), pp. 155-156.

6. Daryl W. Motte, "Recruiting and Selecting Franchisees," in *Franchising Today* (1965), ed. Charles L. Vaughn and David B. Slater (Chestnut Hill, Mass.: Boston College Press, 1965), pp. 50-51.

7. Ibid.

8. Ibid.

Chapter 6
Training Franchisees

1. James E. Barrett, "The Case for Evaluation of Training Expenses," *Business Horizons*, April 1969, pp. 67-72.

2. Ibid., p. 68.

3. Ibid., p. 69.

4. John H. Stevens, "Training and Supervision," in *Franchising Today 1966-1967*, ed. Charles L. Vaughn and David B. Slater (Albany, N.Y.: Matthew Bender and Company, 1967), pp. 277-278.

5. Ibid., p. 279.

6. Charles L. Vaughn, *Franchise Industry Training 1967-1968 (FIT)* (Chestnut Hill, Mass.: Center for the Study of Franchise Distribution, 1968); Charles L. Vaughn and Joseph D. O'Brien, *Franchise Industry Training (FIT)* (Chestnut Hill, Mass.: Bureau of Business Research, 1966).

7. John W. Stokes, *How to Manage a Restaurant or Institutional Food Service* (Dubuque, Ia.: Wm. C. Brown Company, 1978).

8. *Management Source Publications for Small Business* (New York: Dun & Bradstreet, not dated).

9. Paul and Marlene A. Wasserman, eds., *Training and Development Organizations Directory* (Detroit, Mich.: Gale Research Co., 1978).

Chapter 7
Financing the Franchise Operation

1. Jay L. Doty, "Financial and Real Estate Problems," in *Franchising Today 1972*, ed. Charles L. Vaughn (unpublished).

2. Phil David Fine, "Money for Franchisor-Franchisee Operations," in *Franchising Today 1971*, ed. Charles L. Vaughn (unpublished), pp. 102-103.

3. Ibid., pp. 104-105.

4. Ibid., p. 106.

5. Ibid., pp. 107-108.

6. William M. Lendman, "Going Public: 1969," *Franchising Today* (1970), ed. Charles L. Vaughn (Lynbrook, N.Y.: Farnsworth Publishing Company, 1970), pp. 60-61.

7. Ibid., pp. 61-62.

8. Ibid., p. 59.

9. Jack C. Massey, "Going Public: 'Our House is Made of Glass,' " in *Franchising Today 1967-1968*, ed. Charles L. Vaughn and David B. Slater (Lynbrook, N.Y.: Farnsworth Publishing Company, 1968), pp. 106-107.

10. Lendman, "Going Public," pp. 65-66.

11. Ibid., p. 67.

12. Robert O. Snelling, "Why and How Snelling and Snelling Went Public," in *Franchising Today* (1970), ed. Charles L. Vaughn (Lynbrook, N.Y.: Farnsworth Publishing Company, 1970), pp. 70-97.

13. Doty, "Financial and Real Estate Problems."

14. Thomas L. Holton, "Franchisor Accounting Practices: A Sound Approach," in *Franchising Today 1971*, ed. Charles L. Vaughn (unpublished), pp. 117-118.

15. Doty, "Financial and Real Estate Problems."

Chapter 8
The Real Estate Program

1. Bedros Peter Pashigian, *The Distribution of Automobiles, An Economic Analysis of the Franchise System* (Englewood Cliffs, N.J.: Prentice-Hall, 1961).

2. Ibid., p. 25.

3. Saul B. Cohen and William Applebaum, "Major Considerations in Evaluation of a Store Site," in *Guide to Store Location Research with Emphasis on Super Markets*, ed. Curt Kornblau (Reading, Mass.: Addison-Wesley Publishing Company, 1968), p. 83.

4. Forest B. Raffel, "Analyzing Franchise Locations," in *Franchising Today 1967-1968*, ed. Charles L. Vaughn and David B. Slater (Lynbrook, N.Y.: Farnsworth Publishing Company, 1968), p. 199.

5. Don Case, "Executing a Real Estate Program in Today's Competitive Market," in *Franchising Today 1969*, ed. Charles L. Vaughn (Lynbrook, N.Y.: Farnsworth Publishing Company, 1969), p. 80.

6. S. Joseph Loscocco, "Location Analysis and Selection," in *Franchising Today 1967-1968*, p. 196.

7. Case, "Executing," p. 80.

8. John Gorman, "Developing the Real Estate Program," in *Franchising Today* (1970), p. 246.

9. S. Joseph Loscocco, "Developing the Real Estate Program with Sky-Rocketing Costs," in *Franchising Today* (1970), p. 234.

10. Curt Kornblau, "A Guide to Source Material for Store Location Research," in *Guide to Store Location Research*, p. 80.

11. Raffel, "Analyzing Franchise Locations," p. 201.

12. William Applebaum, "The Analog Method for Estimating Potential Store Sales," in *Guide to Store Location Research*, pp. 232-243.

13. Francis R. Cella, "Computerized Site Selection," in *Franchising Today 1969*, pp. 84-95.

14. Gorman, "Developing the Real Estate Program," pp. 248-251.

15. Phil David Fine, "Real Estate Financing," in *Franchising Today 1966-1967*, ed. Charles L. Vaughn and David B. Slater (Albany, N.Y.: Matthew Bender and Company, 1967), pp. 129-134.

16. William Applebaum and others, *Guide to Store Location Research.*

Chapter 9
Franchisor-Franchisee Relations

1. William T. Morgan, Jr., "Franchisor-Franchisee Relationships," in *Franchising Today* (1970), ed. Charles L. Vaughn (Lynbrook, N.Y.: Farnsworth Publishing Company, 1970), p. 280.

2. Ibid., pp. 283-284.

3. Leonard Korot, "Franchisee Unrest: Some Manifestations, Causes and Remedies," in *Franchising Today 1971*, ed. Charles L. Vaughn (unpublished), pp. 163-177.

4. Bruce James Walker, "An Investigation of Relative Overall Position Satisfaction and Need Gratification among Franchised Businessmen" (Doctoral dissertation, Graduate School of Business Administration, University of Colorado, 1971).

5. See, for example, Association of National Advertisers, *The Measured Effectiveness of Employee Publications* (New York, 1953). Subsequently the General Electric Company, with the author serving as project director, conducted a series of communication studies at all levels within the company, but these studies are not published.

6. Walker, *Need Gratification*, pp. 222-223.

7. Charles L. Vaughn, "Recruiting and Selecting Franchisees," in *Franchising Today 1967-68,* ed. Charles L. Vaughn and David B. Slater (Lynbrook, N.Y.: Farnsworth Publishing Company, 1968), pp. 292-314.

8. Urban B. Ozanne and Shelby D. Hunt, *The Economic Effects of Franchising.* Report Prepared for the Small Business Administration, Graduate School of Business, University of Wisconsin (Washington, D.C.: U.S. Government Printing Office, 1971), p. 122.

9. Ibid., p. 122.

10. Bruce J. Walker, "Franchisee Satisfaction," *Franchise Journal Management and Marketing* 5, no. 7 (1972):14-18; Bruce J. Walker, "Franchisee Satisfaction, Part 2," *Franchise Journal Management and Marketing* 5, no. 10 (1973):8-11, 30; Bruce J. Walker, "How Franchisees View Their Positions and Franchise Packages," Speech for Southern Marketing Association Meetings, November 1972.

11. Walker, "Franchise Satisfaction," Part 1, p. 9.

12. Walker, "How Franchises View Their Positions and Franchise Packages," p. 6.

13. Daryl W. Motte, "Franchisor-Franchisee Relations to Prevent a Hostile Environment," in *Franchising Today (1970)*, pp. 275-278.

14. Charles L. Vaughn, "One Dissident Group: An Illustration of Franchisor-Franchisee Problems," *The Cornell Hotel and Restaurant Administration Quarterly* 17, no. 3 (1976):9.

15. Motte, "Franchisor-Franchisee Relations."

16. Theodore F. Pearlman, "Franchisee Relations," in *Franchising Today* (1970), pp. 285-287.

17. Joseph Selame, "Communications through Design," in *Franchising Today* (1970), p. 289.

18. Ibid., p. 290.

19. Matthew L. Lifflander, "Enforcement of the Franchise Agreement," in *Franchising Today, 1966-1967*, ed. Charles L. Vaughn and David B. Slater (Albany, N.Y.: Matthew Bender Company, 1967), p. 351.

20. Ibid., p. 351.

21. Lifflander, "Enforcement," p. 352.

22. Jerrold G. Van Cise (chairman of the special committee), "The Boston College Center's Special Committee on Unfair and Deceptive Practices in Franchising: The Chairman's Final Report," in *Franchising Today 1969*, ed. Charles L. Vaughn (Lynbrook, N.Y.: Farnsworth Publishing Company, 1969), pp. 291-351 (App. B), which list the committee membership and give the final report, as well as a proposal for a National Mediation Panel.

23. Statement by Charles L. Vaughn, "Proposed Trade Regulation Rule: 'Disclosure Requirements and Prohibitions Concerning Franchising' " (Washington, D.C.: Federal Trade Commission Public Hearing), 22 February 1972, p. 9.

Chapter 10
International Franchising

1. Robert A. Weaver Jr., "International Licensing," in *Franchising Today 1966-67*, ed. Charles L. Vaughn and David B. Slater (New York: Matthew Bender and Co., 1967), p. 62.

2. Matthew L. Lifflander, "International Aspects of Franchising," in *Franchising Today* (1965), ed. Charles L. Vaughn and David B. Slater (Chestnut Hill, Mass.: Boston College Press, 1965), p. 101.

3. U.S. Department of Commerce, *Franchising in the Economy 1976-1978* (Washington, D.C.: U.S. Government Printing Office, 1978), p. 5.

4. Weaver, "International Licensing," p. 62.

5. David D. Seltz, "New Breakthroughs in International Franchising," in *Franchising Today 1972*, ed. Charles L. Vaughn (unpublished).

6. Lifflander, "The Outlook for Franchising Abroad in the 1970's," in *Franchising Today 1971*, ed. Charles L. Vaughn (unpublished), p. 307.

7. Joseph C. Stehlin, "International Aspects of Franchising," in *Franchising Today* (1965), p. 107.

8. Lifflander, "International Aspects of Franchising," p. 102.

9. Daryl W. Motte, "Recruiting and Selecting Franchisees," in *Franchising Today* (1965), p. 50.

10. Matthew L. Lifflander, "The American Franchisor's Challenge—International Opportunities," in *Franchising Today* (1970), ed. Charles L. Vaughn (Lynbrook, N.Y.: Farnsworth Publishing Company, 1970), p. 378.

11. Seltz, "New Breakthroughs in International Franchising."

12. Lifflander, "The Outlook for Franchising Abroad in the 1970's," p. 310.

13. "Fast Food Still Top 'Export' from America," *Service World International*, January/February 1975, p. 65.

14. U.S. Department of Commerce, Industry and Trade Administration, *Franchising in the Economy 1976-1978* (Washington, D.C.: U.S. Government Printing Office, 1978), p. 7.

15. Donald W. Hackett, "U.S. Franchise Systems Abroad: The Second Boom," *Marketing: 1776-1976 and Beyond, Proceedings of the American Marketing Association* no. 39 (Chicago: American Marketing Association, 1976), ed. Kenneth L. Bernhardt, pp. 253-255; Bruce J. Walker and Michael J. Etzel, "The Internationalization of U.S. Franchise Systems: Progress and Procedures," *Journal of Marketing* 37 (1973):38-46; Philip B. Dwoskin, "Foreign and Domestic Prospects for the U.S. Fast Food Franchise Industry," *Agricultural Economic Report No. 358* (Washington, D.C.: U.S. Department of Agriculture); J. Irwin Peters and Vernon J. Grubisich, "Franchising in Europe: Variables in Location Selection," a paper presented at the Academy of Marketing Science Conference, Akron, Ohio, May 1977.

16. Lifflander, "The American Franchisor's Challenge—," p. 378.

17. Dwoskin, "Foreign and Domestic Prospects," p. iii.

18. "Dynamic Growth Marks Canadian Franchisors as Total Sales Increase by 123.4% in 1977," *Foodservice & Hospitality Magazine*, 10, no. 9 (1978):41.

19. Ibid., p. 42.

20. M. Mendelsohn, *The Guide to Franchising* (Oxford: Pergamon Press, 1970), pp. 66-78.

21. Ibid.

22. Philip B. Dwoskin, "Fast Food Franchises: Market Potentials for Agricultural Products in Foreign and Domestic Markets," in *The Marketing and Transportation Situation, February 1975* (Washington, D.C.: U.S. Department of Agriculture), p. 26.

23. Franchising Business Study Team to the U.S.A., *Growth of Franchising in Japan* (September 1972), p. 1.

24. For example, Philip B. Dwoskin and Nick Havas, *Japan's Fast Food Industry: Export Potential for U.S. Products* (Washington, D.C.: Foreign Agricultural Service, U.S. Department of Agriculture, 1975).

25. Ibid., p. 2.

26. "Fast Food Still Top 'Export' From America," *Service World International*, January/February 1975, p. 31.

27. Dwoskin, and Havas, "Japan's Fast Food Industry . . . ," p. 6.

28. Address is Fédération Française du Franchisage; 31, Rue St. Augustin, 75002 Paris, France. Telephone: 073-18-73.

29. Bruno Tietz and Günther Matthieu, *Das Franchising als-Kooperationsmodell fur den Mittelständischen Gross: und Einzelhandel* (Saarbrücken, Germany: Universität des Saarlandes, June 1978), p. 52.

30. Herbert Gross and Walther Skaupy, *Franchising in der Praxis. Fallbeispiele und Rechtliche Grundlagen* (Dusseldorf und Wien: Econ Verlag, 1976).

31. Walter Skaupy, "The Current Status of Franchising in Germany," *Commerce in Germany* 214 (1971):7-8.

32. Ibid., p. 7.

33. Ibid., pp. 7-8.

34. Charles L. Vaughn and Alan M. Wright, *Book Review: Franchising in der Praxis. Fallbeispiele und Rechtliche Grundlagen* by Herbert Gross and Walter Skaupy (Dusseldorf und Wien: Econ Verlag, 1976), in *Journal of Retailing* 22, no. 4 (1976-1977):80-83.

35. Alfred Görge, *Organisation und Management. I. Die Internationalisievung von Franchise-Systemen.* (Göttingen: Vandenhoeck & Ruprecht, 1979).

36. Gross and Skaupy, *Franchising in der Praxis*, chap. 22, pp. 241-263.

37. U.S. Department of Commerce, *Franchise Opportunities Handbook* (Washington, D.C.: U.S. Government Printing Office, 1977), p. 155.

38. Ibid.

Index

Author Index

Subject Index

About the Author

Charles L. Vaughn chaired the seven annual international management conferences on franchising held at Boston College and edited or coedited the series of *Franchising Today* books resulting from the conferences. He received the Ph.D. from The University of Chicago and the B.S. from the Kansas State Teachers College of Emporia. Dr. Vaughn has been a researcher, speaker, expert witness before the courts and government agencies, and consultant on franchising since 1964. He taught graduate and undergraduate courses in franchising and general marketing at Boston College and headed the Office of Special Programs there until his academic retirement in 1977. He is now president of the Vaughan Company, Needham, Massachusetts.